Wendell Mortimer, Jr.

Southern Pacific narrow gauge caboose hop between Keeler and Owenyo on October 6, 1949, by Donald Duke.

Southern Pacific Narrow Gauge
by Mallory Hope Ferrell

"... the loneliest and most improbable of all short lines"
—*Lucius Beebe*

Published by: Pacific Fast Mail
P.O. Box 57, Edmonds, Washington
98020

Other Railroad Books by Mallory Hope Ferrell:

Rails, Sagebrush & Pine
    A Garland of Sumpter Valley Days

The Gilpin Gold Tram
    Colorado's Unique Narrow Gauge

The 1871 Grant Locomotive Works
    Centennial Catalog Reproduction

Silver San Juan
    The Rio Grande Southern

Tweetsie Country
    The East Tennessee & Western North Carolina

West Side
    Narrow Gauge In The Sierra

Colorado & Southern Narrow Gauge
    The Bear Trap Stack Era

©**1982 by Mallory Hope Ferrell**

All rights reserved, including those to reproduce this book, or parts thereof, in any form without written permission of the Publisher, PFM Publications.

Library of Congress #82-80930

Front Endsheet: Photograph by Johnny Krause
Rear Endsheet: Photograph by Donald Duke

Dustjacket Painting by: Mike Pearsall

Lithographed in Canada by:
  Evergreen Press, Ltd.
  Vancouver, B.C.

Typography by:
  The Type Merchant
  Everett, Washington

Photograph by Richard F. Thomas.

Southern Pacific Narrow Gauge is dedicated
to my long time friend and fellow photographer
Richard F. Thomas.
His coverage of SP narrow gauge is exceeded
only by his friendship.

ACKNOWLEDGMENTS

When one writes of another time and place, you quite naturally have to depend upon the memories, recollections and illustrations of those who were there, or had the forethought to take note of the things of which history is made. For Southern Pacific Narrow Gauge, I am again indebted to a number of old friends and some new ones, who have shared their photographs and memories.

Those who provided materials on the early days of the Carson & Colorado and Nevada & California included Hugh Tolford; Ken Kidder; Guy Dunscomb; Cornelius Hauck; Jim Johnson of the Southern Pacific; Ellen Guerricagoitia of the University of Nevada Library; the staffs of the Nevada State Museum, Nevada State Historical Society, Paula West of the Wyoming State Archives, and Pamela Crowell of the Nevada State Museum.

Full color paintings were done by Jan Rons; Mike Pearsall and Jim Finnell, while color photography is from Wendell Mortimer, Jr.; Lawrie Brown and the William Kaminsky collection.

More outstanding camera work was provided by Donald Duke; Gerald M. Best; Wendell Mortimer, Jr.; Richard Thomas; Will Whittaker; Al Phelps and John Krause. Additional credits go to Richard H. Kindig; Fred Hust; Gary G. Allen; Bert Ward; Robert Lee Behme; Robert W. Brown; Malcolm McCarter and Mac Owen. Don Duke made prints available from the Walt Thrall and Frank Petersen negatives in his collection. The late Lucius Beebe and Charles Clegg added still more photographs as did the late Jim Wren and Grahame Hardy.

Additional artwork was created by Mike Pearsall; Carl Fallberg; Howard Fogg and Joe Dale Morris. Mike Pearsall also served as art director and driving force behind the book. The fine scale drawings are by Al Barker, Herman Darr and Ken Pruitt. All of the illustrations represent countless hours of research and work.

Thanks are extended to David Morgan and Fred Hamilton of *Trains* Magazine; Robert Hanft; Kyle Wyatt of the California State Railroad Museum; Don Drew of Pacific Fast Mail; Tom Armstrong, Georgia Waite, Afton Frederick, and Stanley Paher.

Finally a word of appreciation to my wife Gloria and children Susan, Mal, Kim and Eric, for giving me the peace of mind and time to research and write.

To each of you, and to those others whose names appear in the credits, it has indeed been a pleasure retracing the now abandoned grades with you. Your help, cooperation and willingness to share is deeply appreciated.

—*Mallory Hope Ferrell*

TRAIN TIME

Dedication 5
Acknowledgments 6
Foreword 9
Preface: Desert Commotions 17
Chapter 1: The Slim Princess 19
Chapter 2: Bonanza In The Desert 59
Chapter 3: Mixed Train From Mina 73
Chapter 4: Narrow Gauge To Nowhere 97
Chapter 5: Twilight On The Narrow Gauge 191
Chapter 6: Like The Lost Tribe — Rosters 203
Roster 207
Index 266
Bibliography 271
Southern Pacific Narrow Gauge At A Glance ... 265

Southern Pacific narrow gauge's nine-spot trails a five car consist as she heads home to Keeler, California in the late afternoon of December 18, 1948. [Photograph by Donald Duke.]

FOREWORD

In the lexicon of the Old West, few names conjure-up more dreams of glory than that of the Carson & Colorado Railroad. Henry Yerington and the moneybags of the Bank of California built it; Lucius Beebe enshrined it; Carl Fallberg satirized it; while time and the Washoe winds have all but erased its path.

It has been called, and fittingly so, the "Slim Princess" owing in part to the fact that her rails were spaced a mere three feet apart. It was also said to have been built "300 miles too long or 300 years too soon." But nevertheless, it survived in part even the greatest of the Nevada short lines . . . the famous and fabulously rich Virginia & Truckee. It was in fact, the V&T and her wealth that financed the Carson & Colorado, not only providing its northern connection at Mound House, Nevada, now only a memory; but its visionary plan of connecting the Carson River with the distant Colorado River and all the silver and gold towns that would spring-up between. Originated, planned, pushed, financed and built by the Virginia & Truckee Railway in the early 1880's, the Carson & Colorado was all too soon a waif, unwanted and then finally unloaded on the unsuspecting but all powerful Southern Pacific . . . just two months before news of the Tonopah gold boom resounded across the great basin and over-shadowed the queen of the Comstock herself, Virginia City.

Ore from Cerro Gordo, Candelaria and Tonopah rolled over the Carson & Colorado, but never to the extent that had been hoped. Wells, Fargo & Company's express rode the rocking cars too, but the big silver and gold camps never materialized. Struggling through sagebrush, Sierra snows, across Mount Montgomery Pass and over the alkali desert, the C&C was subjected to name changes, name calling and partial standard gauging, finally ending its days as an isolated narrow gauge line in California's Owens Valley, just on the east side of the lofty Sierra Nevada. The final years saw Southern Pacific lettered on its cars, but under flaking paint could be read the names of the Nevada & California, Central Pacific and Carson & Colorado, while journal box covers and other metal parts proclaimed them to have been cast in the huge shops of the V&T at Carson. Still other cars and engines ended their days on the valley run between Laws and Keeler, after having served on the likes of the Florence & Cripple Creek, South Pacific Coast and Nevada-California-Oregon.

Following the turn of the century, the Owens Valley was robbed of its water by a distant, yet thirsty Los Angeles. With the loss of water, the ground dried up and cracked. The once rich mines had already played out and many farmers and ranchers just quit trying and left the valley. The final years saw the once grand narrow gauge making thrice-weekly runs down the desert floor, serving the needs of Zurich, Aberdeen, Kearsarge, Manzanar, Owenyo and Dolomite in its seventy mile coming and going between Keeler and Laws. Oddly enough, not one single town boasted a population in excess of 300 souls, while most could not muster more than a few dozen citizens on a July election day!

Still the Southern Pacific narrow gauge struggled through the sand in the desolate yet beautiful valley . . . hauling a mixed consist of borax, talc, soda ash and whatever else its agents could drum-up to fill the wooden cars. The ranchers around Laws provided a few carloads of cattle now and then, usually in the autumn, but no longer did the three and four engine "Stock Extras" blast up Mount Montgomery Pass and out across the valley in the shadow of 14,501 foot Mount Whitney. Just over the Panamints was Death Valley, which at 282 feet below sea level placed the highest and lowest points in the continental United States within the confines of Inyo County.

When the end finally came in 1960 the amazing thing was not that a part of the Old West had vanished, but that it had lasted so long. This then is the story of the Southern Pacific's Owens Valley narrow gauge. Operating in a land of barren contrasts, the slim gauge defied economics, geography and progress to become the last of her breed in the far west. Drifting across the desert sands, smoking for all who came to watch, trailing a diminutive and ancient consist, this was the Southern Pacific narrow gauge.

—*Mallory Hope Ferrell*

Noted artist Howard Fogg helped to immortalize the Carson & Colorado's "Bodie & Candelaria Express" of the early 1880's, with this watercolor (above), which was commissioned by Lucius Beebe. The unique and unlikely narrow gauge, with its inverted crossbuck was captured (right) in her final decade by Donald Duke at Mt. Whitney siding.

LUCIUS BEEBE ENSHRINED IT...

The Carson & Colorado Railroad was originated, planned and built by the Virginia & Truckee Railway, whose morning run between Carson City and Minden, Nevada was captured (above) by Lucius Beebe in July, 1946. It was Beebe and his partner, Charles Clegg, who enshrined both roads in their writing and photography, much of it accomplished while living aboard their private car "Gold Coast" in the V&T's Carson yards. They are shown (left) being served some gourmet delight aboard their second car "The Virginia City", by stewart Clarence Watkins. Photographer Clegg made the classic view (opposite) of narrow gauge S.P. ten-wheeler 8 with ten cars and a caboose-coach, enroute between Laws and Owenyo just after World War II had ended.

...CARL FALLBERG SATIRIZED IT!

Artist Carl Fallberg, famous for his cartoon series, "Fiddletown & Copperopolis" in Railroad Magazine *and a book by the same name, satirized the Carson & Colorado in a loving and humorous manner. Fallberg started sketching the F&C to relieve the boredom of an east coast Marine camp during World War II. This drawing was the first of many.*

1876. LIGHTNING 1876.
EXPRESS!
New Arrangement, May 1st!

THROUGH TRAINS DAILY BETWEEN

VIRGINIA AND SAN FRANCISCO
VIA VALLEJO.

Passengers go Through Direct Each Way, between **VIRGINIA CITY** AND **SAN FRANCISCO,** via. **VALLEJO.**

Tickets Sold, and Baggage Checked To any point on either Line.

ONLY ONE TRANSFER. BAGGAGE CHECKED THROUGH.

DINNER on Boat from San Francisco, and Breakfast at Carson going East.

H. M. YERINGTON,
Gen'l Sup't V. & T. R. R.

E. NILES,
Gen'l Ticket Agent, V. & T. R. R.

EXPRESS FROM San Francisco.	JOINT TIME TABLE. VIRGINIA & TRUCKEE AND CENTRAL PACIFIC.	EXPRESS FROM Virginia.
Ar've 9.30 A. M.	--Virginia City.--	Leave 7.00 P. M.
9.18 "	---Gold Hill.---	7.13 "
8.40 "	-Mound House.-	7.45 "
Dp. 8.00 " Ar. 7.35 "	----Carson.----	8.25 " 8.40 "
6.45 "	--Steamboat.--	9.31 "
6.15 V. & T. TIME	------Reno.------	10.05 C. P. TIME
4.10 A. M.	----Truckee.----	12.00 AM
9.15 P. M.	---Sacramento.--	6.30 "
6.10 "	----Vallejo.----	9.10 "
Leave 4.00 P. M.	-San Francisco.-	Ar've 11.10 AM

SLEEPING CAR daily between Carson and Vallejo.

BREAKFAST on Boat from Vallejo going West.

A. N. TOWNE,
Gen'l Sup't C. P. R. R.

T. H. GOODMAN,
Gen'l P. & T. Agt., C. P. R. R.

PREFACE...DESERT COMMOTIONS

Looking down from the cockpit of a 727 at 37,000 feet, the Owens Valley appears much today as it must have looked to the pioneers and trappers of the early 1800's. Frontiersman Jedediah Strong Smith was the first white man to explore the area. In 1826, on a return trip from California, Smith found the long valley, wedged between the lofty Sierras, and the Inyo Mountains. Fed by runoff from the Sierra, the Owens Valley was green, save for the sagebrush of the east side. Even today, the prevailing winds dump their moisture laden clouds on the Pacific slope of the Sierra Nevada, leaving the area to the east largely barren. Smith made note of placer gold found near Mono Lake, two decades before Marshall's discovery at Sutter's Mill in 1849. Trappers and explorers like Joseph Reddeford Walker (1833) and a group from John C. Fremont's party (1845) entered the valley, happy to find water after hundreds of miles of harsh, sun-scorched sand, alkali flats and rocky mountain barriers. Owens Lake, on the southern end of the Valley, was named by Fremont in honor of Lt. Richard Owens, a member of the expedition. Following the discovery of gold in California, many pioneers attempted an ill-advised short cut through Death Valley, often with disastrous results. These groups included the Jayhawkers, Arcane, Bennett, Bier and Manly parties. Their stories have become a part of the legend of the Old West.

In 1852 Lieutenant Tredwell Moore on the trail of a renegade Indian, discovered gold in a ravine near Mono Lake. Leroy Vining also found gold near the town which today bears his name. By 1859 Mormon miners were at work near Mono, while nearby Dogtown was being settled. William J. Bodey found gold north of Mono and the town of Bodey (later Bodie) was founded. It would produce millions and its false front buildings still stand as a monument to the mines and miners. Soon silver strikes were made at Darwin, Kearsarge, Big Pine Creek, Benton and Mammoth. But they were brief-lived and for the most part the area continued to be the domain of the Piutes and the Bristlecone Pine, at over 4,600 years, the oldest living things on Earth.

Soon the discovery of the Comstock, centered around Virginia City, far overshadowed any developments in the isolated Owens Valley. In 1861, Samuel Bishop drove some 600 head of cattle from Fort Tejon, and founded the settlement of Bishop Creek. Lone Pine was settled as a trading center and supply point for the famous Cerro Gordo mines that same year. Fort Independence was established on July 4, 1862 and became the seat for the new county of Inyo, when it was formed in 1866. The Cerro Gordo silver strikes were followed by new strikes at Panamint and Union, while Bodie was teeming. Thus was the situation in 1880. With the mines of the Comstock reaching greater depths, with higher expenses and the prospect that they would soon "play-out," the promoters, miners, merchants and moneybags began to look elsewhere.

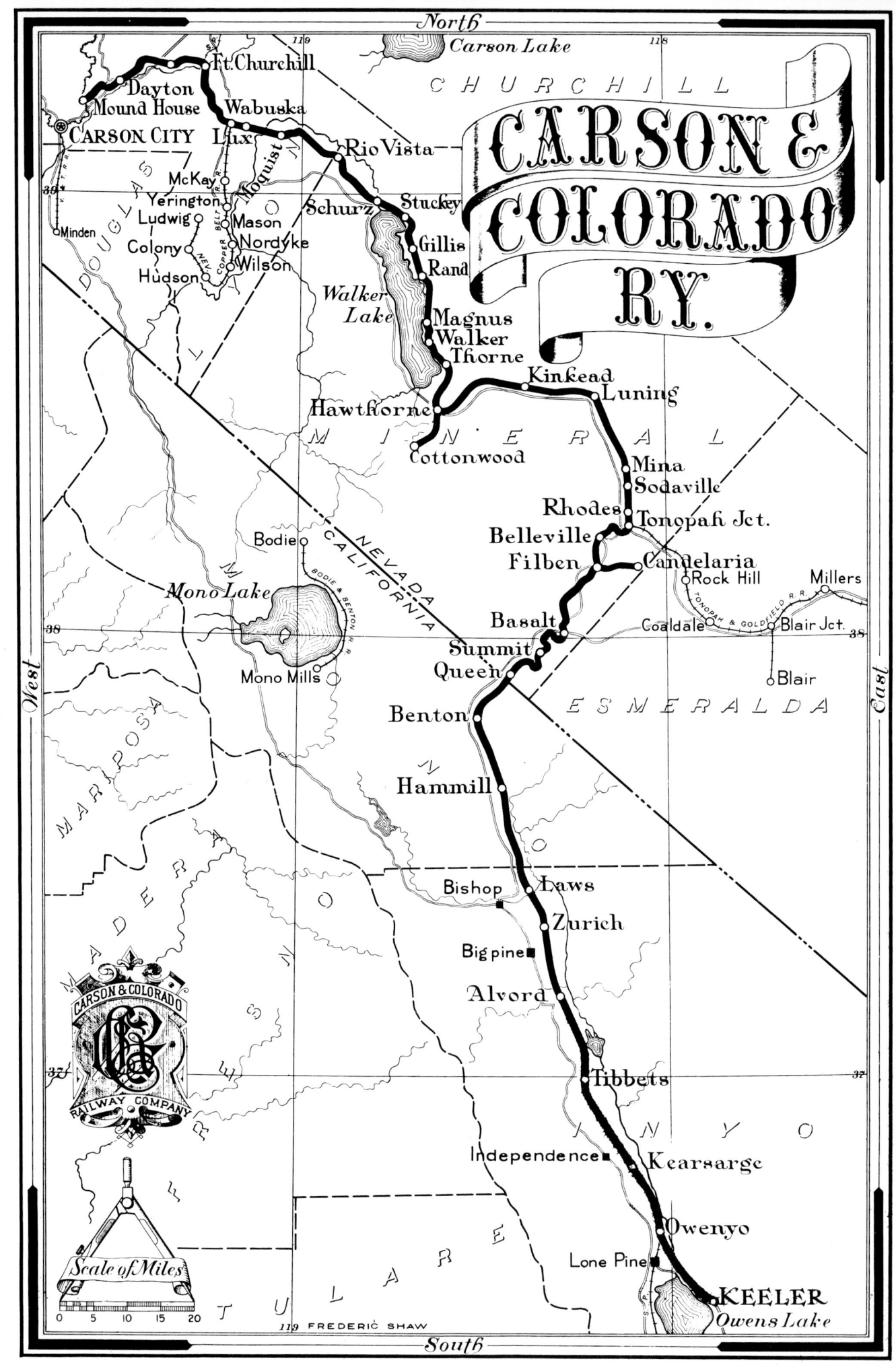

Map by Frederic Shaw from Grahame Hardy Collection.

THE SLIM PRINCESS

Nowhere else was there anything quite comparable to the Carson & Colorado's narrow gauge line. Steeped in the traditions of the Old West and the glimmerings of gold and silver bonanzas, it steamed through the beautiful land of barren contrasts, far outliving its reason for being and its equally narrow counterparts to become the last slim gauge common carrier in the far west.

The story of this line in its early days provides an insight into a spirited era of overnight fortunes, limitless enthusiasm and wild schemes that abounded in the Great Basin and rose and fell like the sparkle in a prospector's pan.

As early as 1871, a Carson City (Nevada) newspaperman had written, "Let us have a railroad from Carson City to the Colorado." In the seventies a lull in mining activity had settled upon the Comstock and Virginia City, but to the south reports of rich strikes filtered in from the sagebrush. Down in California, the Cerro Gordo and others in the Panamint Range near Death Valley stirred the imaginations of visionaries and promoters alike.

By the late 1870's several surveys had been made by the Virginia & Truckee Railway for a line south from Carson City. The first of these was made in 1876 for an extension to Genoa, and another to Wellington and on toward Bodie. No construction work was done on these plans. In 1878 preliminary surveys were made for another line to Bodie and detailed work was started the following year.

In January, 1880 the Virginia & Truckee sent out a survey crew from Mound House to run a line along the Carson River to Fort Churchill, south through the Mason Valley to Walker Lake and on to Bodie.

Ambitious William Sharon, who had risen from Virginia City agent for the Bank of California to become a United States Senator and one-third owner of the V&T, with winning persuasion convinced moneybags Darius Ogden Mills, bank president and major owner of the V&T, to build a narrow gauge railroad south to tap the mining camps that most surely would spring up like double eagles on a faro table.

The Carson & Colorado Railroad Company was incorporated on May 10, 1880. Henry Marvin Yerington was named President and General Manager, while Duane L. Bliss was Vice President. Bliss had been Sharon's Bank of California cashier at Gold Hill and was already associated with Yerington in the highly successful Carson & Tahoe Lumber & Fluming Company, which supplied timbers, finished lumber and cord wood to Carson City, Virginia City and other abuilding towns from the Lake Tahoe cutting areas. The C&TL&F firm utilized its own three foot gauge railroad from the mill at Glenbrook to the top of Spooner Summit, where a spectacular flume was built down to the Virginia & Truckee's wood yard in Carson. The directors of the new road included, in addition to Yerington and Bliss, D.A. Bender of the

A few examples of C&C memorabilia: tickets, passes and checks printed in an era of flourishing handwriting and typography. [All: Author's Collection]

V&T and S.P. Smith, who was D.O. Mills' agent. Neither Mills nor Sharon were directors of the new narrow gauge, but it was common knowledge that they, together with Nicholas Luning, controlled all but a few shares of the stock.

The announced destination of the Carson & Colorado was the silver mining camp of Candelaria, with eventual extension to an as yet undetermined point on the Colorado River. The Virginia City *Evening Chronicle* reported in April, 1880, that President Yerington stated, "the line would eventually be extended to a point in Colorado." However, it appears the reporter misunderstood Yerington, as there is no other evidence that the line was projected in that direction. A map appearing in the *Chronical* on April 9, 1881 shows the line heading directly south from Candelaria, through Columbus, Silver Peak and ending in the desert near the California state line, with branches to Lida and Bodie.

A factor in the rush to organize the Carson & Colorado Railroad was the survey work being pushed by J.C. McTarnahan in the summer of 1880 for the Western Nevada Railroad. The road would begin at Wadsworth (on the Central Pacific, east of Reno) and head south through the desert to Walker Lake, with branches to Bodie and Candelaria. When John T. Davis went to New York to raise funds for the new road in February, 1880, D.O. Mills learned of the project and wired Henry Yerington to begin construction on the Carson & Colorado immediately! The Western Nevada line was later reorganized as the Nevada-California-Oregon Railway and built a narrow gauge line north out of Reno to Lakeview, Oregon.

At a few minutes past noon on May 31, 1880, a special V&T train arrived at Mound House, ten miles east of Carson City. Aboard were Henry Yerington, Superintendent Robert L. Laws and 80 workmen. President Yerington walked out along the wooden stakes that marked the route and at 1:00 p.m. turned the first shovel of sand and announced, "I now in the name of the Carson & Colorado Railroad turn the first sod, may the road be carried on to successful issue." By the time the special left, Laws' crew, consisting mainly of unemployed Comstock miners, were at work on the grade. A great deal more than was generally known rested on the new narrow gauge road. The revenues of the parent V&T were declining with the Comstock. The previous year saw only one-fifth as much ore brought down the hill from Virginia City to the mills along the Carson River, as had been carried in previous years.

By late June, the 300 man grading crew was working through Dayton, while 200 Chinese were at work in Churchill Canyon. The orientals were so generally disliked by anglo crews that they were brought in from Wadsworth to avoid trouble. The white workers were paid $1.75 per day, but .75¢ was deducted for board. Many of these men had previously made up to $4 per day in the Comstock mines and mills and dissatisfaction and unrest was widespread. Graders at Camp Three (just east of Dayton) staged a strike for higher wages on July 1st. Marching west, they soon numbered "about a hundred" men as they descended on Camp One at Mound House. There some fifty workmen were "fired on the spot" and put on a special V&T work train by Superintendent Laws. The rest of the men returned to work at $1.75 per day, happy to at least have a job! Grading was pushed to the head of Walker Lake by late August.

Actual railroad supplies began arriving at Mound House in September. Here rails, spike kegs, ties and tons of supplies were piled up where the V&T and C&C would meet. By the end of October the grading crews had reached the site of Hawthorne and the Celestial laborers had been discharged, much to the ire of their gang boss Ah Quong. Carson & Colorado 4-4-0 number 1 was off loaded at Mound House on October 27, 1880. Track layers were already approaching Adolph Sutro's Ranch, just east of Dayton. The track left Mound House on a wide, sweeping curve, and headed east into the sagebrush and sand. Passing through Dayton, a small milling town of some 400 souls nestled beside the Carson River, the line crossed to the south side of its namesake and followed the canyon for the next 20 miles to the site of Fort Churchill (1861-1869), before turning south through a narrow canyon and into the Mason Valley. The citizens of Pizen Switch had renamed the spot Greenfield and then seeing that they would be some dozen miles from the C&C, quickly renamed the town Yerington in an effort to get the narrow gauge re-routed. The ploy did not work and Yerington would wait another three decades before the Nevada Copper Belt Railroad was built. The C&C did build a depot at Wabuska to serve the area. Continuing south, the line crossed the Walker River and followed it through the sagebrush country to Schurz. Following the prehistoric shoreline of Walker Lake for some 20 miles, the line was built on a level grade to the south end of the lake, where it dropped down into the lake valley.

It was here that Henry Yerington would lay out the townsite for his Division Point of Hawthorne. Already a cluster of tents had been erected near the junction of the new wagon road and the railroad grade, and the "town" was called Milbrae. The settlement included Jenks General Store, Mrs. White's Boarding House and a butcher shop operated by A.J. White. Hawthorne was named for W.A. Hawthorne, the contractor for the wagon road to Bodie, in the fall of 1880.

Each day saw the departure of six cars of rails and twelve cars of ties from the C&C interchange at Mound House, as the "Candelaria" steamed out of town. By mid-December, 1880, track gangs had spiked-down 14 miles of trackage as the "front" advanced behind the grading crews.

Near Schurz, the Carson & Colorado Railroad had to negotiate with the Piute Indians for a route across their Reservation. In return for a right-of-way, the C&C agreed to carry the Indians and their goods for free. As it turned out, the Piute had to ride atop the swaying freight cars. The C&C also installed spigots on locomotive tenders to provide free water . . . the C&C management was all heart!

On January 8, 1881 the first excursion was run from Mound House to Churchill Canyon, some 29 miles. Passengers were hauled aboard flatcars by Number 1, the "Candelaria." A freight train was run on January 28th, hauling supplies for Capt. Canavan's Naileigh Copper Mine. Baldwin locomotives Number 2 "Bodie" and Number 3 "Colorado" were in service and freight and passenger equipment began arriving from eastern car builders.

The tracks were spiked down to Hawthorne on April 18, 1881. Here the town had been laid-out, some 100 miles from Mound House. Hawthorne's townsite company was owned by the railroad and the first passenger train to that point was an excursion from Mound House to show off the new town and sell lots to the residents of Carson and Virginia City. Some 1,000 people rode open cars through the dusty desert. Nevertheless, the town grew. By August thirty houses had been

The Virginia & Truckee's morning "up" train to Virginia City, pauses on the Crown Point Trestle near Gold Hill, Nevada with Baldwin 4-4-0 Number 11, the "Reno". This trestle was constructed in 1869 and was 500' long and 85' high.

built and the new depot was being finished on F Street. The railroad built an enginehouse, shops, and the toll road westward over the mountains to Bodie. The company also planted trees. The new town became the Esmeralda County Seat, replacing the fading mining camp of Aurora in 1883.

Construction was pushed south from Hawthorne during the summer of 1881, heading up out of the valley in an easterly direction to Soda Springs Valley before turning south again on an easy grade to Soda Springs. This point would later be called Sodaville and would be the transfer point for the Tonopah gold rush in 1900.

Beyond Sodaville the Carson & Colorado turned west and leaving Excelsior Flat Valley, climbed the east slope of the Candelaria Mountains to Belleville. Service to Belleville was begun on the last day of 1881. This was the first sizeable settlement along the C&C since Dayton, 144 miles back.

The line from Mound House to Belleville had been through largely dry sagebrush country with few streams and little heavy grading or fill work. Construction had been on public lands, except across the Piute Reservation, with a minimum of expense to the railroad's owners. Laws' crews had spiked-down 150 miles of 35 pound narrow gauge trackage in a year and a half. Some rails were rolled as early as 1866 in Holland, while others came from Sheffield, England. These older rails had originally been purchased by the V&T and used by the C&C when rail shipments from eastern steel mills fell behind the demands of the tracklayers.

Timetable Number Seven, issued on January 1, 1882 showed Train One, the "Bodie and Candelaria Express," leaving Mound House daily at 9:30 a.m. and arriving in Belleville at 7:20 that evening. The northbound "San Francisco & Virginia Express," Number Two, departed Belleville at 7:45 a.m. and arrived at Mound House at 6:00 p.m., where passengers transferred to a connecting V&T train. Connections with the stage line for Bodie were made at Hawthorne, arriving in Bodie at 10:00 p.m.

The Slim Princess' tracks were pushed from a junction with the main line (Filben) on a 2.26% grade up the Canyon during the next two months, along the west slope of a rocky ridge and across a 292 foot long 50 foot high wooden trestle into Candelaria. A big celebration was held as the "Bodie" brought the first passenger train into the mining camp on February 28, 1882. Agent J.N. Barstow joined some 300 people in cheering as the 4-4-0 pulled her short consist into town. Regular service was extended from Belleville a few days later, with the "Bodie & Candelaria Express" arriving at 8:00 each evening.

A few weeks later, in March, 1882, the newly opened Candelaria depot was blown over by a strong wind. It flipped over into the canyon early one morning. Two men inside were shaken, but uninjured. The station was winched back to the same spot, but anchored to the foundation this time!

The Carson & Colorado's trackage at Candelaria was located high on the hillside above the town. The depot itself was located some distance from Main Street. The town boasted of 27 saloons and not a single church soon after the railroad arrived. The Northern Belle Mining Company immediately began shipping out ore over the C&C to their two 20 stamp mills at Belleville, while the Mount Diablo sent its ore to be processed at its Sodaville mill. The C&C used specially built four-wheel ore cars for this service. Nearly as important as the ore shipments were the cordwood, salt and other supplies hauled to the various stamp mills. Each stamp required 1,000 cords of pine each month to power its boiler.

The same year that the C&C arrived in Candelaria, the Candelaria Water Works & Mining Company built a large stamp mill at the head of Main Street and brought in water from the White Mountains in a 27 mile long pipeline. The C&C hauled out in excess of 65 tons of ore per day despite the local mills' competition.

The C&C was a financial success, despite the lack of thriving communities along its line; the road was turning a profit. By the end of 1882, gross revenues totaled $442,254, with a net profit of $111,103. Both Bodie and Candelaria were at their peak. Candelaria's major producers were the Northern Belle, Mount Diablo and Argentum Mines, which yielded $1,205,457 in silver ores the year the narrow gauge arrived. At Bodie the Standard Consolidated and the Bodie Consolidated Mining companies were the major producers. The town could count more than 1,500 people with more arriving daily. By the end of 1881 the mining camp had its own railroad, The Bodie Railway & Lumber Co. It is not surprising to find none other than Henry Yerington was behind this narrow gauge logging line that supplied lumber and timber to the rip-roaring camp made famous by Bret Harte's "Bad Man From Bodie".

No public notice had been given by the Carson & Colorado as to its intended final destination. There had been speculation for many months that the line would be extended into Southern California, but nothing official. However on December 1, 1881 articles of incorporation had been quietly filed in California for an extension of the line from the state line to Mojave on the Southern Pacific's line between San Francisco and Yuma. When the C&C reached Candelaria, the company announced that the line would not build beyond this point for "some time", but would eventually build branches to Bodie (from Hawthorne) and into Mono County, in the northern part of the Owens Valley.

On March 25, 1882 General Freight and Passenger Agent D.A. Bender announced that the C&C would build over Mt. Montgomery Pass and into the Owens Valley, toward Mojave. Bender went on to say that the road was profitable and had great potential for both mining and agriculture. It is interesting to note that the railroad was not ignoring farm traffic at this early date, as has been suggested by some historians. It is safe to assume that the quick profits and overnight bonanzas associated with silver mining made better "copy" than hay and grain shipments.

The mining camps in the Inyo Mountains, which border the Owens Valley on the east, had already created some excitement, namely at Panamint just west of Death Valley and at Cerro Gordo, high on the mountainsides above Hawley (soon to be renamed Keeler). The Darwin Mines were also producing silver, lead and zinc. Additional traffic was to be found in the soda and potash deposits near Owens Lake. High freighting costs had prevented their development in previous years.

As early as 1864, Francis Marion "Borax" Smith had been mining borax at Columbus (near Belleville), but he abandoned these operations in 1875 because of a lack of dependable transportation. In 1867 salt was being recovered from Teels Marsh and shipped to Virginia City by camels that had been imported from Africa. Despite Smith's failure with the Columbus operations, he later went on to greater glories in the borax business and built the narrow gauge Death Valley Railroad, the Tonopah & Tidewater Railroad, and played a major part in the development of the "Great American Desert."

In order to construct the Carson & Colorado into Owens Valley, two new companies were formed: Carson & Colorado Railroad, Second Division, which would build from Belleville, Nevada to the California state line and the Carson & Colorado Railroad, Third Division, to build south from the state line. Both companies were wholly owned by the original railroad and all trackage was operated under lease.

The extension was started in the spring of 1882, leaving the existing line two miles south of Belleville at a point called Junction (later Filben). The line was built on the gentle slope which opened onto Teels Marsh, and climbed a rocky canyon before beginning a winding three percent grade to Mt. Montgomery Pass. The Pass* was crested at 7,138 feet — higher than the Central Pacific's crossing of the Sierra at Donner Summit. Heading downgrade on the south side of the pass, a 247' tunnel was bored on the 2.3% grade down to the valley floor.

Benton station was reached in January, 1883, and served the nearby mining town. The tracks then dropped down into the Hammil Valley and on a gradual descent into the Owens Valley at Laws. Laws station was built to serve the nearby mining supply and farming community of Bishop Creek (now Bishop) on the west side of the valley. Laws was reached in mid-March, and was named for Robert C. Laws, the C&C's Superintendent.

Construction work south from Laws went at a rapid pace, with some 400 men on the job under the direction of Chief Engineer James T. Oliver, who had been placed in charge of all C&C location work south of Belleville. Workers spiked-down three-quarters of a mile of track per day and an excursion was run from Mound House to the end of iron on July 4, 1883. At the end of track, near Lone Pine, the excursionists went by wagon to Independence for the celebration. The locomotive's tender

*Mt. Montgomery Pass was also called McBride's Pass, and Buena Vista Pass.

was reported to have carried "a dozen gaudily painted Indians" on the trip down from Hawthorne. The C&C depot serving Independence was named Citrus (later Kearsarge).

The remaining 70 miles of trackage from Laws to Hawley on the shore of Owens Lake was completed in July 1883. This line did not pass through a single established town between Belleville and Hawley (143 miles).

No explanation was given by the C&C for the route selected through the Owens Valley. It seems likely that the decision was based on economic factors. The populated western side of the valley was also bisected by numerous small streams that flowed down from the nearby Sierra. By locating the trackage on the east side, much bridging and grading was avoided and there would be no threat of washouts. Water had been a problem on the northern part of the line, where Carson River flooding around Dayton had put the line under water on several occasions.

Lone Pine had been hit by an earthquake in 1872, which had killed 26 people and opened up a large void in the valley floor. But, whatever the reason for putting the tracks on the desolate east side of the valley, the people in the established towns were not happy about it! Of the existing communities (Lone Pine, Independence, Big Pine and Bishop Creek) only Lone Pine was to ever see rail service. A line was graded between Laws and Bishop Creek, but tracks were never spiked-down. Likewise a line from Benton Station to Benton was talked about, but never built.

As completed, the Carson & Colorado Railroad extended 293 miles from Mound House, Nevada to Hawley, California; with a six mile branch from Junction to Candelaria. The line had been built at a minimum cost, a maximum distance in a short period of time. Heavy grading had been avoided as much as possible. There were but two large trestles, on the Candelaria branch and only one tunnel, just south of Mt. Montgomery Pass. The maximum grade of 2.77 percent had been reached just north of Belleville, while the crossing of the summit was made with a 2.30 percent gradient. (Grade on the twisting Candelaria branch had been held to 2.33 percent.) The road boasted eight wood burning Baldwin 4-4-0s, six wooden passenger cars, and 138 freight cars.

Upon completion of the line, an Inauguration Special was run the entire length of the road on July 12, 1883. Aboard the special were Henry Yerington, accompanied by Darius Mills, William Sharon and other officials of the C&C. After riding through desert heat from Mound House to Hawley, Mills is quoted by both Kneiss and Beebe as turning to his companions and saying: "Gentlemen, either we built this line 300 miles too long, or 300 years too soon."

Regular train service was begun on August 1, 1883. At Hawley a new enginehouse, turntable, and depot were under construction. Captain James M. Keeler started steamboat service on Owens Lake in order to deliver cordwood from the Sierra foothills to the mill at Hawley. The C&C management was impressed enough to rename the end of the line Keeler. High up in the Inyo Mountains above Keeler, the Cerro Gordo was producing silver ore and could now afford to ship lower grade ores over the C&C to Belleville's mills.

The managements of the Virginia & Truckee Railway and the Carson & Colorado Railroad were closely interlocked. Henry Yerington was general manager of the V&T and president of the C&C. D.A. Bender was general passenger and freight agent for both roads and the C&C shared the Carson City main office with the V&T. Robert L. Laws, the superintendent of the C&C, was not an employee of the V&T and his office was in the narrow gauge road's Hawthorne depot. Of course, D.O. Mills, William Sharon and Nicholas Luning owned most of the stock in both roads. It is interesting to note that while Yerington and Bliss sat on the boards of both roads, (and Mills after 1892) that no other person sat on the boards of both lines.

The directors of the C&C upon its completion in 1883 were:
    Henry M. Yerington (also president)
    Duane L. Bliss (also vice-president)
    W.D. Tobey (Bliss' brother-in-law)
    Lloyd Tevis (president of Wells Fargo Bank)
    John Forbes
    S.P. Smith

Major repairs and car building for the C&C were handled at the huge stone shop of the parent road in Carson City. Narrow gauge equipment had to be loaded aboard a flatcar for the ten mile trip from Mound House to the Carson shop.

Completion of the Carson & Colorado Railroad seems to have signaled a decline in the mining prosperity of the region it served. Agriculture appears to have benefited more from the construction of the "Slim Princess". Huge quantities of hay as well as meat and vegetables were shipped over the narrow gauge to the mining districts. Soon cattle ranches sprang up in the valleys, with sheep and cattle shipments providing the C&C with a good source of traffic.

After 1883, the once rich silver mines at Candelaria began to play out. 1885 was the big year for Bodie, although mining continued on a smaller scale for years. The overnight stop, which was once made at Candelaria was pulled back to Hawthorne, and then to Sodaville as the mining fortunes declined. Candelaria's population went from 750 (1880) to 595 (1890) and to 160 (1900). The National Belle Mine closed in 1884 and soon the Mount Diablo and Argentum had also quit.

All through this period, the question was repeatedly asked by the area's press: "When would the C&C extend its tracks to Mojave?" Each time the question was asked, the C&C sidestepped the answer.

In June, 1887, D.A. Bender was quoted as saying the extension

Virginia City

The Queen of the Comstock provided the mineral wealth that financed both the Virginia & Truckee and its narrow gauge offspring the Carson & Colorado. The V&T's "Reno" awaits departure time (above) during the 1880's. [Nevada State Museum] Nearby was the Consolidated Virginia Mining Company, with V&T combine 16, Central Pacific's Palace Car 2 and a V&T Kimball coach. [Huntington Library]

Lake Tahoe Narrow Gauge

In order to supply lumber, mine timbers and cordwood to the Comstock mines, mills and towns, the Carson & Tahoe Lumber & Fluming Company was organized by Henry Yerington of the V&T and Duane Bliss, who was William Sharon's Gold Hill cashier. The highly successful operation saw timber logged from around Lake Tahoe and brought from the mills at Glenbrook to the top of Spooner Summit by a three foot gauge railroad. A flume took the products down to the V&T's wood yard at Carson City, where the Number 9 switched loads (right) in 1876. The C&T&L&F's "Tahoe" is shown on the line's switchback in 1876. [Author's Collection and Nevada State Museum.] The "Tahoe" is shown (opposite) with her crew in a pair of views from the early 1880's at Glenbrook. [Guy Dunscomb Collection.]

would be built, but on September 28th a reporter for *Railway World* was successful in obtaining an interview with D.O. Mills in which Mills was quoted as saying: "We don't know ourselves. There is no doubt its extension would be a great benefit to Reno. Of course, it will be extended, it is merely a question of time."

The line was extended that year, but only two miles south of Keeler to the old Cerro Gordo boat landing. (Jiggerville) This construction was necessary to comply with the original charter, but caused a brief flurry of rumors that the C&C was building toward Mojave.

In 1887 a long spur track was built five miles north of Keeler to Israel Luce's Inyo Marble Works. The only major business provided by this addition was 200 cars of white marble shipped out in 1890 for construction of the Mills' building in San Francisco.

In 1888 an enginehouse and turntable were constructed at Belleville, the result of a brief upturn in mining.

In 1890 the only major addition to the Carson & Colorado was constructed. On August 17th, beginning with an extension to the Hawthorne wye track, crews started the 7.30 mile Cottonwood Branch. The line was completed that fall and began to haul cordwood for both the mines, mills and the railroad itself.

The C&C was reorganized in 1892, with the capital stock left intact, but the funded debt reduced from $4,380,000 to $2,000,000, and the interest rate reduced from six to four percent. It was at this time that the three companies that built the road were consolidated as the Carson & Colorado Railway. Darius O. Mills became a Director, replacing Duane L. Bliss. George Whitell, another Tahoe lumberman became Vice President, while Yerington, Bender and Smith stayed in their previous positions. New members to the C&C board were: W.M. Randol, J.M. Allen, John W.C. Maxwell and W.S. Wood. This reorganization was essentially a financial maneuver as Mills still owned the road, Sharon was dead and operations continued unchanged under Superintendent Laws.

The Carson & Colorado itself reflected the steady decline in mining and resultant loss of traffic, constantly losing money after 1885. Revenues continued to decline through the 1890's. While operating expenses were being met, no interest was being paid on stocks and bonds. Maintenance was neglected and the company made do with the original equipment, as funds were not available for new cars and locomotives. By 1897 the road took in only $131,096, less than a third of its 1883 earnings. The decline of silver prices as result of the Silver Panic of 1893 did not help the V&T nor the C&C.

No directors' meetings were held between May, 1896 and March, 1900. Mills was in his New York office trying to forget he ever built the C&C.

So, as the century ended, the Carson & Colorado Railway continued to struggle through the desert — illogical, improbable, ill-conceived and unlikely, it traveled its yard wide trackage and awaited the big bonanza.

Mound House

The initial point of construction for the new narrow gauge Carson & Colorado Railroad was a point on the high desert known as Mound House. At this junction with the Virginia & Truckee, ten miles east of Carson City, the new C&C was projected and built almost 300 miles into the barren vastness on the east side of the high Sierra. An early construction train of the C&C with 4-4-0 Number 3 waits at Mound House in 1882. The cars are filled with lumber, rails, ties, Wells, Fargo Express and soon the combine and coach will be filled with passengers from the connecting V&T train which has just pulled in from Carson. [University of Nevada.] The smaller view shows the V&T's own facilities at Mound House just before C&C construction began. [C.E. Watkins from Guy Dunscomb.]

C&C Interchange
A mixed train of the Carson & Colorado waits at Mound House (opposite top) in 1882. The standard gauge V&T tracks are on the left, headed toward Virginia City. The C&C boxcar is lettered "Wells, Fargo & Company Fast Express." [University of Nevada.] The Mound House depot had seen better days (opposite, lower) and was no longer in use by the 1930's. [Louis Stein.] The C&C's 4-4-0 "Colorado" pauses at Mound House (this page) with a short consist, which includes a "tin flatcar" (No. 49) and caboose coach in 1883. [A.E. Barker Collection.]

Trouble at Dayton
A Carson & Colorado 4-4-0 and her train has derailed and wrecked in Daney Canyon in 1881-82. The "Ernie Birdsall", a Baldwin 2-4-2T from the Lyon Mill & Mining Company, at nearby Dayton, has come to the scene with a rescue train as officials and onlookers view the mess. The two C&C cars on the track are "tin boxes", part of a group of all metal cars bought by the C&C. [University of Nevada Collection.] The Dayton depot is seen in the smaller view. The structure has since been moved, but still exists, while the depot sign hangs at a local service station. Dayton had been a Pony Express station in the 1860's. [Author.]

Construction Train at Wabuska
As the Carson & Colorado's railhead was pushed forward during 1881, construction materials were hauled greater distances from Mound House. Daily construction trains brought in rails, ties, timbers and supplies. By early spring rails had reached Wabuska, and C&C Number 3, the "Colorado", is shown (above) with a mixed train on fresh track. The same engine is shown (opposite) passing through Wabuska in 1883. [Both: Hugh Tolford Collection.] As the tracks were laid across the high desert toward Hawthorne, workmen lived in construction trains such as the one shown (opposite lower) in 1881. [A.E. Barker Collection.]

The first excursion train to reach the site of Hawthorne, Nevada was run on April 14, 1881 for the purpose of auctioning lots in the new town. The train is shown on the north edge of town that day. [Stanley Paher Collection.] The "Darwin" is seen at Hawthorne in the mid-1880's with her crew. [A.E. Barker Collection.]

Hawthorne

Hawthorne became the C&C's operating headquarters and soon boasted extensive facilities. Number 6, the "Hawthorne" pauses (above) at her namesake town in about 1900. [Author's Collection.] The layout included twin enginehouses and coaling dock. Eucalyptus trees were planted by the C&C to provide shade. The terminal is seen (opposite) in 1901. [Ken Kidder.] Number 5, "Belleville", takes on coal in c.1900 in a photo from the Gerald M. Best Collection. The twin enginehouses are shown (opposite, lower) in May, 1896. [Author's Collection.]

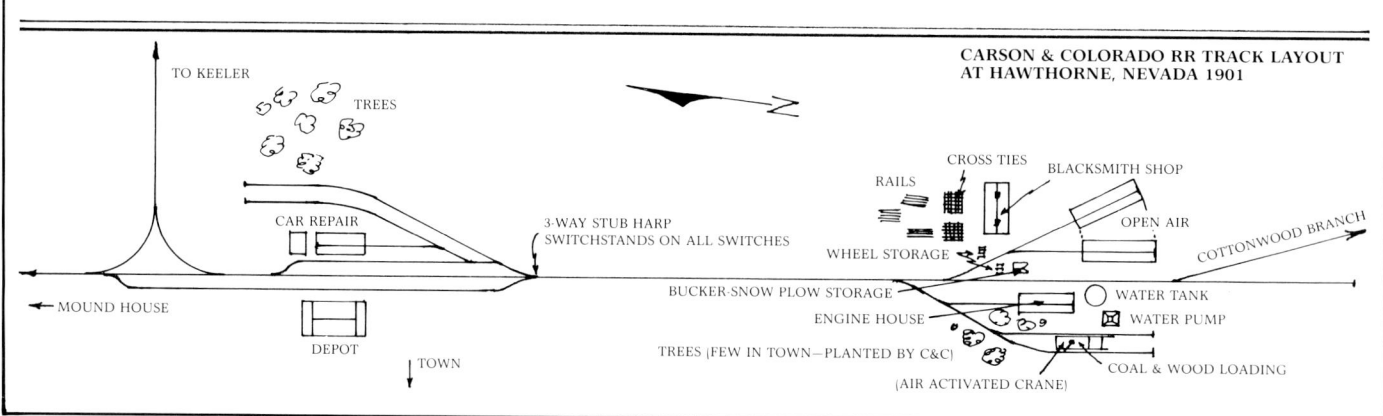

CARSON & COLORADO RR TRACK LAYOUT AT HAWTHORNE, NEVADA 1901

CARSON AND COLORADO RAILROAD.

TIME TABLE No. 7.

To take Effect on Sunday, January 1st, 1882, at 7.45 A. M.

For the Government and Information of Employés only.

1. Bodie and Candelaria EXPRESS.		Miles from Mound House.	STATIONS.	Miles from Belleville.	2 San Francisco & Virginia EXPRESS.	
9.30	A. M. LV.	0	Lv MOUND HOUSE Ar	150	6.00	P. M. AR.
10.00		6	DAYTON 6.0	144	5.25	
10.45		18	CLIFTON 8.0	132	4.45	
11.20		26	FT. CHURCHILL 2.0	124	4.12	
11.26		28	WASHOUT 10.0	122	4.05	
12.00	M.	38	WABUSKA 4.0	112	3.25	
12.15 / 12.30	P. M.	42	CLEAVER 3.0	108	3.10	
12.40		45	MASON 9.0	105	3.00	
1.10		54	RIO VISTA 4.0	96	2.25	
1.25		58	RESERVATION 7.0	92	2.10	
1.47		65	SCHURZ 13.0	85	**1.47**	
2.30		78	GILLIS 22.0	72	1.00	P. M.
3.40 / 4.10		100	HAWTHORNE 10.0	50	11.45 / 10.45	
4.43		110	STANSFIELD 3.2	40	10.05	
4.53		113	KINKEAD 11.8	36	9.55	
5.33		125	LUNING 6.0	25	9.15	
5.56		131	NEW BOSTON 6.0	19	8.55	
6.15 / 6.30		137	SODA SPRINGS 6.0	13	8.35	
6.50		143	RHODES 7.0	7	8.15	
7.20	P. M. AR.	150	Ar BELLEVILLE Lv	0	7.45	A. M. LV.

J. R. KING, Train Dispatcher, is authorized to move trains by Telegraph or otherwise.
Full Faced Figures denote meeting and passing places. Trains run Daily.
The attention of Trainmen is particularly called to the Rules and Regulations printed on the back of this card, as they will be strictly enforced.

H. M. YERINGTON, Gen'l Supt.   W. H. CRISLER, Master Transportation.   R. J. LAWS, Asst. Supt.

Belleville Mills

The milling town of Belleville, Nevada was reached by the C&C's tracks in late 1881. It was the first sizable established town on the railroad since Dayton, some 144 miles back. The National Belle Mills processed ore from Candelaria. The twin mills are shown (above). The C&C depot and water tank are located on the flat, beyond the town, where a 4-4-0 is turning on the wye. A C&C 4-4-0 is shown switching the National Belle in 1882, with a string of four-wheel ore cars. [Both: University of Nevada.] Timetable Number 7 was the first to show the service to Belleville. [Author's Collection.] The branch to Candelaria left the main line at Fiben, where a stub switch and harp switchstand saw service into the 1930's. [Gerald M. Best.]

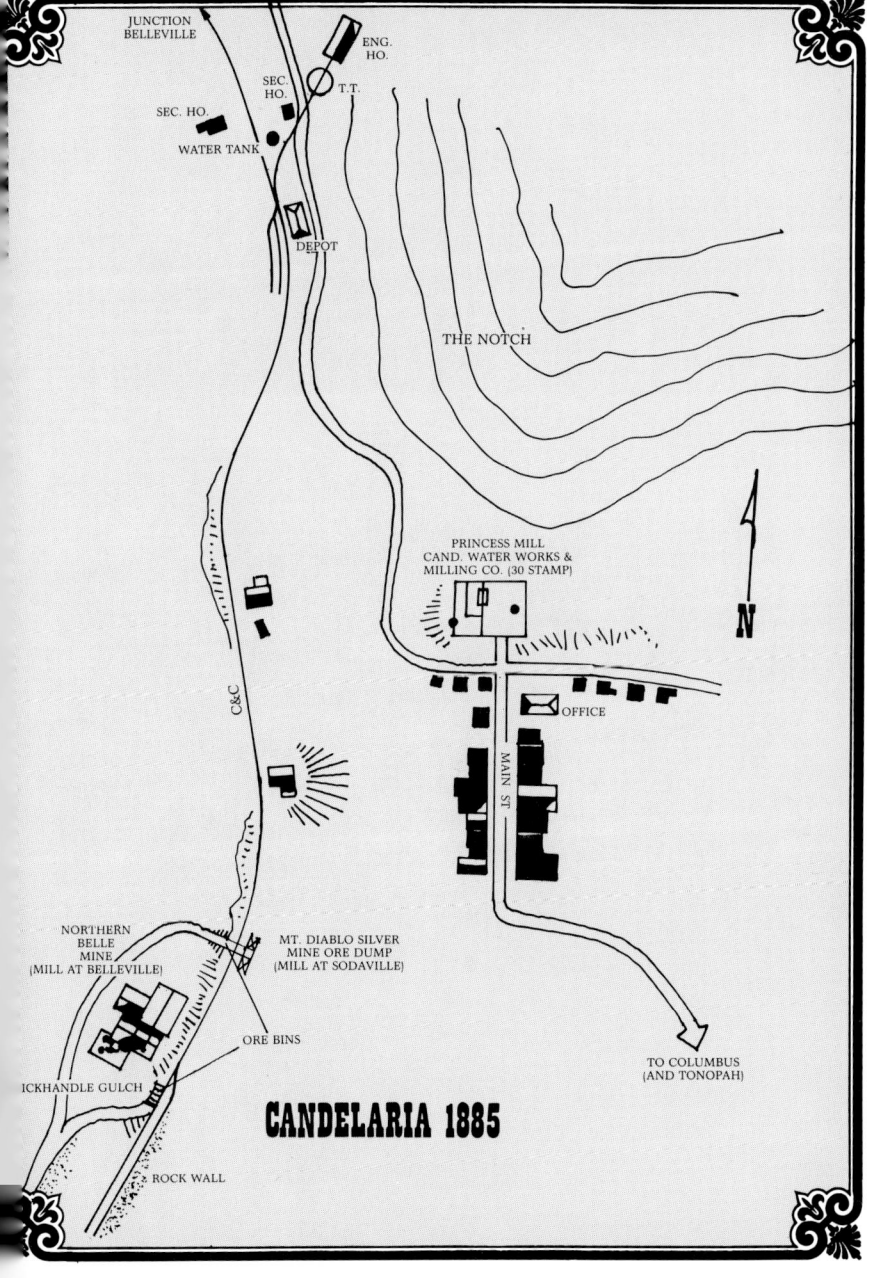

Candelaria Silver

After a steep climb up a 2.26% grade, the Carson & Colorado's tracks reached the silver camp of Candelaria in February, 1882. The tracks were high above the camp on the hillside. The above view looks down on the town in 1882. [Hugh Tolford Collection.] At left a C&C 4-4-0 leads an ore train across the 292 foot long, 50 foot high trestle on the branch in 1885. The cars were former V&T ore cars that have been regauged for the C&C. The C&C train (opposite, lower) works the Northern Belle Mine and the Mt. Diablo Silver Mine dump that same year. The wooden ore cars are numbered 1-14. [Both: University of Nevada.] Northern Belle ore went to their two 20 stamp mills at Belleville; while Mt. Diablo ore was sent over the C&C to the Sodaville mill.

Candelaria Depot
The Candelaria depot was located on the hillside above the town. The building was blown off its foundations by a windstorm shortly after construction in 1882. Number 7, the "Benton", poses with her crew in 1884 (above). Wood burning Number 5, the "Belleville" was photographed (opposite top) in 1896. Candelaria boasted 27 saloons and not a single church. The town's main street is shown (opposite lower) in 1893. The Candelaria Water Works & Mining Company Mill was built at the head of the street in 1882, while the C&C depot was on the hillside to the left [Hugh Tolford Collection.]

Completion of the C&C appears to have signaled a decline in Candelaria's silver mining fortunes. The National Belle Mine closed in 1884 and was soon followed by the Mt. Diablo and Argeutum. However mining continued on a reduced scale for many years. Three miners prepare to go underground (opposite top) at the Holmes shaft in 1890. They were Captain Ashby, Fred Corkill and Johnny Lawler. Candelaria's main street looked quiet (opposite lower) in 1893. The camp was still served by the C&C, with the "Churchill" shown at the depot in 1898 with a passenger train. The crew was Bill Robinson, Engineer; Charles Meadows, Mail Clerk; Fred Barnes, Conductor; John McGillis, Fireman and Frank Regan, Brakeman. (Hugh Tolford Collection) Winter on the branch often required a snow bucking train to clear the line such as the one shown in the 1880's. [Stanley Paher Collection.]

Montgomery Pass
Mount Montgomery Pass was crested at 7,138 feet above sea level in 1882, but not without difficulty. The line from Belleville used a twisting right-of-way on a 2.77 percent grade. Just south of the pass, a 247 foot tunnel was bored on the 2.3 percent downgrade. The tunnel is seen (above) with a mixed train behind the "Hawthorne" in 1888. [Hugh Tolford.] Today the portals are largely obscured on the desolate pass. [Wendell Mortimer.] A four car mixed train is depicted (opposite top) nearing Mt. Montgomery Pass in the 1880's. Just south of the pass, the line crossed into California, and the same train shown on the opposite page is seen again at the state line marker, with an interesting assortment of passengers and crew. [Hugh Tolford Collection.]

Bodie & Hawley Express
With the completion of the Carson & Colorado to Hawley in 1883, the daily passenger (mixed) train was named the "Bodie & Hawley Express". Bodie was not on the railroad and Hawley was soon renamed Keeler. The northbound run to Mound House was named the "San Francisco & Virginia Express". The nature of the mixed consist "express" can be seen (above) as it prepares to depart Hawthorne, with Number 6. [Hugh Tolford.] The "Hawthorne" is shown (opposite lower) at Keeler in 1885, while the top view shows "C&C employees at the Wells, Fargo & Co. office" at Keeler in 1887. Next door was the Palace Saloon. [Author's Collection.]

Inyo Development Company

Keeler was not only the end of the line for the C&C, but the desert town had its own three foot gauge feeder. The Inyo Development Company was formed in 1885 by D.O. Mills to recover soda ash from Owens Lake. In 1902 the firm purchased a former Eureka & Palisade 2-6-0 from the Bodie & Benton, and had the Mogul rebuilt by the Virginia & Truckee's Carson Shop. The I.D.C. locomotive is seen enroute to Keeler (above) in 1902. [Ken Kidder Collection.] The engine had a front plate that stated "Rebuilt by V&T Ry Carson", and is seen (opposite lower) at Hawthorne that same year. [Author's Collection.] The Inyo Development Company used four wheel "ore" cars that were built by the V&T (opposite top) for the Owens Lake operation. The view was made in 1904 and shows two foot gauge push cars and tracks in the foreground. [Hugh Tolford Collection.]

Carson & Colorado's Number 3 waits at Tonopah Junction in 1905. The "Colorado" has been converted to burn coal, and has an extended smokebox with straight stack, air brakes and converted gas headlight. [Wyoming State Archives.]

❷
BONANZA IN THE DESERT

With the decline of silver mining, the glitter of the Comstock was all but gone, and with it the glory of the once proud Virginia & Truckee and its slim gauge offspring the Carson & Colorado.

When the Southern Pacific Railway offered Darius Ogden Mills $2,750,000 for the desert narrow gauge in March 1900, Mills promptly accepted. By this time Sharon and Luning were long dead and Mills, never happy with the line, had discounted rumors of rich strikes in the southern deserts. Mills had by this time retired to New York where he was content to "play" with his banking, hotel and railroad investments and live off the spoils of a now fading Comstock.

However, the reports were accurate this time. District Attorney Jim Butler, of Nye County, Nevada, enroute to his ranch on May 17, 1900 had been delayed on business in Belmont and was forced to camp out on a ridge in the San Antonio Mountains, 70 miles south of Sodaville. The next morning he noticed an outcropping of ore and took a sample with him. Butler later gave the ore specimen to a friend, who sent it to a school teacher at Austin, who assayed the rock. The school teacher wrote to Butler saying that the ore contained large quantities of gold. Butler returned to the discovery site and started digging the ore. The discovery was the greatest bonanza since the silver strikes on the Comstock. The new "boom" town of Tonopah sprung up near Jim Butler's find.

Word of the new bonanza came less than two months after the Southern Pacific's purchase of the Carson & Colorado. Collis P. Huntington, the last of the "Big Four," and President of the SP visited the C&C line in late May, 1900. The *San Francisco Call* reported that "it is undoubtedly the intention of Huntington to extend the road to Reno, where it will join the Central overland". The June 1, 1900 edition of the *Call* stated that the C&C route would result in a "shortening of about 350 miles from the Southern part of the state to the East", and that the SP intended to change the track to standard gauge.

Almost overnight, the gross revenues of the Carson & Colorado Railway shot upward. From a low in 1899 of $146,238 the revenues had reached $466,205 by 1903. Soon the income of the narrow gauge totaled more in a single year than in the entire decade of the 1890's. This huge increase in traffic also proved to be a windfall for the Virginia & Truckee as freight and passengers destined for the new mining camps moved over the V&T line from Reno to Mound House. Here the freight was reloaded to the three foot gauge for the run through canyon and desert country to Sodaville, nearest rail point to the Tonopah gold fields.

Soon the platforms at Mound House and Sodaville were full of shipments to the new camps and the C&C was taxed to handle the traffic. On the V&T traffic was backed-up on sidings along the line, while the SP was reported to have "over 400 carloads sidetracked at Sparks", awaiting delivery to the V&T and C&C.

The need for standard gauging was apparent as shipments filled depots and overloaded platforms along the line from Mound House to Sodaville. Wells Fargo & Company Express shipments were getting through however, and one enterprising man sent 2,000 bricks by express over C&C to Goldfield! The shipper paid a premium price for his bricks; reportedly the express bill was $682. Soon an embargo was placed on the C&C and lasted two and a half months before the beleaguered road could get caught up.

Beginning in September, 1900 the C&C began converting their eight 4-4-0s from woodburners to coal. The diamond stacks were replaced with straight stacks and modifications were made to the firebox grates, smokebox and tenders in the V&T's huge stone "fort" at Carson City. With the declining demand for cordwood, the Cottonwood Branch out of Hawthorne was abandoned. (Rails removed in August, 1902.) Conversion of the engines was completed in the fall of 1901.

During the middle week of February, 1901, Carson & Colorado Superintendent Robert L. Laws was out on the line between Mound House and Wabuska, surveying the line for a possible third rail. After the SP take over, Laws was retained in his previous position, while the railroad's name was also unchanged. The SP named J. Kruttschnitt as General Manager; Jas. Agler, Manager and G.F. Richardson as Superintendent of Transportation of their Carson & Colorado Railway.

Down in the Owens Valley the National Reclamation Service and local ranchers and farmers were building an irrigation system in 1903 that soon turned the barren desert into a green agricultural area. But Los Angeles, 250 miles to the southwest, would soon purchase the water rights and build an aqueduct from the Sierras that would see the valley return to its desert profile.

Failing in an attempt to purchase the Virginia & Truckee Railway from D.O. Mills, the SP made plans to build its own standard gauge line from Hazen, on the main line, to Fort Churchill on the C&C, thus bypassing the famous short line completely.

On February 19, 1904 the first rails for the Tonopah Railroad were spiked into position at Tonopah Junction. This narrow gauge railroad was completed to Tonopah on July 23rd of that year, and operated into the C&C's yards at Sodaville via trackage rights. The Tonopah Railroad ordered 15 freight cars built by J.S. Hammond's California Car Works, in San Francisco; and several 2-6-0s built by the Baldwin Locomotive Works in Philadelphia. However, service was started with a used 2-8-0 from the Nevada-California-Oregon Railway and an array of three foot gauge cars from the Carson & Colorado and the recently standard gauged South Pacific Coast line from Alameda to Santa Cruz, California. At the height of the boom, additional motive power was brought in from the Denver & Rio Grande.

Standard gauging the C&C from Mound House to Tonopah Junction was begun in October, 1904 by Japanese labor crews. The 4' 8½" rails were laid outside of the narrow gauge tracks with longer crossties being substituted every few feet. As the dual gauge was pushed forward, the transfer point was relocated. Wabuska was reached by the four rail track in late February, 1905; later Schurz and then Hawthorne on June 24, 1905. Sodaville was reached in July.

As the dual gauging progressed, some trackage realignments were also made, namely the reduction of some sharp curves at Mound House, Dayton and a 15.8 mile relocation that bypassed Hawthorne.

The Southern Pacific sent some one thousand men to Hazen in April, 1905 to begin work on the 28 mile line to Fort Churchill. The grading and track crews advanced rapidly across the flat cattle country and the line was completed on September 1, 1905. A new terminal and town was established at Mina, nine miles north of Tonopah Junction. The Tonopah Railroad converted its tracks to standard gauge in one day — Sunday, August 14, 1905, allowing passengers and freight to ride all the way to Tonopah without a transfer to the slim gauge. The Tonopah Railroad had lasted only one year and one month as a narrow gauge pike. The Tonopah line gained trackage rights over the old C&C from the Junction to Mina, while beyond that point the road was still three foot gauge all the way to Keeler.

Sodaville, Nevada had long been a milling town and station on the Carson & Colorado, but became a "boom" town in 1901, as the closest rail connection to the Tonopah Gold Rush. This was Sodaville's main street in 1902. [Hugh Tolford Collection.]

On May 11, 1905 the entire Carson & Colorado Railway became a part of the new Nevada & California Railway, which was formed by the SP to effect a through line from Hazen, Nevada to Mojave, California. (Salt Lake Division timetable Number 7, January 1, 1906 was the first to show the old C&C as a part of the SP, under the N&C herald.)

The selection of Mina as a servicing point was no accident. When the SP took over the C&C in 1900, Hawthorne had been the main operating base with dual enginehouses, shop, wye and operating offices in the depot. With the Tonopah discovery, a turntable, roundhouse and water tank were built at Sodaville. Following construction of the Tonopah Railroad in 1904, this line used the C&C tracks from Tonopah Junction to Sodaville, utilizing the C&C facilities there. As Tonopah business increased, it became apparent that the Sodaville terminal would have to be expanded. However, local rancher Bob Stewart had given a land speculator an option on the surrounding terrain and its water rights, and he was demanding $100,000 for the option. The SP simply backed up 3.8 miles and established a brand new town at a point where good water and cheap land was available. The year 1904 saw further gold discoveries at Goldfield and even more traffic over the line. Hawthorne not only lost its place as a railroad center in 1905, due to the line relocation, it lost its status as the Esmeralda County seat when booming Goldfield was selected in 1907. (It again became a county seat when Mineral County was formed in 1911.)

Mina had several hundred residents by the end of 1905, most of them were railroad employees and their families. The yards along Front Street were filled with dual gauge trackage, with narrow gauge

The Tonopah Gold Rush saw the S.P.'s Carson & Colorado Ry. hard pressed for equipment. This narrow gauge Baldwin 4-4-0 was the former San Joaquin & Sierra Nevada Number 1026. She was found at Hawthorne in October, 1904. [Hugh Tolford Collection.]

locomotives being serviced in the eastern end of the eleven stall enginehouse.

In 1908 Cerro Gordo's silver mine staged a brief revival. The town, located high up in the Inyo Mountains above Keeler, had once seen a population of several thousand. It was at this time that a spectacular cable tramway was constructed from the mine down to the tramway terminal on the N&C, south of the Keeler depot. This particular excitement, one of many at Cerro Gordo, was brief-lived. The camp still stands, like a sentinel between Owens Valley and Death Valley, its equipment kept greased by a caretaker. Largely abandoned, it waits for the day when the miners will return.

The Southern Pacific finally made good on Henry Yerington and Darius Mills' promise of the 1880's when it began construction of a line from Mojave in the summer of 1908. But the line, built as a part of the N&C, was standard gauge, and lacked the spirit that had forged the old Carson & Colorado. "The Jawbone" line joined the N&C narrow gauge at Owenyo, which first showed up on C&C timetables as a short desert spur track, 15.9 miles north of Keeler, in 1903. Unlike Mina, Owenyo had no dual gauge trackage. "The Jawbone" was completed in 1910, and was instrumental in hauling supplies for construction of the aqueduct system from the valley to Los Angeles.

After much name calling, some name changing and a brief turn-of-the-century return to the old days of ore hauling and mining booms, the remaining 159.7 miles of narrow gauge was left to its own means. Unwanted and almost forgotten, its diminutive trains still scaled the pass and rolled off the desert miles, making do with mixed trains and mixed consists. The bonanza was over.

TONOPAH GOLD RUSH!

The gold strikes at Tonopah created an influx of people and supplies after the turn of the century, as the towns of Tonopah and Goldfield sprang up out on the Nevada desert. Most of the miners and supplies came in over the Carson & Colorado and the narrow gauge Tonopah Railroad which was opened in July, 1904. The yard at Tonopah is filled with three foot gauge cars lettered for the C&C, Tonopah RR and South Pacific Coast in this 1905 scene. [Wyoming State Archives.] Motive power was brought in from the SPC, and San Joaquin & Sierra Nevada, roads recently standard gauged. The 1026 of the SJ&SN was found at Sodaville in 1905. [Hugh Tolford Collection.]

Photographs of Tonopah during the brief one year period in which the Tonopah RR was narrow gauge are rare. In this pair of glass plates, exposed in 1905 by Cheyenne photographer J.E. Stimson, the yards are visible at left center, with several locomotives working the three foot gauge. [Wyoming State Archives.] The Tonopah Railroad's Number 1 (top), was outshoped by Baldwin in 1904. [Broadbelt Collection.]

TONOPAH R.R.

During the Tonopah Rush, equipment from throughout the west was brought in to haul supplies into camp and the ores out. As with all mining "booms", more materials, machinery, lumber, food and other supplies were hauled into the mining camp, than products of the mines were hauled out. In this view, ore is stacked for shipment on the Tonopah platform. Denver & Rio Grande 2-8-0, Number 66, works the yard, which is filled with Tonopah RR and Carson & Colorado cars. A Tonopah Railroad 2-6-0's capped stack is visible at left. [Wyoming State Archives.] Baldwin Number 4 was delivered in 1904 and sold to Oregon's Sumpter Valley Railway, when the Tonopah was broad gauged in August, 1905. The C&C combination-caboose appears in the center of the 1905 view, and later served as the station at Millers, Nevada. The car is now at Laws, California. [Both: Author's Collection.]

Standard Gauging

Standard gauging of the Carson & Colorado by the Southern Pacific was begun from Mound House to Tonopah Junction in October, 1904. Narrow gauge San Joaquin & Sierra Nevada Number 1024 (2-6-0) works with a pile driver on the Carson River Trestle near Dayton (above). The flatcar (565) is from the South Pacific Coast. [Chester Barton, Stanley Paher Collection.]
By late winter standard gauge rails had been spiked-down (below) and S.P. 4-4-0 1339 was working the same trackage. [Hugh Tolford Collection.] An early standard gauge passenger train (opposite top) pauses at Dayton in 1905 with S.P. 1058, a 4-6-0, and a 4-4-0 as road engine. The siding is still narrow gauge. [Chester Barton, Stanley Paher Collection.] Things did not go too smoothly on the new 4'-8½ line, as witness S.P. 2158, which has derailed on soft track near Mound House in 1905. [Hugh Tolford Collection.]

Locomotives 18, 14 and 8 triple-head a twenty car stock extra over Mount Montgomery Pass in a December, 1936 photograph by Jim Wight. [Gerald M. Best Collection]

❸
MIXED TRAIN FROM MINA

With the Tonopah and Goldfield gold strikes came standard gauging for portions of the old Carson & Colorado's trackage. First to be broad gauged was the Mound House to Sodaville section, which received 4'8½" spaced rails outside of the three foot tracks between October and September, 1904. It was at this time that the original line was relocated to the east, bypassing the old division point of Hawthorne.

Failing in an attempt to purchase the Virginia & Truckee, the Southern Pacific sent a large crew to Hazen, Nevada to build a 28 mile connection with the C&C at Fort Churchill. This line was begun in April and completed on September 1, 1905. In effect, it eliminated the V&T from the Tonopah Gold Rush traffic. Within two months after the completion of the cut-off from Hazen to Fort Churchill, the Mound House Post Office was closed.

On May 11, 1905 the Southern Pacific had formed the Nevada & California Railway Company to take over all lines (completed and projected) between Hazen, Nevada and Mojave, California, including the Carson & Colorado. The first N&C timetable was issued on January 1, 1906.

The "Jawbone" Branch of the Southern Pacific was constructed north from Mojave between 1908 and 1910. It connected with the narrow gauge Keeler line at Owenyo. At this time the Gallows turntable at Keeler was dismantled and moved to Owenyo. The main shops for the narrow gauge remained at Mina.

The Jawbone Branch was completed in October, 1910. This standard gauge line, as well as the narrow gauge, carried materials for the construction of the huge Los Angeles Aqueduct system. It is ironic that this pipeline would eventually rob the Owens Valley of its water and the narrow gauge of its farm traffic. Connecting passenger service from Los Angeles was begun on October 22, 1910, arriving at Owenyo at 8:50 p.m. At Owenyo a connection was made with the narrow gauge for Mina and Keeler. When the connection was missed, passengers stayed-over at the Owenyo Hotel, not noted as one of the finer hostels in the West. Daily service was dropped a few years later and by 1916 the narrow gauge was carding a mixed train daily between Mina and Keeler (except Sunday) and Sunday only service between Keeler and Laws. During the 1920's a sleeper was tried on the overnight run between Los Angeles and Owenyo, connecting with the narrow gauge mixed trains from Mina.

The N&C was sold to the Central Pacific Railroad on March 1, 1912. In the brief period between 1905 and 1912, a number of cars were re-lettered for the N&C, but photographs from this time are rare. After 1912, equipment was lettered for the Southern Pacific, with the rare exception of a few cars that were still lettered for the Central Pacific. (The SP absorbed all CP properties on October 1, 1945.)

In 1928-29 a seven mile line relocation was built between Monola and Aberdeen around the new Tinemaha Reservoir on the Owens River. Business was so good during the early months of 1929 that the Owenyo transfer dock was employing 60 men. Timetable Number 35, issued in 1929, showed six mixed trains and two scheduled freight trains operating on the narrow gauge. However, the stock market crash on far off Wall Street that year put an end to all that.

With the purchase and standard gauging of the Nevada-California-Oregon Railway in 1927 by the Southern Pacific, a number of cars and locomotives were sent to the Mina-Keeler narrow gauge. Obtained was a "new" Business Car, which had been the N-C-O's "Fairport," and had begun service on the Denver, South Park & Pacific. The N-C-O car became C.P. 20 on the Southern Pacific narrow gauge and replaced the aging C&C "Esmeralda", which was retired at Keeler. The Southern Pacific narrow gauge also obtained 15 boxcars, 22 stock cars, 34 gondolas, 5 tank cars and a Schenectady-built 4-6-0 that had seen service on the Florence & Cripple Creek in Colorado.

During this period, the SP narrow gauge had its own group of "feeder" lines. At Keeler, the Cerro Gordo Mines Company operated an aerial tramway that connected the mines with the narrow gauge, just south of the depot. Further down the tracks was the Inyo Development Company's three foot gauge railroad. Motive power for this line was provided by a former Eureka & Palisade 2-6-0 (Baldwin #3701-1875) that had been obtained from the Bodie & Benton. Following an extensive rebuilding in the V&T's Carson City Shops, the mogul was run over the C&C's tracks to Keeler for delivery to her new owners in 1902. The number plate of the I.D.Co. Number 1, bore the lettering: "Rebuilt by V&T Ry. Carson". Inyo Development also had 2.6 miles of portable two foot gauge track on which push cars were used to haul soda.

The Inyo Development Company was formed in 1885 by Darius Ogden Mills and some of his C&C associates. Mills named L.F.J. Wrinkle to supervise the recovery of soda ash from Owens Lake. The V&T shops constructed a group of iron three foot gauge ore cars for the I.D.Co. In 1920 the firm was leased to the Natural Soda Products Company. This firm had been formed in 1915 by Noah Wrinkle, son of the Inyo Development Company's superintendent. The kilns at Keeler were fired by coke, and limestone used in the processing of the soda ash came from a quarry at Dolomite, just north of Keeler. The rail connection to the former I.D.Co. line was broken in 1926, while Natural Soda Products operated until 1952.

Slightly over four miles north of Keeler are the remains of another cable tramway. Old maps show this line went to the Saline Valley Salt Marsh, behind the Inyo Mountains, but little else is known of the operation. The six car siding here was called Tramway (MP 572.2).

The Candelaria branch, officially abandoned in 1905, was torn up in 1934. The line had seen only occasional ore shipments during the previous thirty years, and the Great Depression had closed the last mine. That same year saw the little used connection with the Virginia & Truckee at Mound House abandoned, as rails were removed between that point and Churchill.

Mina, Nevada had not even been a station on the original Carson & Colorado Railroad, but had been founded in 1905 during the Tonopah Gold Rush. Sodaville, the closest station to the Tonopah-Goldfield mines, had served as the supply point for the first few years. The narrow gauge Tonopah Railroad had been completed in July, 1904 from Tonopah Junction (5.5 miles south of Sodaville) to the new boom town of Tonopah. The Tonopah RR ran over the Carson & Colorado's tracks to Sodaville. When sufficient land for expansion could not be obtained at Sodaville, the railroad simply backed up 3.8 miles north and established the new town of Mina. Here were ample water supplies and cheap land, and it was here that the Southern Pacific built its large dual gauge yards and facilities. When the Tonopah Railroad was standard gauged on August 14, 1905, it was granted additional trackage rights into Mina and shared the two story depot there with the Espee's own standard gauge as well as the narrow gauge line to Keeler.

By 1938, traffic on the narrow gauge between Mina and Laws had dropped to next to nothing. A weekly mixed train handled what few carloads were offered. The autumn stock trains provided exciting action, as three engines blasted up Montgomery Pass, but little revenue . . . not enough to justify the lines' operations. The last train from Mina to Keeler was operated on Wednesday, February 16, 1938. The triple-headed consist carried all the remaining narrow gauge rolling stock with it to the Owens Valley. The mixed train (Number 612) was led by ten-wheelers 18, 14 and 9. A handful of local residents came down in the pre-dawn cold to see the last narrow gauge leave town. For the next 32 years, the SP narrow gauge would operate within the confines of Inyo County, California.

The trackage between Tonopah Junction and Benton was abandoned, but the rails remained in place until they were requisitioned by the United States Navy in 1942. The last train from Mina also spelled the end of passenger service on the SP narrow gauge. The automobile and the paving of parallel U.S. Highway 395 in 1925 had taken its toll. Mixed train revenue had hardly paid to maintain the several small combination cars that had been used in this service for a number of years. These ancient combines continued to trail along behind freight trains in the Owens Valley, serving as a caboose in later years. Also concurrent with the last train from Nevada, the remaining narrow gauge was placed under the supervision of the San Joaquin Division, with headquarters in Bakersfield.

In 1938 the farms and ranches around Monola and Laws produced some 1,600 boxcar loads of potatoes, while cattle rode to pasture aboard wooden stock cars and gondola loads of sugar beets were shipped out of the valley. The 30.8 mile long line north of Laws to Benton saw little service and its rails were removed in 1943.

So from 1910 to 1940, the SP narrow gauge made-do with a slim diet of mixed trains and whatever its agents could drum up in the way of freight to fill the sunburn red cars. The glory days of hauling silver and gold were gone forever.

Nevada & California Ry.

The Southern Pacific formed the Nevada & California Ry. in 1905 to take over all lines between Hazen, Nevada and Mojave, California, including the remaining Carson & Colorado narrow gauge, between Mina and Keeler. On the opposite page, N&C 17 makes an unscheduled stop in the desert in about 1910, near Laws, California. [Donald Duke Collection.] A four engine N&C freight train (above) prepares for departure from Mina on dual guage trackage in 1912. [Guy Dunscomb Collection.] Photographs of equipment lettered for the N&C are rare, as the name was only used between 1905-1912. The triple-headed freight (opposite lower) is working a southbound train near Queen, Nevada, with engines 4, 16, 17. [Dale Darney Collection.]

MINA

After 1905, Mina, Nevada was the junction point between the narrow gauge and the standard gauge; as well as the connecting Tonopah & Goldfield. The Mina depot served all passenger and mixed trains of both roads and was photographed (right) by Al Phelps in 1938. A triple-headed mixed train prepares to leave town (above) in the 1920's. [Guy Dunscomb Collection.] Ten-wheeler 14 was having her pop valve tested in 1936, while the Number 8 waits at Mina the following year. [Both: Gerald M. Best.]

Mina from enginehouse roof in 1935. Doubleheader about to leave for Keeler. [Gerald M. Best]

Boxcar City at Mina in 1906. Cars v SPC, C&C, N&C, Oregonian. [Autho

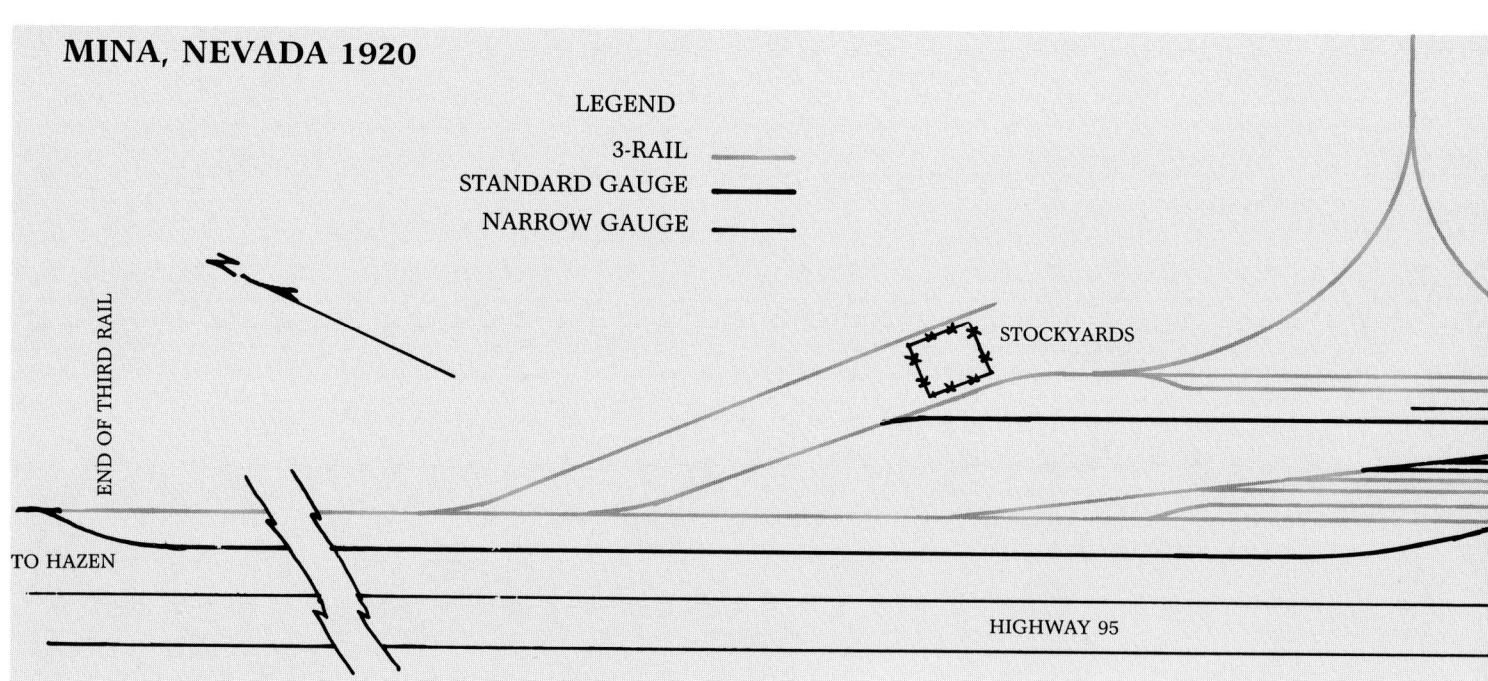

MINA, NEVADA 1920

LEGEND
3-RAIL
STANDARD GAUGE
NARROW GAUGE

END OF THIRD RAIL
STOCKYARDS
TO HAZEN
HIGHWAY 95

Mina Yards, looking south in 1912 [Author's Collection]

*Mina Enginehouse (from rear) in c.19

mer narrow gauge rolling stock from llection]

Mina Enginehouse c.1906. Narrow gauge stalls on left, narrow gauge cars on right. [Author's Collection]

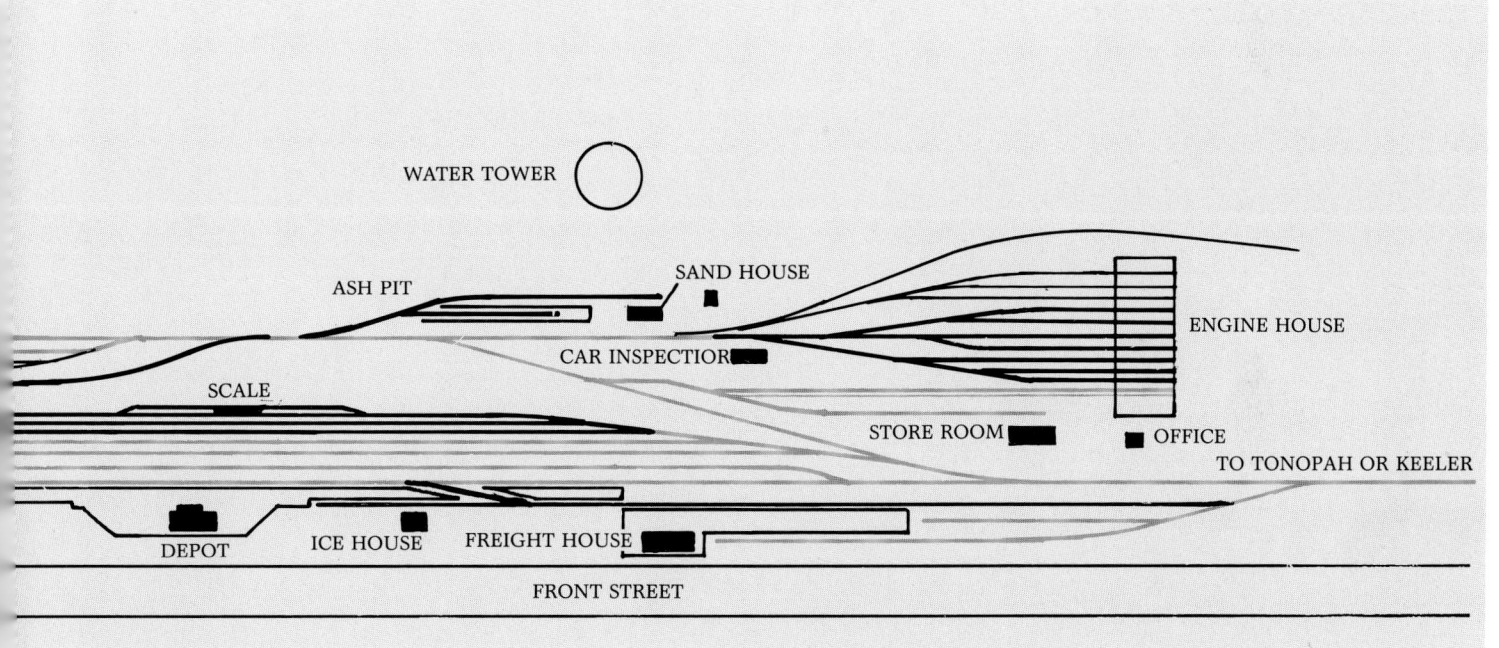

gh Tolford Collection]

SP narrow gauge 9 at Mina 1937. [Ted G. Wurm, from Bert Ward Collection]

Mina Enginehouse

Mina, which had not even been a station on the Carson & Colorado, was founded during the Tonopah Gold Rush. Here the Southern Pacific built a large dual gauge enginehouse, freighthouse, shops and depot. The enginehouse is seen in 1907 (top) with narrow gauge engines 3, 5 and 11 at left. [Hugh Tolford.] Inside the huge house, ten-wheeler Number 8 was found by Ted Wurm in 1937. A doubleheaded mixed train is ready for departure (opposite lower) for Keeler in 1935, with Number 14 and 17. Lined up in front of the Mina enginehouse (opposite top) are engines 8, 17 and 22 in the early morning of December 10, 1936. [Both: Gerald M. Best.]

83

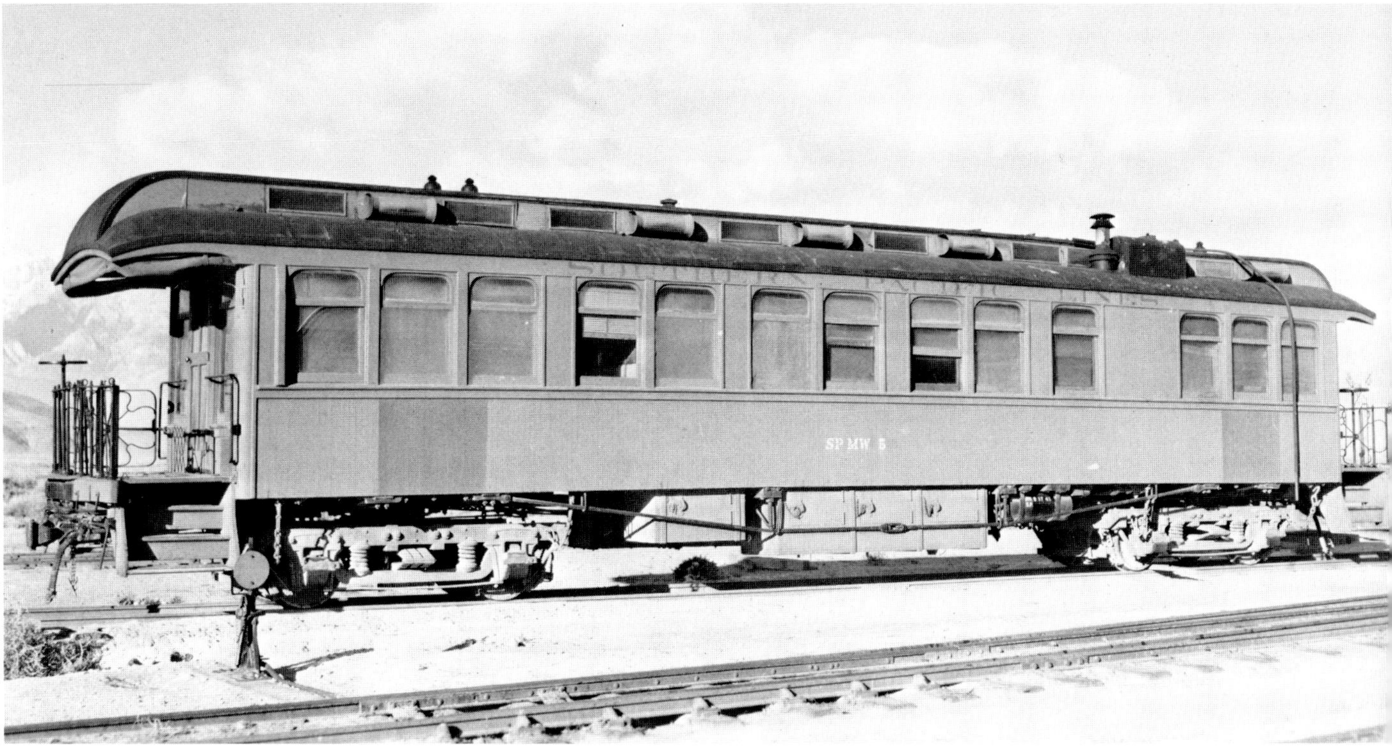
SP MW 5

SOUTHERN PACIFIC LINES
C P
20

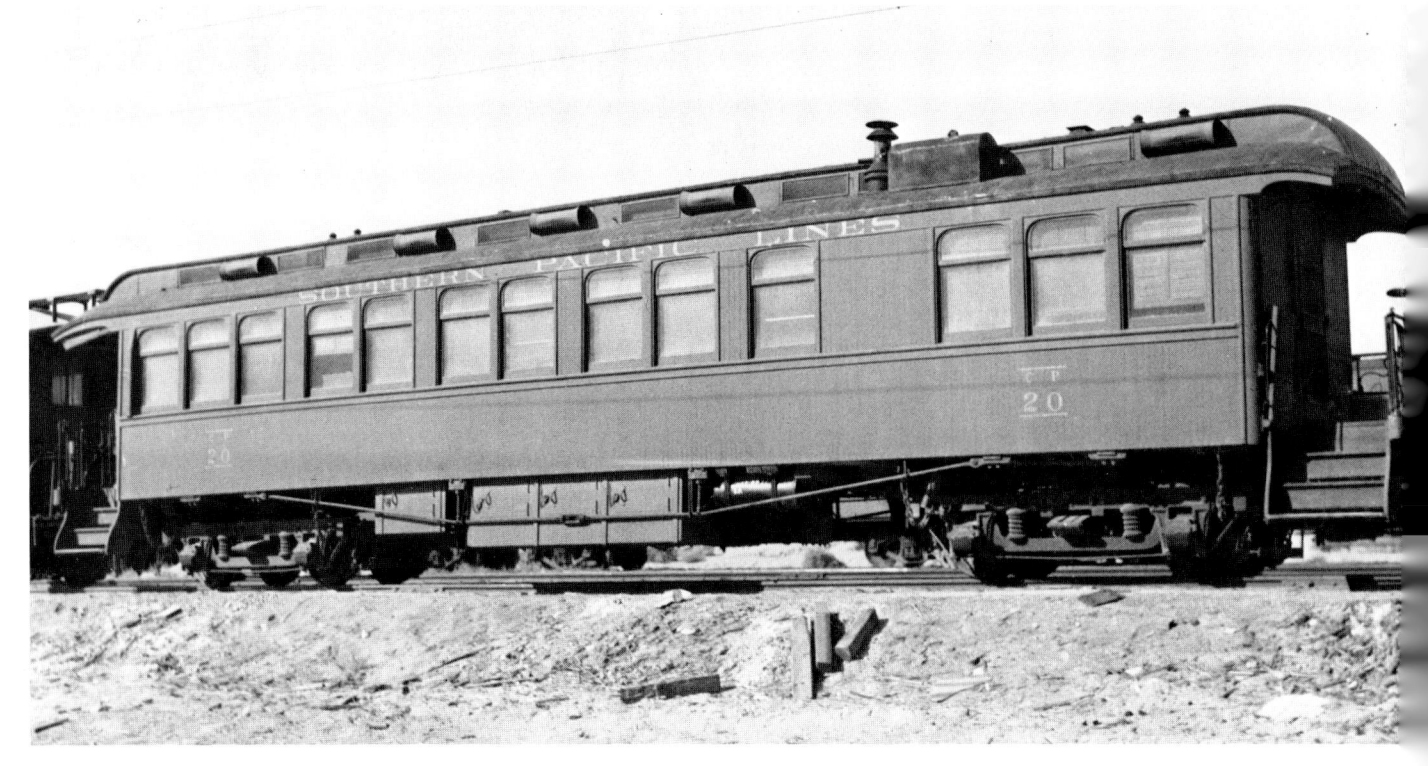

Business Cars

During the lifetime of the narrow gauge, the road operated two officer's cars. The "Esmeralda" was built for the C&C and retired in 1927. She is shown (above) at Hawthorne in c.1905. The "C.P. 20", was acquired from the Nevada-California-Oregon in 1927, where she was the "Fairport". Built by the Denver, South Park & Pacific, the car is shown (left) in the Mina enginehouse, [Jim Wight] and at Owenyo (opposite bottom) in 1939. [Al Phelps.] The car was renumbered MW 5 in 1944 and was found by Gerald M. Best at Owenyo.

Stock Extra
A triple-headed stock extra nears the summit of 7,138 foot Mount Montgomery Pass during World War I. Sheep were transported from summer pastures in th[e] mountains to winter pasture in the Owe[ns] Valley. [Guy Dunscomb Collection.] Another triple-header starts up the pass (left) on December 23, 1936, with engin[es] 18, 14 and 8 pulling twenty stock cars and a combine-caboose. The pass was t[he] highest on the entire S.P. system. [Jim Wight.]

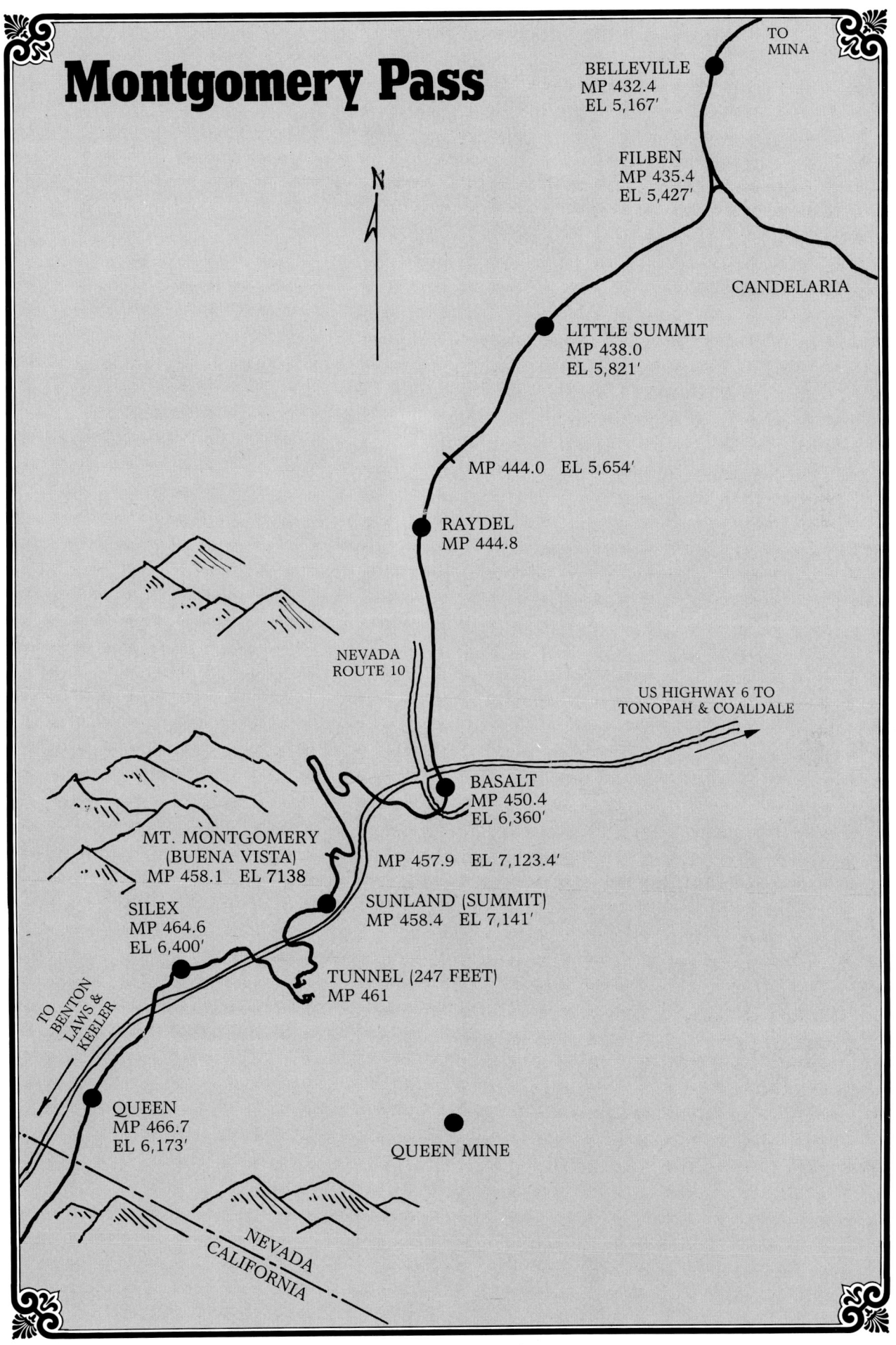

Triple-Header
A "Stock extra" pauses at Mina with ten-wheelers 12, 16 and 18 in the mid-thirties. The train consists of a string of stock cars of various lengths, heights and designs. [Jim Wight.] Stock car 62 was a former Nevada-California-Oregon car and was photographed in 1946 at Owenyo. That same year the car was renumbered 169. [Bert H. Ward.]

Snow on the Narrow Gauge

For a desert narrow gauge, the Keeler line generally had more trouble with drifting sand than snow. However, lofty Mount Montgomery Pass was the exception. At 7,138 feet above sea level, the pass was the highest on the entire S.P. system. For this reason, snowplow pilots were added to several engines by the Mina shop each winter. A three engine mixed train pauses for a brake inspection in January, 1938 (opposite top) with locomotives 9, 17 and 22. The train Number 612, operated from Mina to Keeler on Wednesday only at this time. [Jim Wight from Al Phelps Collection.] Flanger 108 saw infrequent use, when photographed at Mina in 1935. [Gerald M. Best.] The water tank at Basalt, Nevada was being thawed out with a steam hose (above) in December, 1937. [Jim Wight, from Gerald M. Best Collection.] The Basalt tank was photographed later that same winter (below) by Al Phelps.

Southern Pacific 18 heads a short mixed train near Mount Montgomery Pass in 1937 (opposite). The trackage here had seen better days and would be abandoned the following year. The lower view finds the mixed, with Number 17 and a helper at the once "boom town" of Belleville, Nevada in 1935. [Both: Jim Wight from Author's Collection.] Soon the consist will be working hard on the southbound run over the pass. A bridge inspection party (above) was photographed at the remote Mount Montgomery station. [S.P. Historical Collection.]

By the late thirties, traffic between Mina and Laws had dropped to next to nothing. A weekly mixed train handled the few carloads (above). Engines 17 and 9 head the mixed (Train #612) in August, 1937 [Jim Wight, Al Phelps Collection.] Below, Engine 18 on the same train on June 19, 1937. The little train had only a year to run. [Ted Wurm Collection.]

Last Train from Mina

On February 16, 1938, the last narrow gauge train left Mina, Nevada, with ten-wheelers 9, 14, 18 and the remaining three foot cars, for Keeler, California. The consist included the household effects of employees and their families who were transferred to the Owens Valley, and paused in the pre-dawn light.

Stranded by economics, geography and time, the Owens Valley narrow gauge traversed a beautiful and remote land on the east side of the Sierra. Former Florence & Cripple Creek 22 drifts into Keeler in a 1940 photograph by the late Frank J. Peterson. [Donald Duke Collection.]

4

NARROW GAUGE TO NOWHERE

Imagine, if you will, a three foot gauge main line railroad running over seventy miles through the desert on 35 pound rail, serving no town with a population of over 300 souls, nor one with even a retail store. This same narrow gauge is operated by steam power, has no physical connection with any other railroad and its wooden equipment dates from the 1880's and 1890's. Add in a desolate, remote locale, harp switch-stands on stub switches, a friendly crew and you have a glimpse of the Southern Pacific's Owens Valley line after World War II.

In its final decades, the SP narrow gauge was indeed the most unlikely narrow gauge on earth. Thrust across the American wastelands and run by sheer determination, the line ran into the Space Age on 1880 technology. Hauling talc and carrying its weight in alkali dust, the SP narrow gauge ran out her years in a vast and beautiful land, trapped by geography, economics and time.

Following the abandonment of the line to Mina in 1938 and the section to Benton in 1943, the SP narrow gauge became an isolated 70.4 mile road linking Laws with Keeler. Wedged as it were between the lofty peaks of the Sierra Nevada on the West, with the lower Inyo and White Mountains on the East, the line served the remote country on the "back side" of the Sierra. Inyo County not only contained the last narrow gauge in the far West, but also the highest point in the Nation (Mt. Whitney 14,495) as well as the lowest (Death Valley 282 below sea level).

Motive power on the SP narrow gauge after 1940 consisted of a trio of former Nevada-California-Oregon ten-wheelers Numbered 8, 9 and 18. They were built by Baldwin in 1907, 1909 and 1911 respectively and served the line as long as steam lasted. A former Florence & Cripple Creek 4-6-0, that had come to the line via the N-C-O, was held for a while as the standby engine at Keeler. This Schenectady-built ten-wheeler was the only non-Baldwin locomotive on the roster and was a sister engine to the famous Rio Grande Southern Number 20, of Colorado fame.

World War II saw a great upturn in business over the narrow gauge, as previously undeveloped mineral resources were tapped for the war effort. Several reduction mills were built in the valley. The United States Vanadium Company built a mill at Laws, while a smaller plant was constructed at Zurich (Blue Star Grinding Company). Traffic increased to such an extent that there was talk of standard gauging the road. A plan was formulated by the government to retrack the old grade between Tonopah Junction and Laws, to provide an alternate transcontinental route, should the Donner Pass crossing be threatened. However, this "emergency plan" was never put into effect due to the remote nature of the war with Japan. Not so distant, however, were the

Japanese internment camps that were built in the Owens Valley during the war.

Keeler, at the southern end of the SP narrow gauge, was made the engine terminal for the entire line after the connection with Nevada was severed. The town itself was home to some 75 people. The sun shines an average of 360 days a year here and the summer daytime temperature frequently exceeds 110 degrees in the shade. Just across from the large depot, the Desert Club Bar was a popular "watering spot," featuring Lucky Lager Beer. About the only other cool spot in town was beneath the water spout of the Keeler tank.

The railroad facilities at Keeler were of the open air variety. Several carbodys provided storage for spare parts and tools, but the work was done outside in the desert heat that often approximated that of Hades. The thick clouds of dust from the nearby Sierra Talc Company gave a further impression of inferno to the scene. There had once been a single stall, wooden enginehouse here, with a Gallows turntable. The turntable was removed to Owenyo, when the standard gauge Jawbone Line was completed in 1910. The enginehouse burned in 1946, and the turntable was dismantled at Owenyo in 1948. A wye at the south end of town served to turn the equipment in later years.

Just below the frame Keeler Depot was the Cerro Gordo Mines tramway terminal. The town of Cerro Gordo sits high up in the Inyo Mountains, to the east of town. It is reached by a twisting eight mile mountain road, with hairpin curves, switchbacks and 25 percent grades. The aerial bucket tramway had been built from Cerro Gordo to Keeler in 1908, during one of the brief-lived mining excitements. Up at Cerro Gordo the hoisting machinery is still kept greased and ready by a caretaker, who with his wife were the last residents of the camp.

Trackage as late as 1950 consisted of 56 miles of 35 pound rail, intermixed with some 15 miles of 62 pound steel between Keeler and Owenyo. Some sections of original 35 pound rail, rolled in Sheffield, England, were still in the track; while a few rails made in Holland in the 1860's were reportedly in use on some sidings. Harp switchstands and stub switches were in common use until the end of World War II and a few were still in place after that time.

Operations throughout the 1940's and early 1950's followed a similar pattern. Train service was usually run three days a week over the entire line on Monday-Wednesday-Friday. Extra trains were run as needed on other days. Two ten-wheelers were kept in steam at Keeler. One was used on the thrice weekly freights, while the other served as standby. One full crew was assigned to the "Keeler Branch," as the Southern Pacific referred to the former Carson & Colorado. However, in the fall, when large shipments of sheep were sent to the southern ranges; and in the spring when strings of aging cattle cars headed for summer pasture above Laws, it was not unusual to have three engines under steam. Extra crews were dispatched from the Sparks "Extra Board," and made the 300 mile trip from Reno via bus.

A typical run over the SP narrow gauge began in the early morning light at Keeler. In the shadow of the nearby Inyo Mountains, Engineer W.C. "Walt" Ferguson oiled-around the Number 18, as Fireman George Murry filled the tender, beside the Keeler tank. Back in the former combine, now used as a caboose, Conductor J.A. "Jim" Brennan looked over the waybills while brakemen Carl Hanson and Clyde Beckes loaded ice into the car's cooler.

Engineer Ferguson, known as "Fergie," and Jim Brennan were long time veterans of the narrow gauge desert run. Both held enough seniority on the Salt Lake Division to "hold down" plush main line jobs, but they preferred the narrow gauge. While the crews came off of the Salt Lake Division, a carryover from C&C days, the maintenance of the line, its rolling stock and locomotives fell under the San Joaquin Division at Bakersfield.

After some switching at the talc plant, the short consist of sunburnred equipment started northbound on its 17 mile run to Owenyo. It was in this area that the Employees' Timetable warned: LOOK OUT FOR DRIFTED SAND BETWEEN MP 573 and MP 575. A brief switching move was made at Dolomite, where the mine had a few cars loaded and waiting. While the timetable listed Dolomite, Mock, Alico and Mt. Whitney as stations, they were actually only sidings in the desert that served as loading points for talc, pumice, soda, ore and other minerals.

After one hour across the desert, the train arrived at Owenyo, which was by far the largest rail yard on the narrow gauge. Owenyo is a contraction of the words Owens and Inyo. The settlement was established as the junction point between the standard gauge "Jawbone Branch," from Mojave and the narrow gauge in 1910. Most of the town's 74 residents were railroad employees or their families. Owenyo was unique for a narrow gauge/standard gauge interchange point in that there was no dual gauge trackage. Narrow gauge cars were spotted across the platform and the loads transferred by hand. On the south end of the yards was the huge transfer trestle, which allowed the contents of narrow gauge cars to be dumped by gravity into waiting standard gauge cars underneath. Near the depot was a transfer gantry, of the Queen Truss design, that allowed heavy loads to be moved from three foot gauge to broad gauge equipment. Car repairs, formerly made at Keeler, were handled on the Owenyo "rip track," just south of the depot and hotel. Like the Keeler engine shop, the Owenyo car repairers had only a cobalt blue sky for a roof.

Extra 18 West pulled up to the Owenyo depot and the crew went inside for orders. Owenyo Agent W.F. Tommer was in charge here. He hired the platform labor, many of whom were Piute Indians, and in general ran the narrow gauge. Mr. Tommer came to the line back in 1924 and became such a fixture that locals referred to the road as "Mr. Tommer's Railroad." When Tommer retired in 1954, he had completed 52 years of service on the SP and had never missed a day due to illness. The office was full of the clutter of many years. There was a small rock collection in the window, while nearby was the hand crank telephone, with which Agent Tommer kept in contact with the agents at Keeler and Laws, the only other active agencies on the narrow gauge. The magneto powered telephone system was used to activate a series of bells, which signaled the other agents. Train orders were typed out on an ancient Remington, while outside, the order board was always in the stop position. Owenyo's depot also employed Josephine "Jo" Cole as freight clerk. Jo was the only woman on the narrow gauge payroll. The benches outside the depot were usually occupied by one or more retired railroaders at train time. The nearby Owenyo Hotel housed mainly railroad employees, who had bid the narrow gauge desert run. It was not classy, but it was clean. Most of the SP narrow gauge folks lived in nearby Lone Pine.

After switching a few gondola loads onto and off of the transfer trestle, Extra 18 West headed out of town in a plume of oil smoke. Headed northbound, the train contained eight empty boxcars for Zurich and a loaded high car for Laws. A water stop was made at Karsarge (MP 550.1), some 26 miles from Keeler. This now closed depot was once called Independence (in hope the town of Independence would move the five miles to the new site), and for many years was called Citrus. The classic structure stood near what were once groves of fruit trees. The trees were purchased and cut down so that their roots would not take the water away from the ever-thirsty Los Angeles Aqueduct system.

Heading north through Aberdeen, the tracks crossed the Owens River and skirted the edge of Tinemaha Reservoir. Passing through a deep rock cut and across a wooden trestle over the Owens River, the consist steamed through Monola, 51 miles from Keeler. At Zurich, a major loading point, several gondola loads of soapstone were waiting under a loading ramp. After some switching, "Fergie" dropped off the empty gondolas and spotted the loads so that they could be picked up on the return trip.

Laws, the northern terminus for the SP narrow gauge was reached at noon. With an elevation of 4,115 feet, it was quite different from Keeler. The countryside was dotted with farms and ranches and the grassy yards were lined with huge Lombardy poplars and cottonwood trees, planted there back in Carson & Colorado days for shade. The small Post Office served a population of 100, but only a handful are in town today. The grazing cattle hardly looked up as the Number 18 and her train of swaying cars smoked into the picturesque yards, past the water tank, oil tank and pump house and came to a halt near the depot. The yards here contained all that was necessary to keep the narrow gauge in operation. Nearby was the hand operated Gallows turntable, built in 1883 and still in use. Engineer Ferguson and Conductor Brennan went inside the small frame depot to talk with Laws Agent J.S. Parrish about the switching to be done. The crew then took time out for lunch under the eaves of the depot.

After lunch, the crew did a number of switching moves at the mill, on the north end of town. The Huntley Industrial Minerals Company had six loads for Owenyo that day. After setting out the empty boxcars brought up from Owenyo, the loads were switched out and a load of farm produce was added. The 4-6-0 then eased down through the grassy yards and was carefully spotted on the turntable. Everyone pitched in to turn the ten-wheeler. Water was then taken from the Laws tank, before Extra 18 East whistled off southbound with seven highcars loaded with potatoes and potash. The time was 1:48 p.m.

The seven gondola loads of soapstone were picked up from the siding at Zurich. The 18 had some difficulty getting the 14 loads started out of town, but after some stack talk and wheel spinning, her 44 inch drivers got a hold on the light rail and the consist moved off in a picture resembling the burning of Rome.

On the SP narrow gauge, trains heading toward San Francisco were carded as Westbound (north on compass), while those headed away from San Francisco were Eastbound (south on map). It made little difference that there were no rails between Laws and Mina, the Laws depot nameboard still showed the distance to San Francisco as 506.8 miles. At Keeler the distance was shown as 576.5 miles.

A water stop was made at Aberdeen Tank. Here the tank was filled by a windmill powered pump. When the water table was low, or the wind did not blow, it was often necessary to carry along a water car, behind the regular tender in order to make it between water stops. After arrival at Owenyo, the loads of potash were spotted along with the potatoes next to the unloading dock. The soapstone loads were placed on a siding, as the Jawbone local had not yet come in with the empties for these loads. A few switching moves were made up the transfer table and the Number 18 picked up caboose 401 for a "caboose hop" home to Keeler in the late afternoon sun. As the sun dropped below Mt. Whitney, the long shadows covered the valley floor, as the short train steamed southbound. The rapid cooling of the air was noticeable as the 18 was spotted on the Keeler ready track and the crew headed for their cars and a late supper. Looking back, you can see a picture of the SP narrow gauge in the twilight . . .

Caboose Hop
Noted rail photographer Al Phelps was on board Extra 22 West on Thursday, August 17, 1939 as a Keeler to Laws "caboose hop" was made to pick-up company oil. The northbound run paused at Owenyo (opposite lower) to get orders, before heading across the desert for a water stop at Kearsarge (opposite top). After setting out the caboose (above), the crew ate lunch before turning the Schenectady built 4-6-0 on the Gallows turntable. [Photographs by Al Phelps.]

104

Oil Train

Extra 22 East heads south through Black Canyon on August 17, 1939 (opposite top), with five cars of company oil and a pair of flats. Photographer Phelps rode on the roof of caboose 467, which, with its passenger trucks, "rode like a Pullman." The following day, Number 22 prepared to leave Owenyo (opposite lower) with four empties and the caboose. A water stop was made at Kearsarge (above) while the crew talked about "good fishing spots." [Photographs by Al Phelps.] The motive power for these runs was found at Keeler in May, 1940 by Frank J. Peterson (below).

Back Side of the Sierra
Hauling talc and carrying her weight in alkali dust, the Southern Pacific's narrow gauge ran out her years in a beautiful land of contrasts. The Number 18 is framed, on her northbound run out of Keeler, against the mighty Sierra with towering 14,495 foot Mt. Whitney at the right. The classic rail photograph was made by Donald Duke. The smaller view by John P. Carrick finds Number 8 steaming out of Keeler with a short consist.

Keeler Terminal
Following abandonment of the narrow gauge line to Mina, Nevada in 1938, the engine terminal was established at Keeler. Here repairs were made in the open air. The turntable had been moved to Owenyo in 1910 and the single stall enginehouse had burned in 1946. The facilities were captured (above) in the evening light on May 30, 1949. [Fred Hust.] Engineer Walt Ferguson taps a baulky air pump on Number 18 in 1953, while the "shops" are pictured. at top right. [Both: Wendell Mortimer, Jr.]

Open Air Shops

The open air shops of Keeler are depicted on these pages. The temperature here often exceeds 110° in the shade. Ten wheelers 8 and 9 are on the ready track (below) in 1950. [Donald Duke.] Engines 18, 9 and 8 are shown (above) in a Guy L. Dunscomb view made in 1946. A late afternoon sun highlights the flank of the Nine spot (opposite top) in a Donald Duke photograph, while the lower scene shows the terminal area with Owens Lake and the Sierra in the background. [Richard F. Thomas.]

Overleaf: "From Nowhere to Nowhere."
Acrylic on panel 24" × 40" by Mike Pearsall
[Collection of Robert Dezelin.]

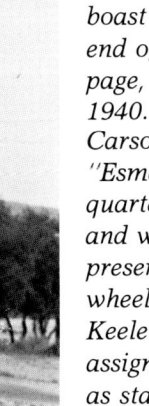

Downtown Keeler

Keeler, once the terminus of a three hundred mile long narrow gauge, could boast of only about 75 residents by the end of World War II. On the opposite page, the "town" is seen, looking south in 1940. [Donald Duke collection.] Former Carson & Colorado business car "Esmeralda" was used as sleeping quarters by the train crews and was later to be moved and preserved. [Al Phelps.] On this page ten wheelers 18 and 9 are under steam at Keeler, in 1953. One engine handled road assignments, while another served as standby, and the spare engine underwent repairs and inspections. [Wendell Mortimer, Jr.]

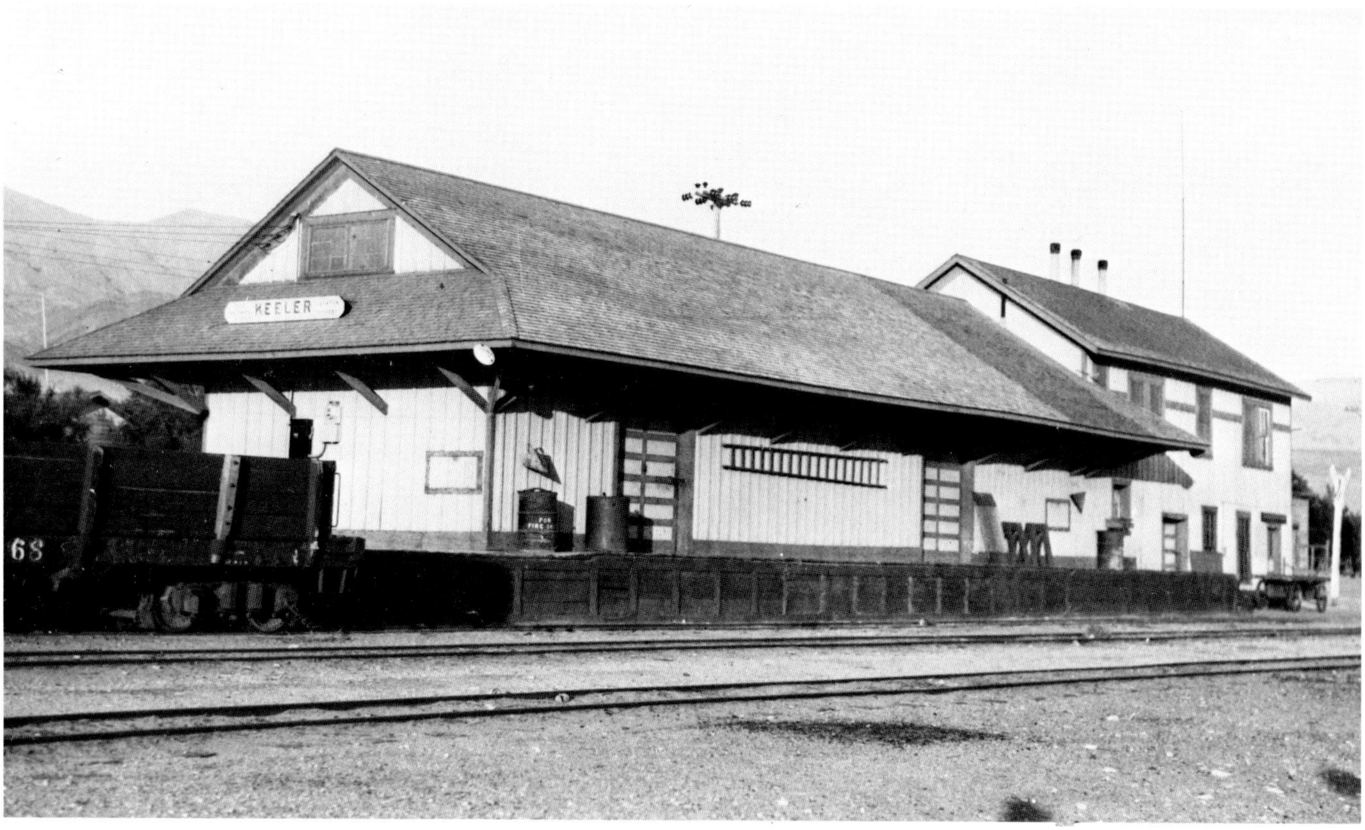
KEELER

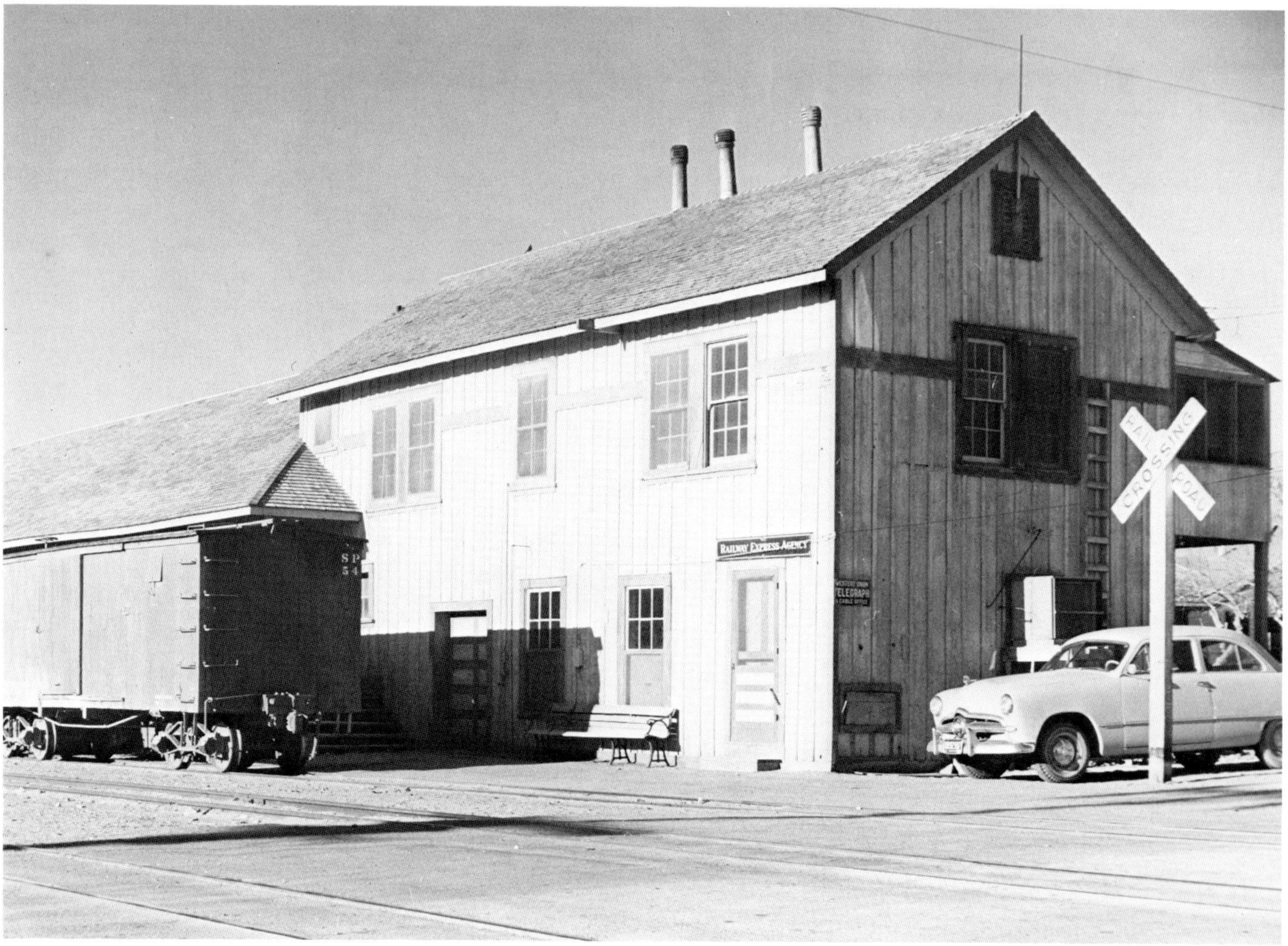
RAILWAY EXPRESS AGENCY
TELEGRAPH
RAIL ROAD
CROSSING

Keeler Depot
The Keeler depot was constructed in the early 1880's by the C&C and received an addition on the south end somewhat later. Located at mile post 576.5 and at an elevation of 3,610 feet, the frame structure remained an open agency until August, 1957. The depot still stands today and is shown in a series of photographs over the years. Al Phelps made the view (opposite top) in 1939, while Robert W. Brown made the photograph (opposite lower) in 1954. On this page is a scene (above) by Donald Duke, while the Number 18 has just arrived (below) on February 10, 1951. [W.C. Whittaker.]

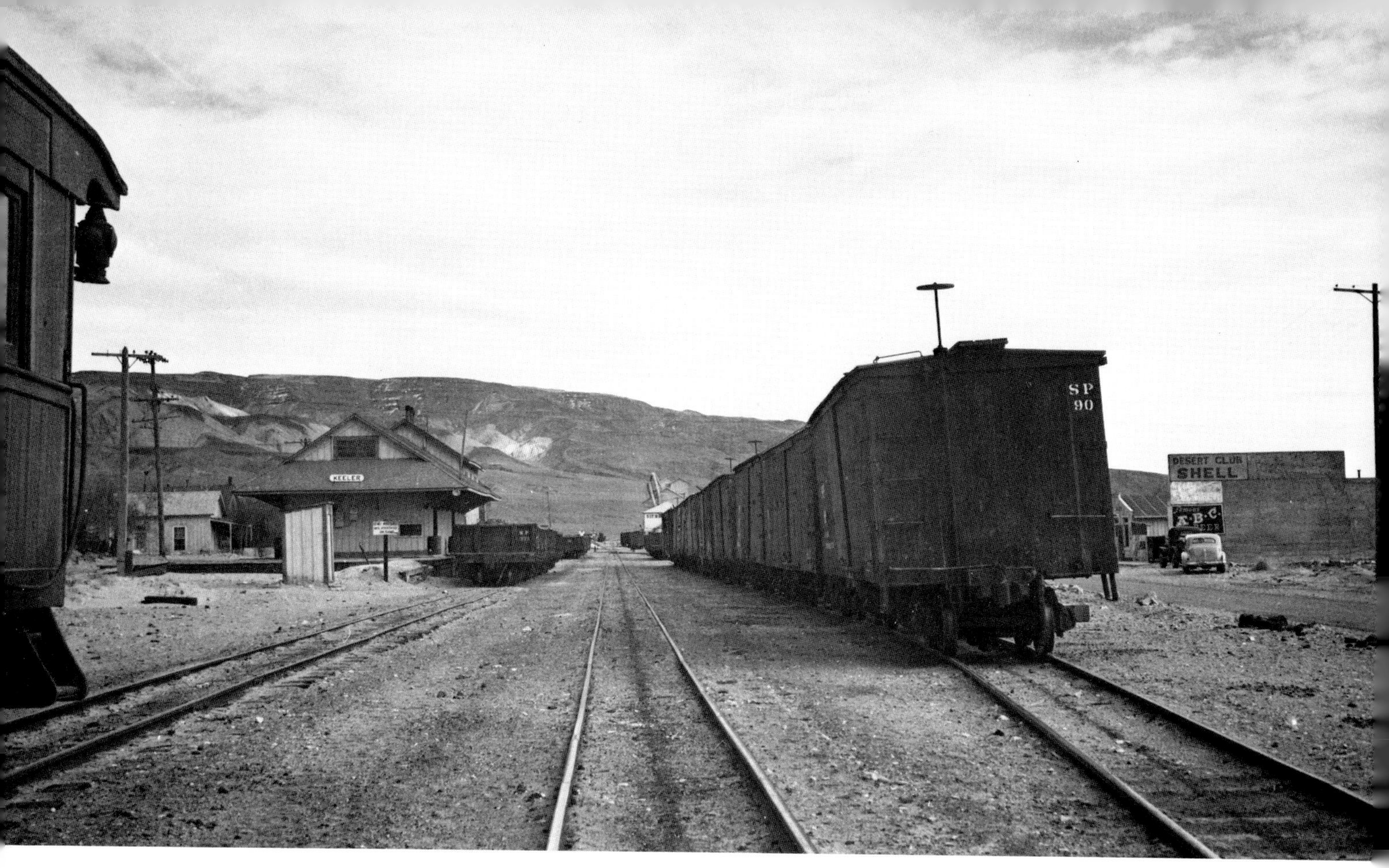
KEELER
SP
90
DESERT CLUB
SHELL

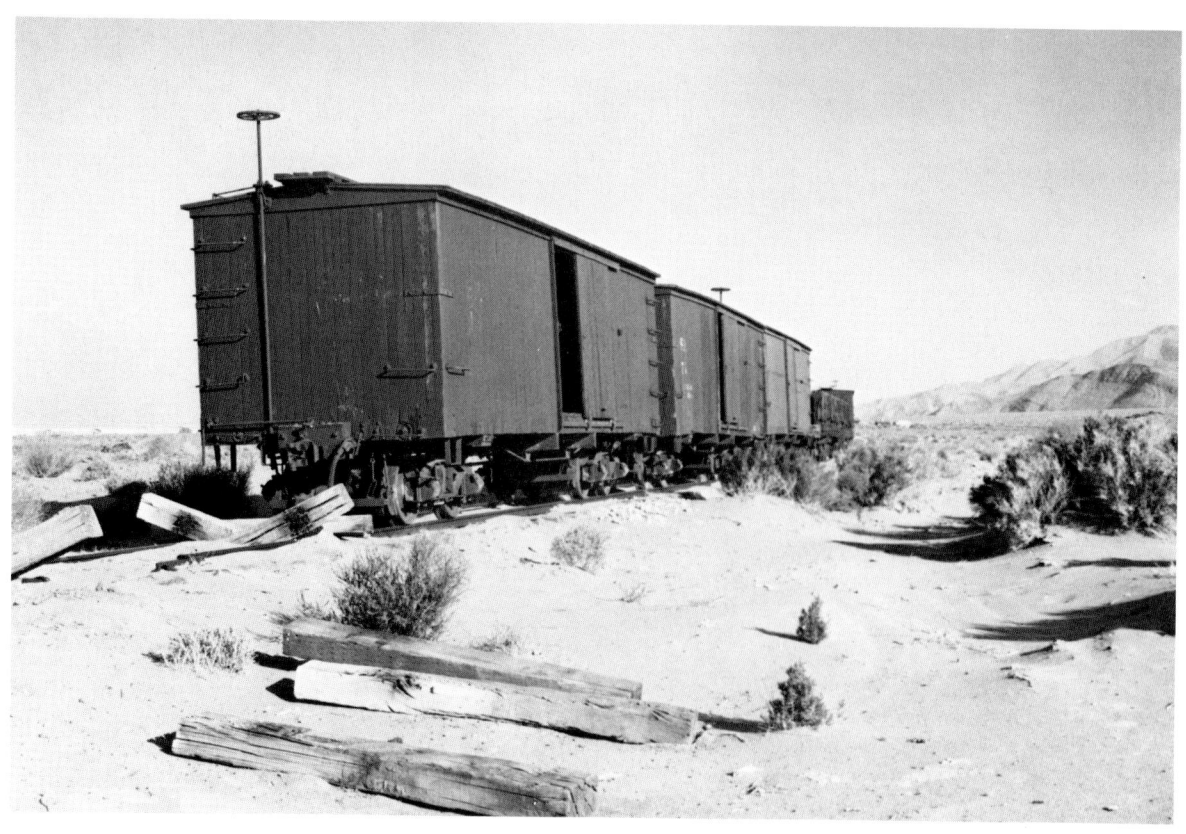

Beyond downtown Keeler (opposite top) were several local industries, including the Sierra Talc Company. [Robert Hanft from Guy L. Dunscomb collection.] The trackage continued south from town, past the abandoned tramway terminal and ended (opposite lower) in the desert sands. [Gary G. Allen.] The tramway of the Cerro Gordo Mines Company had been built in 1908 to connect the silver mine with the railroad. The aerial tramway terminal is shown (below) in 1939 with baggage car 12 and combine 7, both still lettered for the Central Pacific. [Al Phelps.] A closer view of the tramway terminal is found (above) in a 1954 photograph by Robert W. Brown.

Leavin' Keeler

Southern Pacific 18 prepares to leave the Keeler Depot (opposite top) in October, 1949. A stop is made near the shop area in order for conductor Jim Brennan (in doorway) to load ice aboard combine-caboose 401 (opposite lower and above). After checking over the consist narrow gauge Extra 18 West departs in a series of Donald Duke photographs.

Keeler still had three-way stub switches and a few harp switchstands after World War II. When the "Esmeralda" car body was sold, baggage car 12 was placed on a short length of track and was used by crews. The (bottom) view looks south and was made in 1946. [Bert H. Ward.] The above photograph was exposed in 1940 by Gerald M. Best.

Keeler Tank

Ten wheeler 9 eases past the Keeler tank with a five car train in July, 1959. [Mac Owen.] The tank itself is pictured (left) the following year. [Gary G. Allen.] The Nine spot takes water (opposite top) in a Wendell Mortimer, Jr. view. Conductor Jim Brennan stands on the platform of 401 with his dog, while the fireman fills the tank of Number 18 Jim's dog often rode the narrow gauge combine. [Donald Duke.]

123

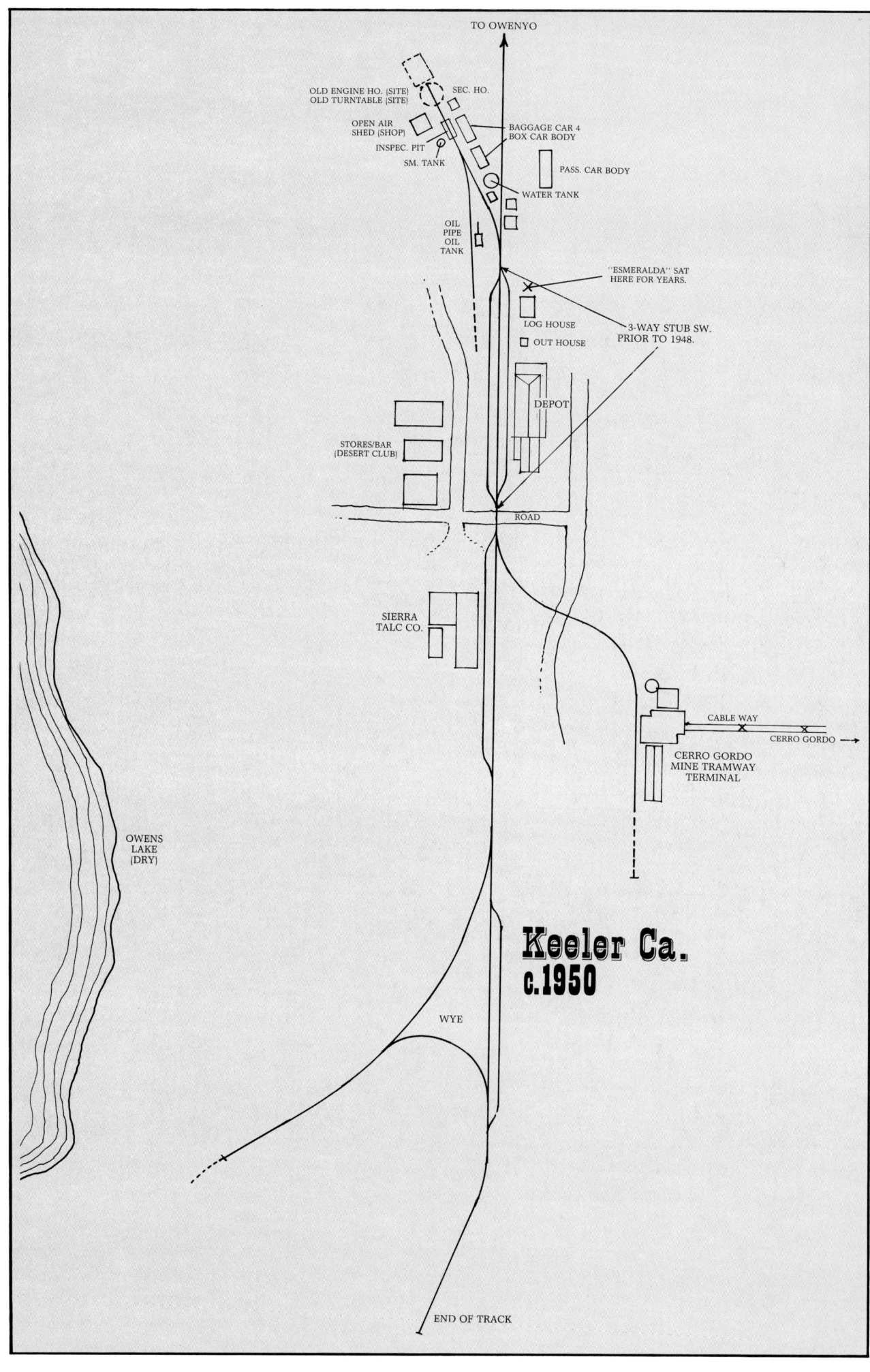

Dolomite Siding

Southern Pacific 18 switches the Limestone Quarry at Dolomite, located six miles north of Keeler at the base of the Inyo Mountains. The date is February 22, 1949 and Donald Duke was on hand to record the action.

Desert Run
Number 18 was captured at speed as she blasted across the desert on her northbound run from Keeler to Owenyo on July 20, 1946. Photographer Bert H. Ward found the consist a few miles out of Keeler.

128

Southern Pacific narrow gauge 18 has paused in the desert due to a "hot box" on the third gondola back in the train. [Bert H. Ward.] The crew is repacking the journal and soon the consist will be on its way again. The 18 is shown (top left) at speed near Mt. Whitney siding in 1952. [Jim Wren.] The siding at Mt. Whitney used harp switchstands and a stub switch in 1948. [Gerald M. Best.]

In its final decades the Southern Pacific narrow gauge was indeed the most unlikely short line on earth. The road was trapped by geography, economics and time, as she ran out the years in a vast and beautiful land. Donald Duke captured the spirit of the line in this composition showing the 18 with her ancient combine on October 6, 1949.

Splender In The Desert
SP 9 heads north from Keeler in the early morning light of a December, 1948 day (opposite top). The action was captured by Donald Duke, near Dolomite siding. A few miles further north the 9 was found by Robert M. Hanft (opposite lower) at Alico siding in October, 1953. [Guy L. Dunscomb collection.] On this page, the Number 18 heads across the Owens Valley on February 22, 1952. An extra passenger car (baggage 12) has been added to the consist to accommodate a group of visiting railfans. [Richard F. Thomas.]

Owenyo

Owenyo, at mile post 559.8, was the junction point between the narrow gauge and the standard gauge "Jawbone Branch" from Mojave. The yards (left) did not contain any dual gauge trackage however. [Wendell Mortimer, Jr.] Number 18 pulls into Owenyo (lower) from Keeler on July 20, 1946. The train is passing the transfer trestle, where ash, talc, soda and other minerals were dumped from the narrow gauge (top) to the standard gauge. [Bert H. Ward.] Combine-caboose 401 stands by the Owenyo depot (opposite), while her crew switches the yard. The word Owenyo is a contraction of the words "Owens" Valley and "Inyo" County. [Donald Duke.]

Owenyo Transfer Trestle

When the standard gauge "Jawbone Branch" was completed to Owenyo in 1910, interchange facilities were constructed at the new junction, as well as a depot and hotel. At the south end of the yard a transfer trestle was built to allow minerals to be dumped from the narrow gauge cars into broad gauge equipment. Number 18 is shown switching the trestle (above) in a Donald Duke view. The trestle is shown in 1939. [Al Phelps.] On the opposite page the layout is seen in a pair of Richard F. Thomas photographs.

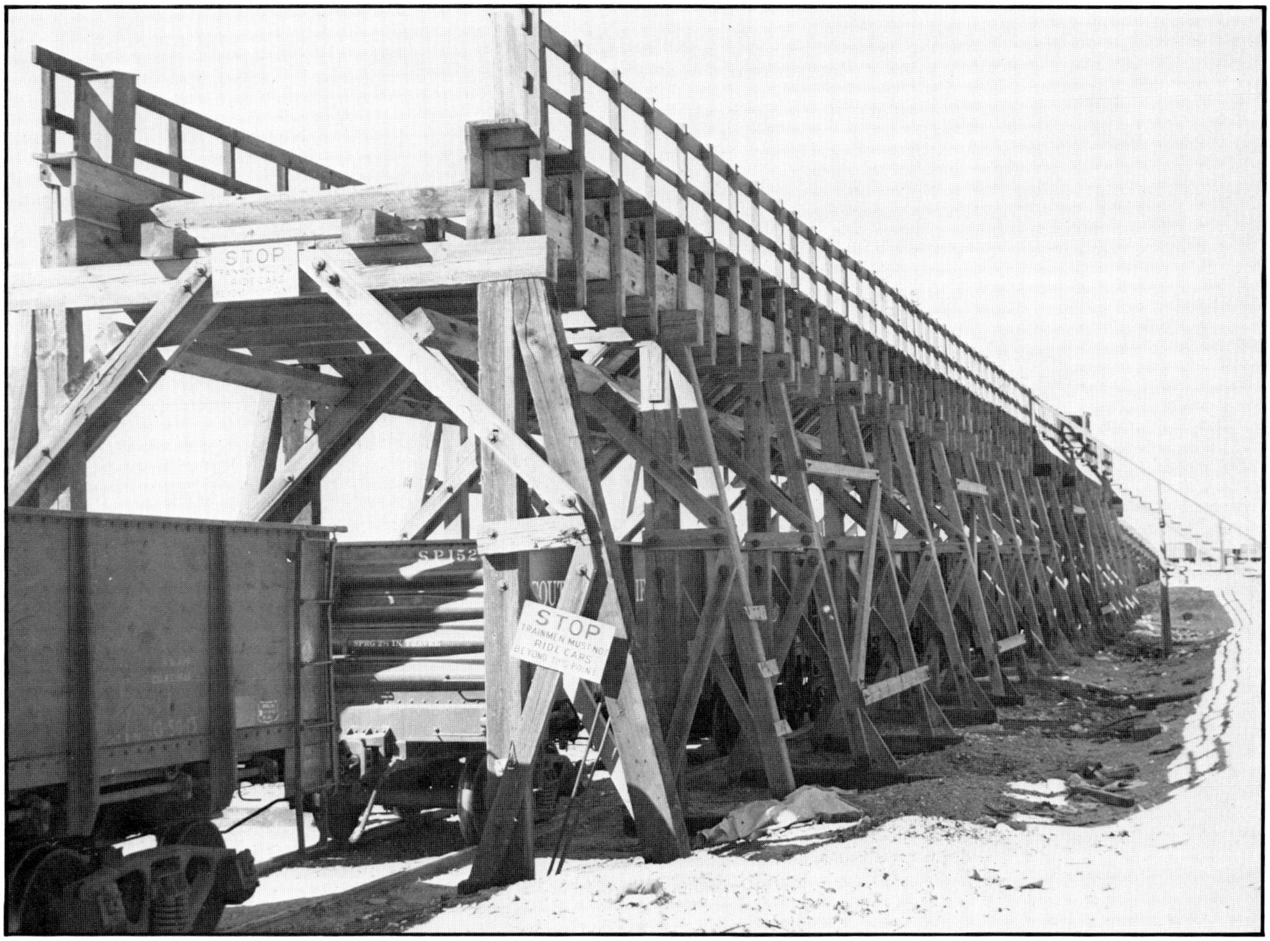
STOP
STOP
RIDE CARS

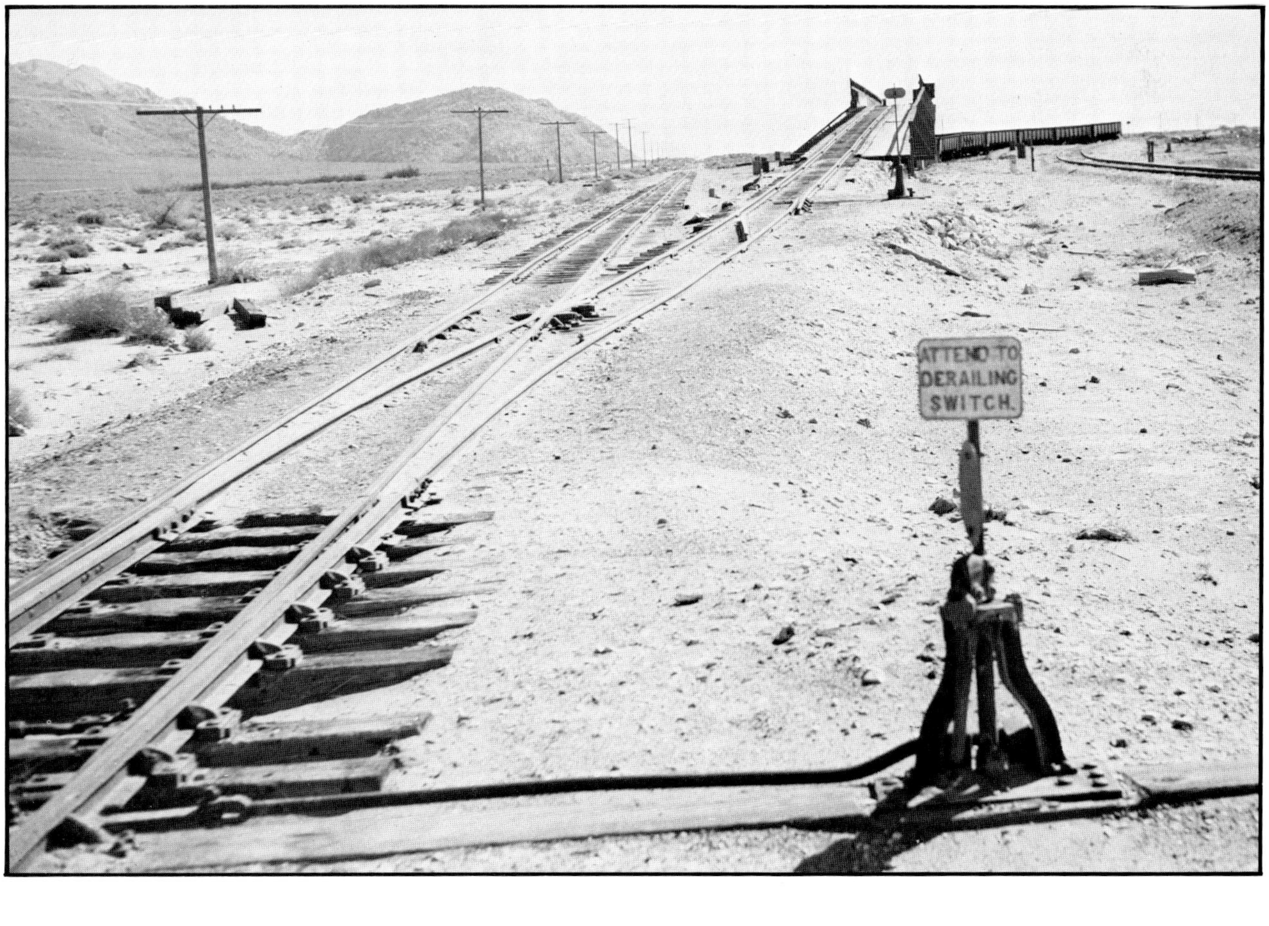
ATTEND TO
DERAILING
SWITCH.

PACIFIC
STANDARD TIME
STANDARD
CLOCK

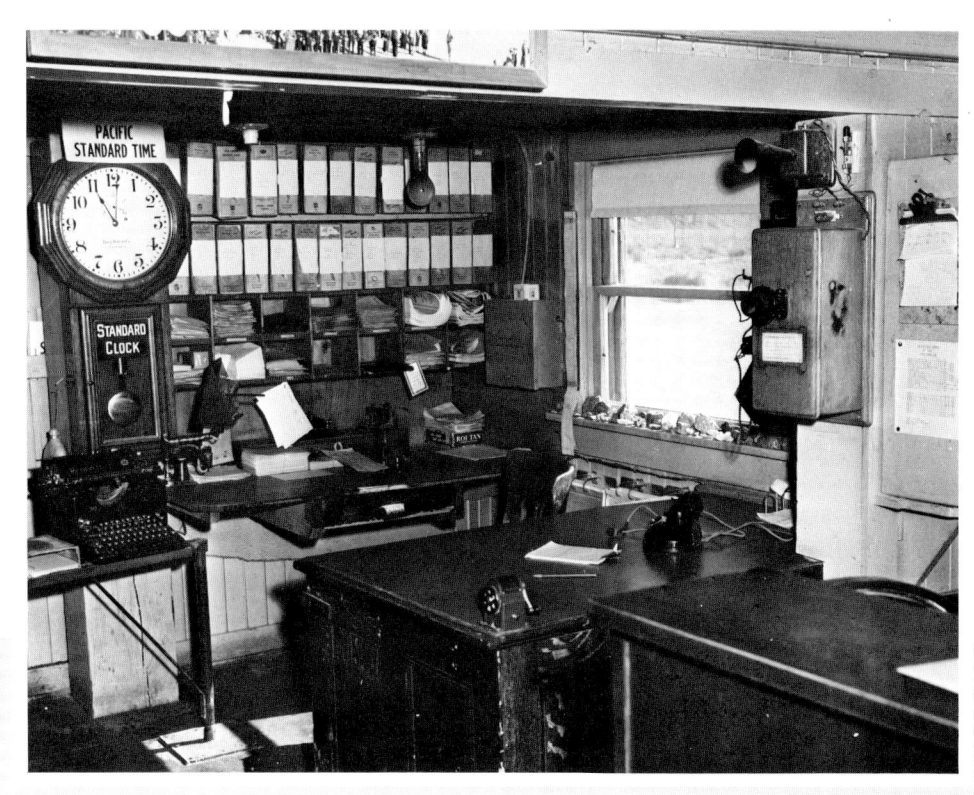

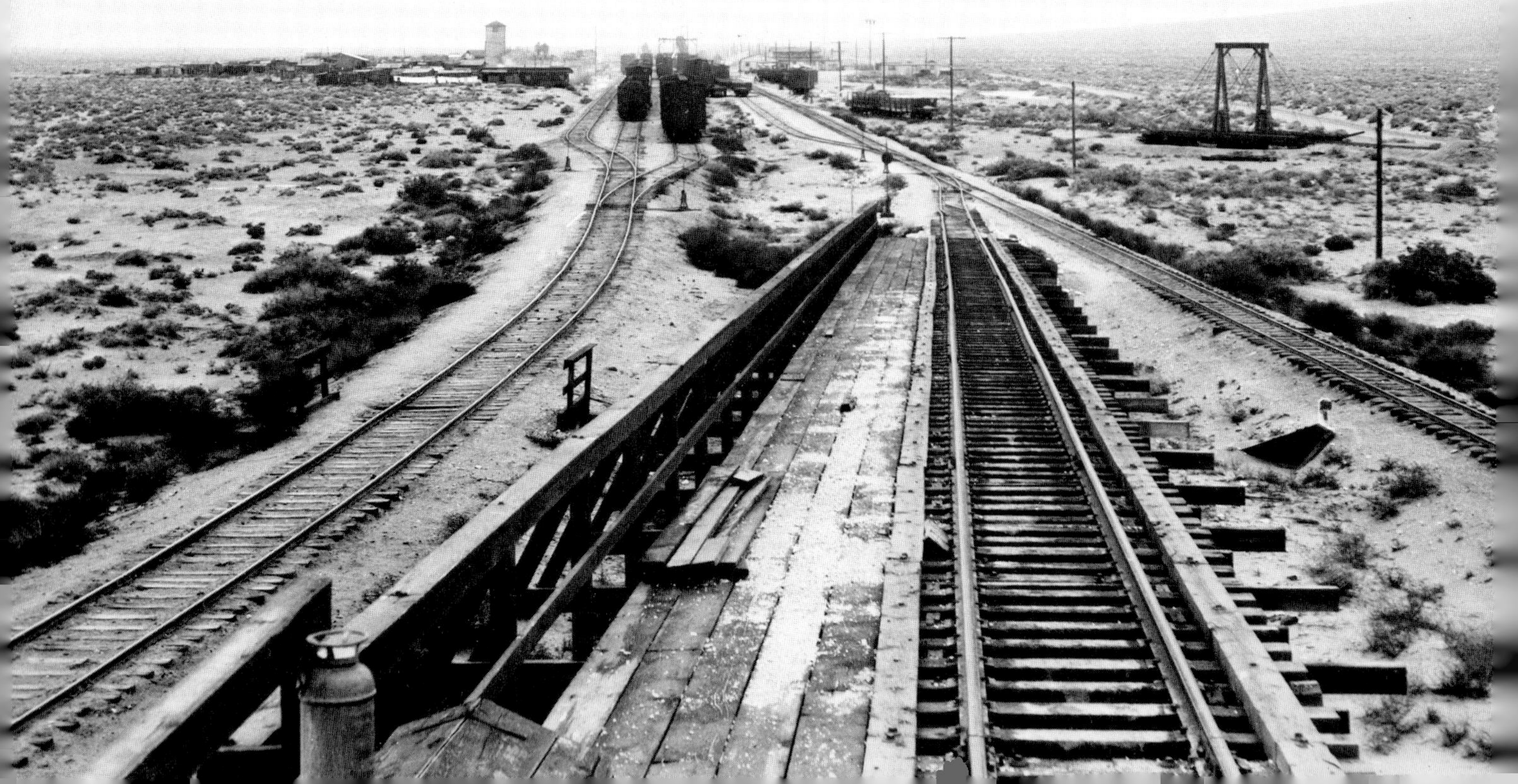

Owenyo...in the middle of nowhere!

While Owenyo was the transfer point between the three foot and standard gauge branches, there was no dual gauge trackage. The 1930's view (opposite below) shows the layout from the transfer trestle. The operations were directed from the small office (opposite top), complete with old crank telephone, ancient Remington, waybills and rock collection on window sill. A northbound train approaches the depot (above) on March 16, 1954, with Number 9. The hotel is just behind the station. [All photos: SP collection.]

Engine 9 switches a string of "A" frame hoppers, loaded with soapstone, onto the narrow gauge-to-standard gauge transfer trestle near the south end of Owenyo, July 1959. [Ektachrome by Wendell Mortimer.]

A northbound freight has just pulled-up to the "non-classic" depot-office that served Owenyo (opposite top). Josephine Cole, the Owenyo freight clerk, was the only woman employee of the narrow gauge. Agent W.T. Tommer stands at the semaphore handles, which were always in the "stop" position. Tommer controlled the operations of the narrow gauge for so long that people referred to the line as "Mr. Tommer's Railroad." [Three views: SP collection.]

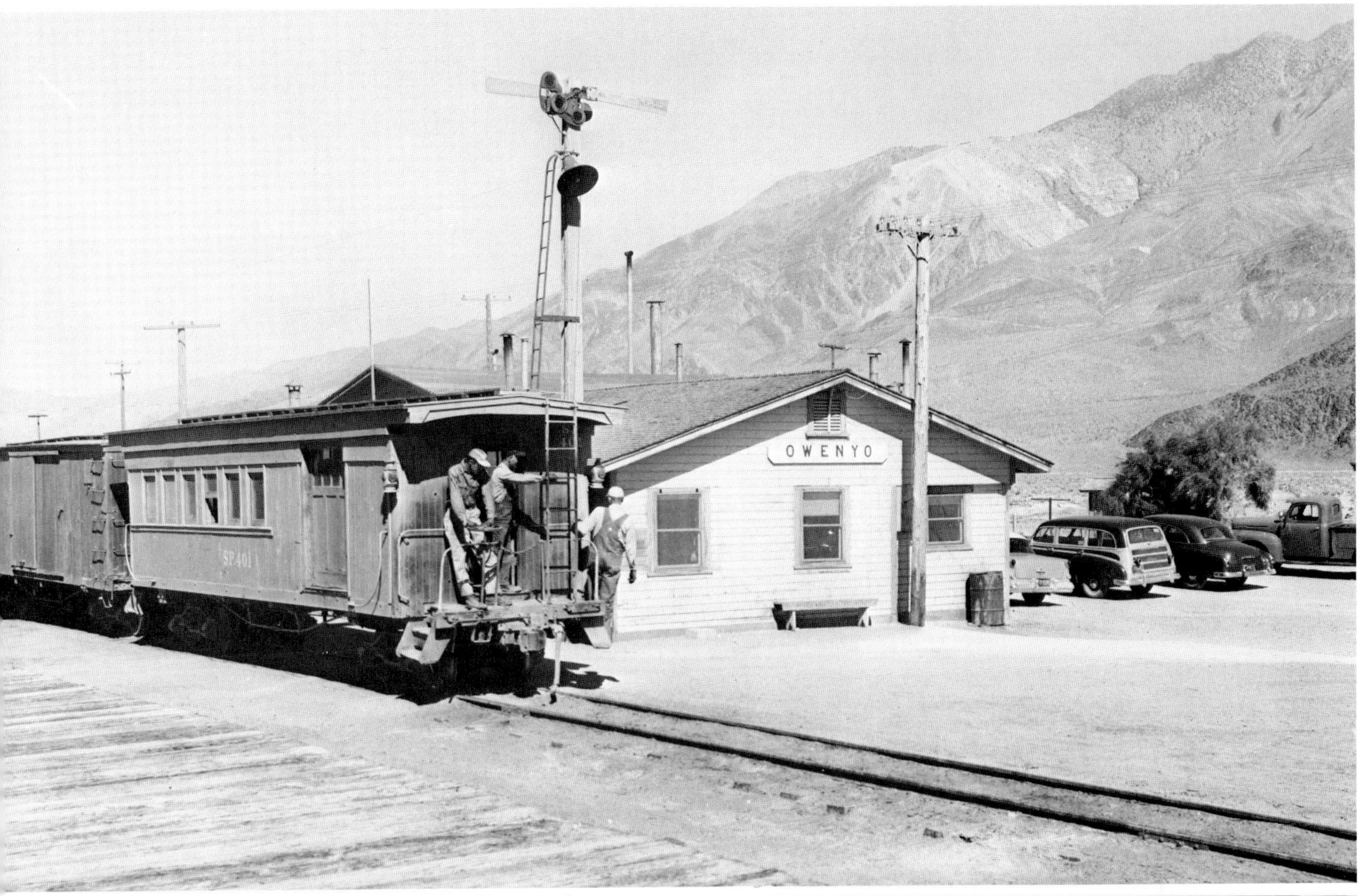
OWENYO
SP401

14 15 16 17 18 19 20
21 22 23 24 25 26 27
28 29 30 31
Southern Pacific

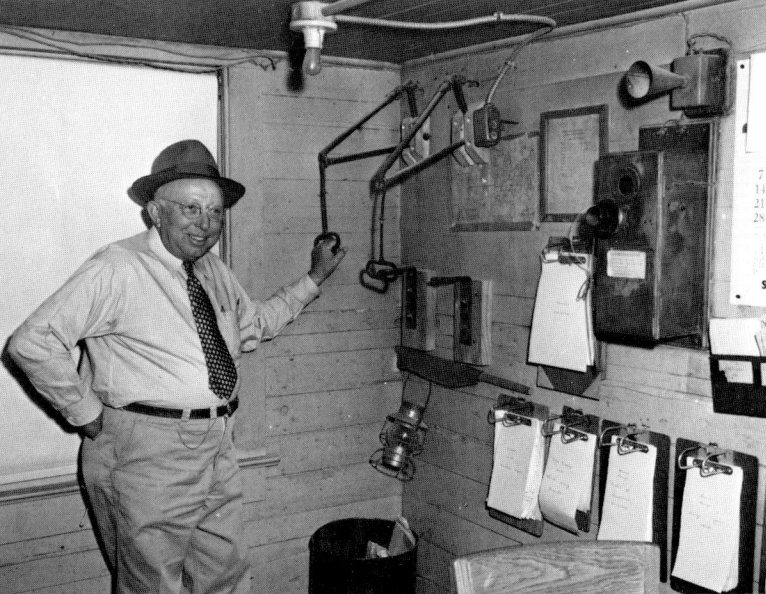

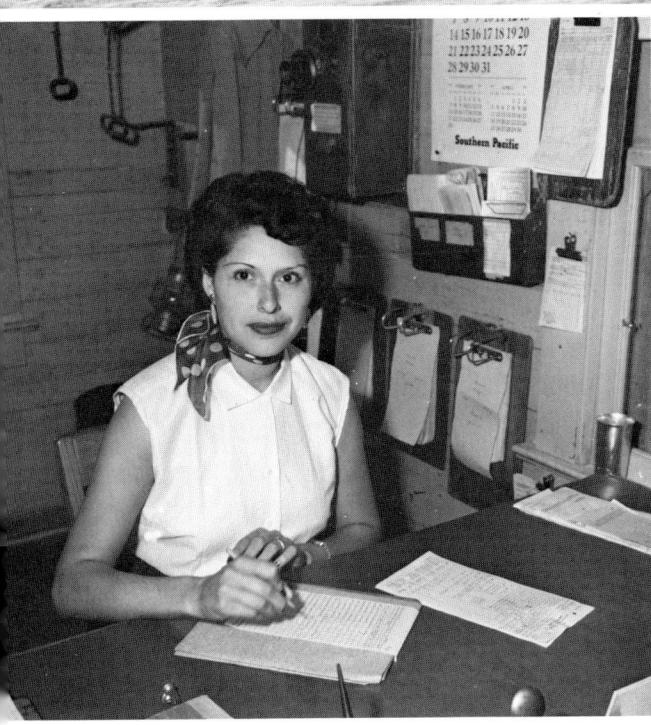

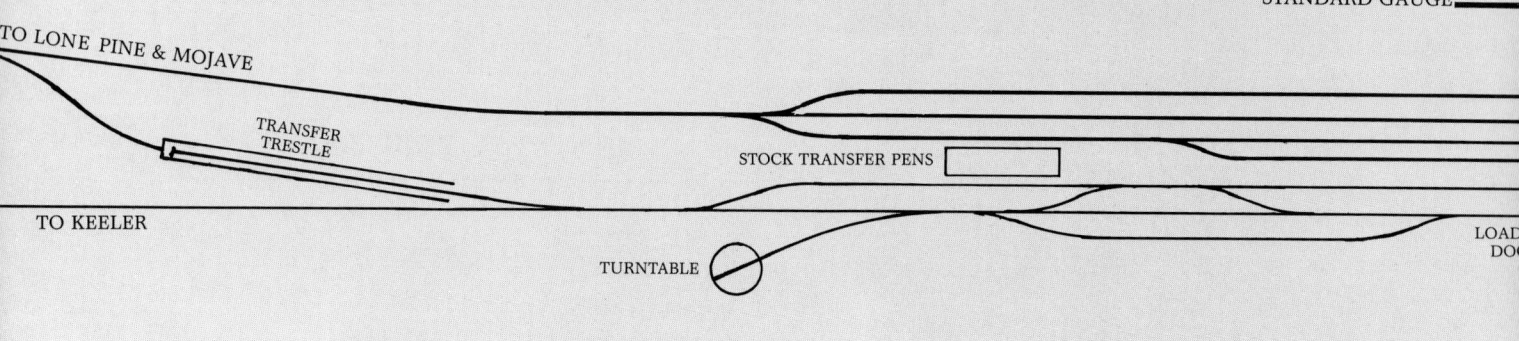

Owenyo Hotel and depot looking southerly August 17, 1939. [Al C. Phelps.]

Owenyo transfer gantry, where materials were transferred between narrow gauge and standard gauge. [Richard F. Thomas.]

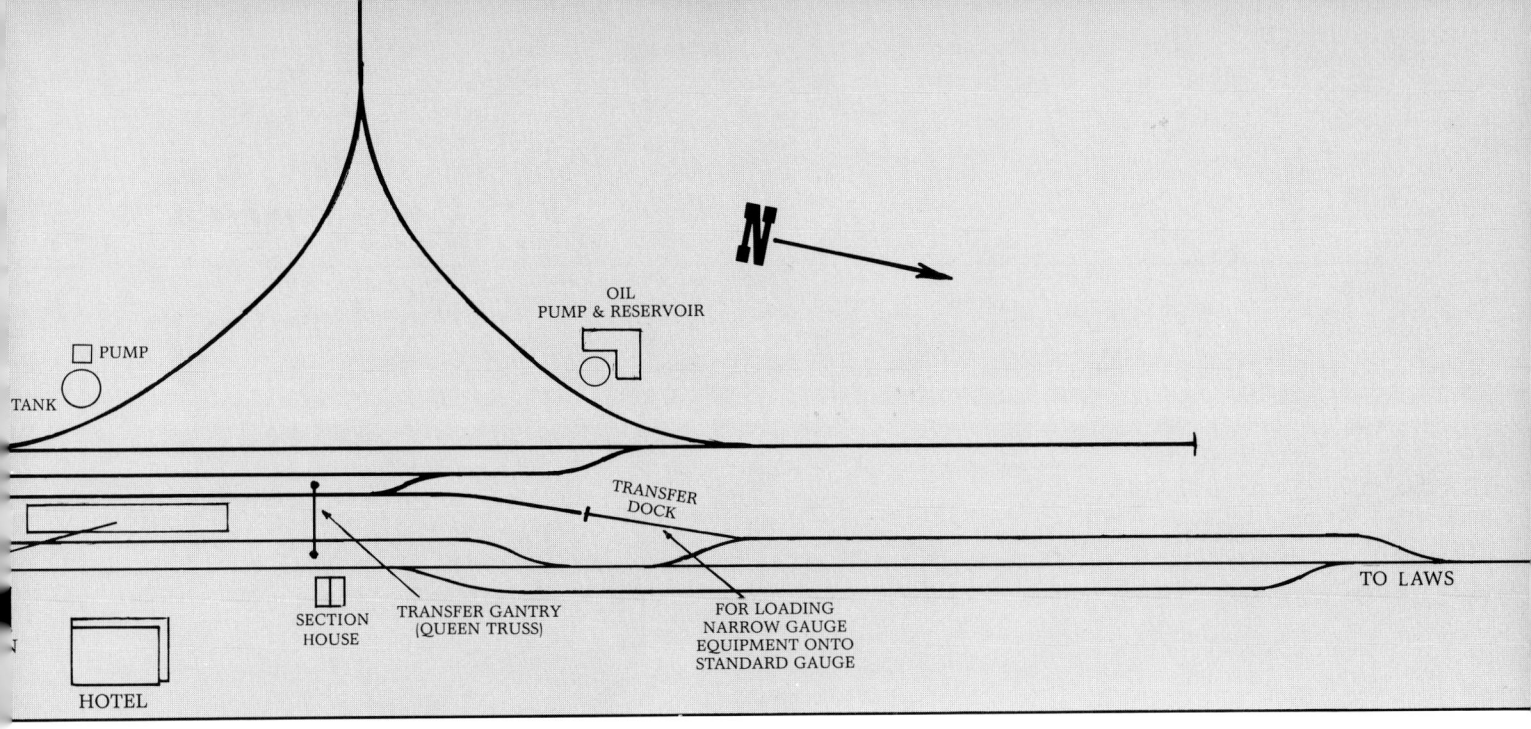

Transfer gantry at Owenyo was hand powered. [Robert W. Brown.]

The gallows turntable at Owenyo was originally used at Keeler. [Bert H. Ward.]

Many shipments destined out of the valley were not suited to the transfer trestle, or gantry crane and had to be moved by hand. Cattle and sheep simply walked from cars of one gauge to those of the other via the livestock transfer (opposite top). [Richard F. Thomas.] In the lower view, bags of gypsum are being moved across the dock, while on this page, the Number 9 switches a string of cars near the depot. [Both photos: SP collection.]

When it was necessary to send a car or locomotive to the shops in Bakersfield, the narrow gauge equipment was loaded aboard a standard gauge flat (above). The Number 9 was bound out of the valley in February, 1951. [Fred Hust.] A special loading trestle (below) facilitated such movements. [Richard F. Thomas.]
On the opposite page, the difference between the gauges is seen as SP 18 smokes away (top) next to the regular "Jawbone Branch" engine in 1951.
[W.C. Whittaker.] Within a few years Alco road switchers had replaced steam on the standard gauge (lower), but not on the slim rails . . . yet! [John Hungerford.]

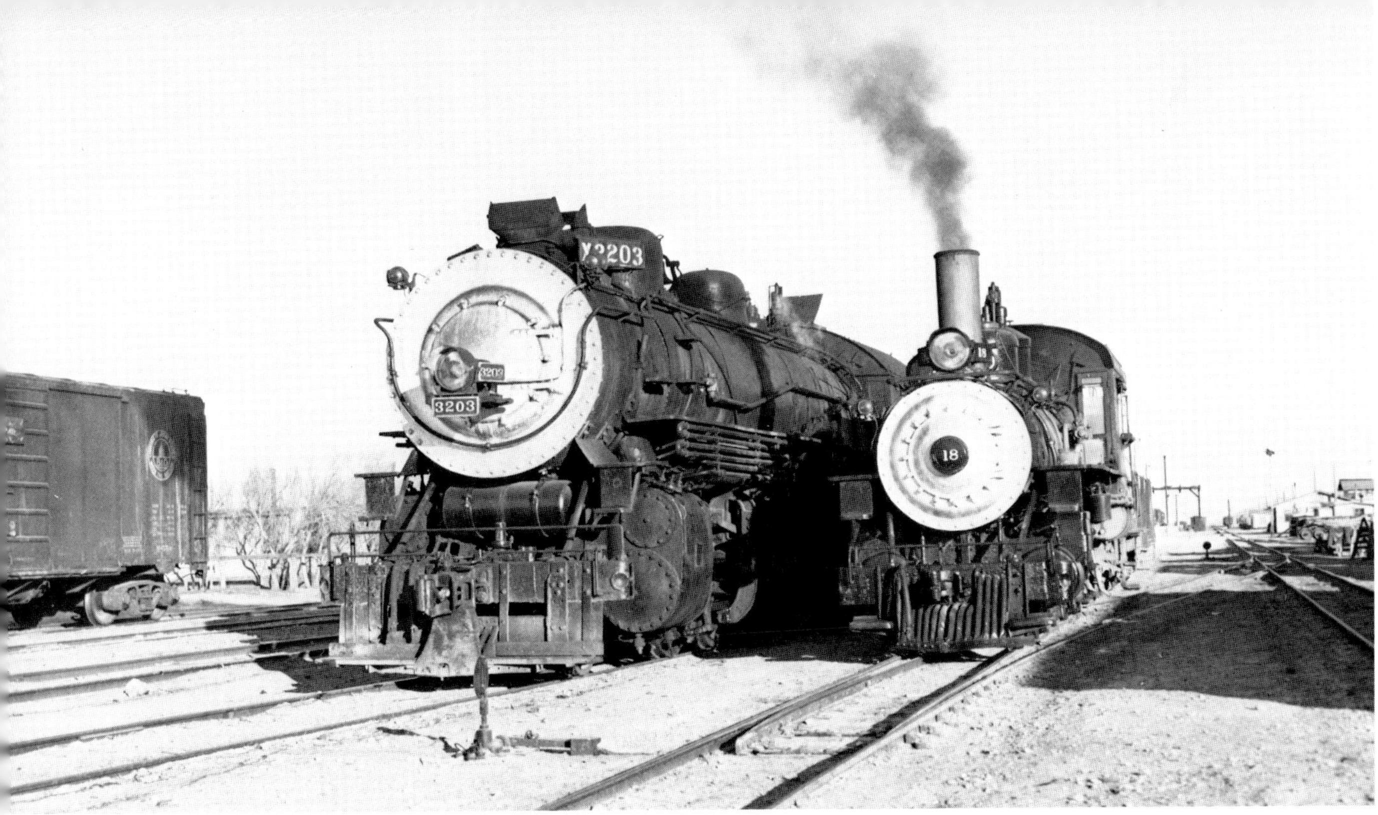
X3203
3203
3203
18

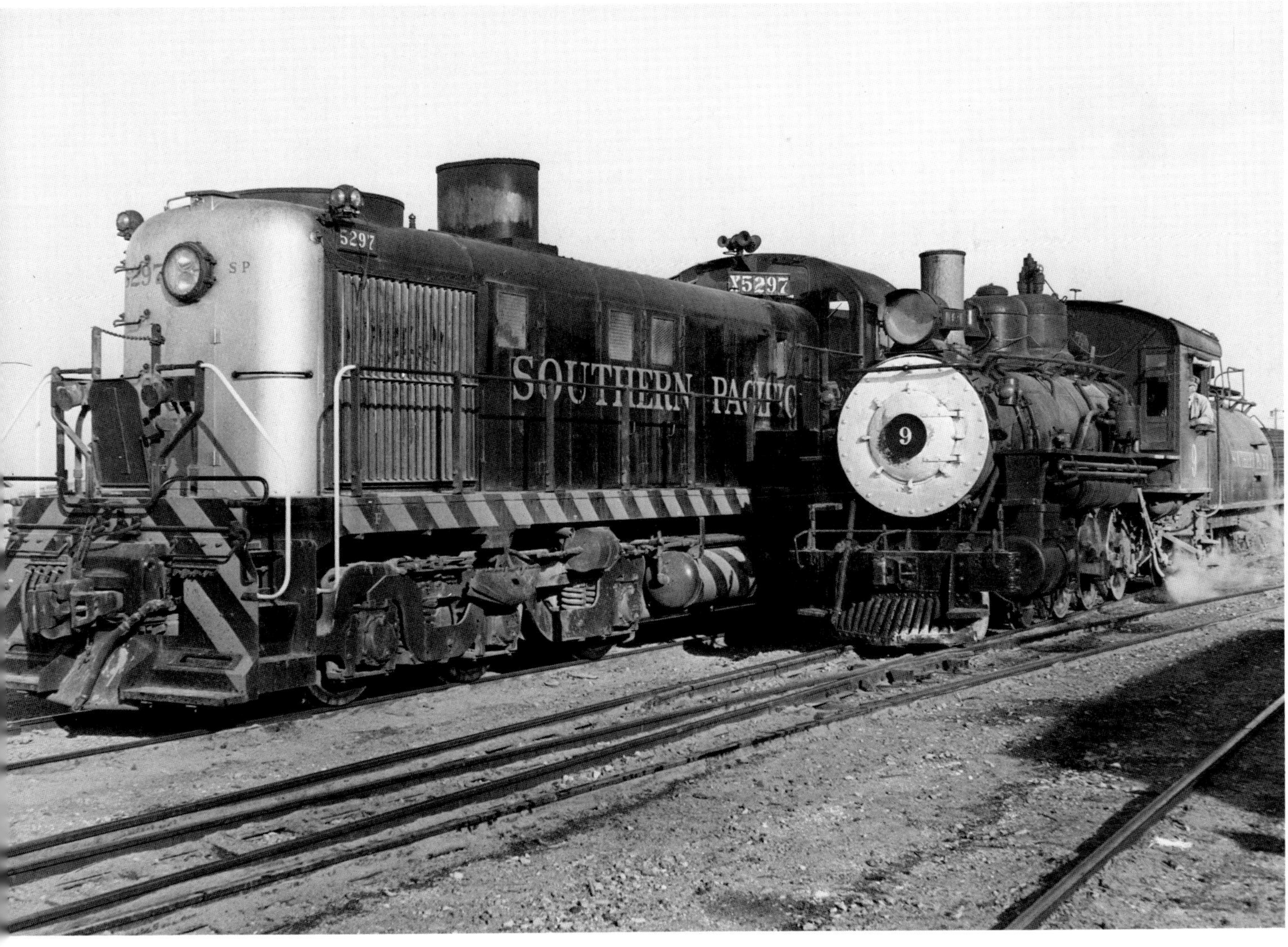
5297
SP
X5297
SOUTHERN PACIFIC
9

Outside Connections

After the completion of the "Jawbone Branch" from Mojave to Owenyo in 1910, connecting passenger service was offered for a few years, then dropped. Connecting passenger service was also offered over the former narrow gauge line north of Mina. A special American Potash & Chemical Corporation employees' train, double-headed behind SP 702 and 4332, was found on the "Jawbone" line at Cantil, California in 1952 (above). The lower view finds 2-8-2 605 with a freight train at Wabuska, Nevada on the former Carson & Colorado grade. Wabuska was the junction point with the Nevada Copper Belt, and one of their wooden boxcars has been spotted on the siding. [Both photographs: Donald Duke.] SP 18 smokes up the morning sky at Owenyo (opposite top) and prepares for a run across the desert with rebuilt combine-caboose 401 in 1953.
[Both photographs: Wendell Mortimer, Jr.]

149

Steamin' Thru The Desert
The desert water stop is made (opposite top) at Kearsarge tank in 1959. The train is returning from Zurich with loads of soapstone. [Lawrie Brown.] The 18 switches at Zurich (opposite lower) in a 1952 view by Wendell Mortimer, Jr. Ten wheeler Number 9 heads across the desert floor of the Owens Valley with a single boxcar and caboose-combine 401 in a 1953 study of railroading on the back side of the Sierra. [Wendell Mortimer, Jr.]

Night Time On The Narrow Gauge
Night operations on the SP's narrow gauge were rare, as trains were generally run only during the daylight hours. However on rare occasions, the slim gauge stayed up past her bedtime. The Number 9 heads home to Keeler (left) in March, 1954 as conductor Harry O'Nan gives a "highball" signal at Owenyo. [SP collection.] The Keeler engine terminal is quiet except for the sound of escaping steam from ten wheeler 9. [Wendell Mortimer, Jr.]

Daybreak finds renewed activity. The Number 9 has just arrived in Owenyo (above) and will soon be headed across the desert for Laws. [John Krause.] The 18 smokes up the Owens Valley (opposite) as she heads northbound out of Owenyo. [Richard F. Thomas.] The 18 was found in the desert by Will Whittaker in 1951.

Snow On The SP Narrow Gauge

While the Owens Valley was noted for the "over 100" temperatures of summer, the line did see an occasional snowstorm blow in from the High Sierra. Engine 8 pauses at Aberdeen on February 23, 1953 (opposite lower) in just such a storm. [Fred Hust.] Photographer Donald Duke found the same Laws bound train taking water at Kearsarge tank (opposite top). By the time the train reached Laws (above) the snow had stopped, but it was still cold work turning the 4-6-0 on the gallows turntable. [Donald Duke.]

157

Kearsarge

The Kearsarge depot is seen (above) in its final years as a freight heads north in 1953. [Wendell Mortimer, Jr.] The 18 was paused for a drink at Kearsarge tank in 1952 [W.C. Whittaker.] The hobo, like the railroad he's walking, appears to have seen better days. [Wendell Mortimer, Jr.]

Photographer John Krause captured the action of SP 9 as she headed northbound out of Owenyo with a long train of high cars (below). Extra 9 East (southbound) has paused in the desert (above) between Zurich and Kearsarge on February 22, 1956. [Fred Hust.]

The depot at Kearsarge once served a large ranching and farming area. Located near Independence, by the original Carson & Colorado, it had been hoped the town would move to the railroad station. This never happened and the depot was torn down in 1955, after having been closed for years. The 18 pauses for water on February 22, 1952 while heading a northbound freight. [Richard F. Thomas.] The depot was photographed in 1948. [Guy L. Dunscomb.]

"Sunset Water Stop" by Jim Finnell
11½" × 15½" acrylic on masonite.

Aberdeen Tank
Ten wheeler 18, which came from the Nevada-California-Oregon, makes a water stop at Aberdeen tank. The tank was filled by a windmill and when there was insufficient wind, it would be necessary to couple on a water car behind the tender, so that the engines could make it between water tanks. [Opposite: Robert Lee Behme, above Donald Duke.]

Southern Pacific narrow gauge 18 has paused at Aberdeen tank on October 6, 1949 in a classic scene by Donald Duke.

Owens River
Between Aberdeen and Monola, the slim gauge rails crossed the usually placid Owens River at two locations. The 18 is seen at the first crossing above Aberdeen (opposite top) in 1952 [Richard F. Thomas.], and at the second crossing (opposite lower) in 1954 [Al C. Phelps.] Don Duke found the #8 blasting over the trestle (above) near Monola, during a period of high water in early spring.

The trackage around Tinemaha Reservoir was relocated in 1928-29 and involved a deep rock cut. The Number 18 is shown blasting through this cut (above) in 1952 with a southbound freight. [Richard F. Thomas.] The 18 heads across the desert near Laws (opposite top) in a Walt Thrall photo made in 1949. [Colorado Railroad Museum collection.] The remote nature of the mainline through the sagebrush and sand is clearly shown in a Wendell Mortimer, Jr. view.

Action With Eighteen

SP 18 has paused at Zurich, where loads of soapstone fill the siding. [Donald Duke.] Zurich was at one time a major shipping point for vanadium and talc. In later years, when the crew tied-up at Owenyo rather than at Keeler, it was not possible to turn the engine. The Owenyo turntable had been removed in 1948. Therefore it would be necessary to back the engine to Laws, where the steamer could be turned on the gallows turntable. Such an operation is pictured (opposite) as the 18 backs her train northbound near Tinemaha Reservoir in 1953. [Wendell Mortimer, Jr.]

171

Smoking Towards Laws
Southern Pacific 8 heads a freight four miles south of Laws, California on a cold February day in 1953. Snow covers the nearby foothills of the White Mountains, and the temperature is hovering at freezing in the valley. Donald Duke was at trackside with his 4x5 graphic to record the scene.

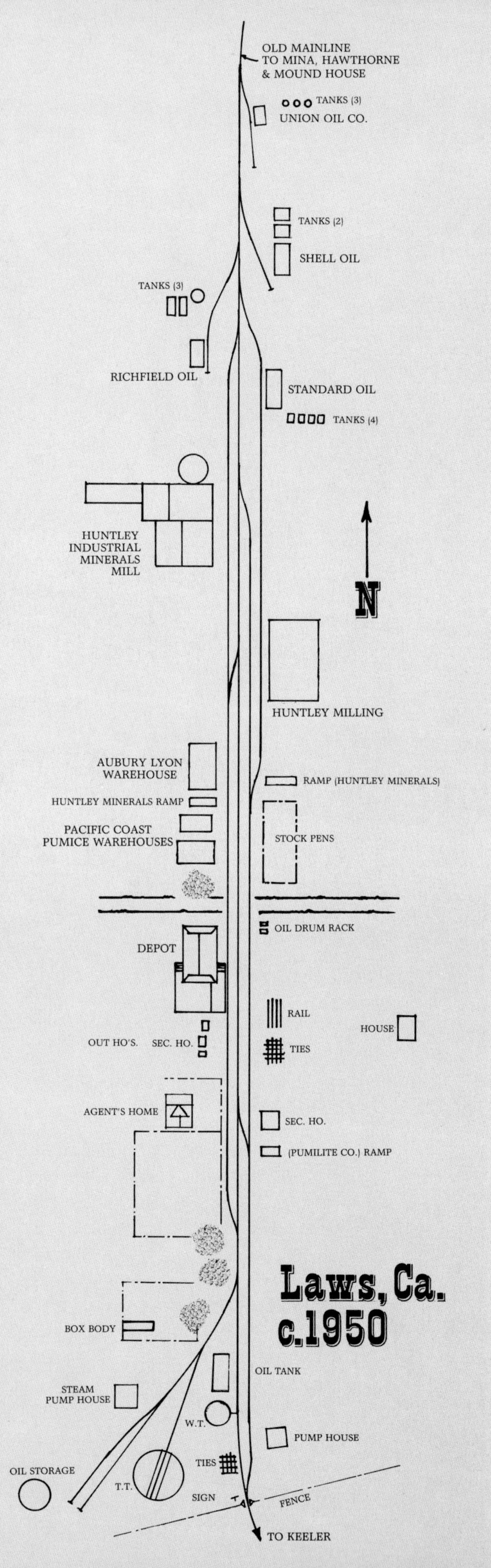

Laws Yards

A northbound freight (Extra 18 West) has just arrived at Laws, California, (right) in the summer of 1953. [Wendell Mortimer, Jr.]

Southern Pacific 18 is shown arriving in Laws in a 1949 photograph by Donald Duke.

The sleepy noontime quiet of Laws has been broken by the arrival of the Southern Pacific's 18 and her train of ancient wooden cars. The depot is deserted (opposite) as the train crew goes about the switching chores. [Donald Duke.] The 18 switches the grass covered rails north of the depot (opposite top and above) in April, 1952. [Both Wendell Mortimer, Jr.] An overall view of the yard (top), looking north, is seen in a 1939 photograph by Al C. Phelps.

Gallows Turntable

The Gallows Turntable at Laws was built by the Carson & Colorado in 1883 and served the narrow gauge until the end of operations. The 18 is turned by her crew (opposite) in 1952. [Wendell Mortimer, Jr.] Donald Duke found the crew getting their backs into turning the table (above) on a bright Owens Valley afternoon. The close-up of the "Armstrong" method of turning an engine was made by Wendell Mortimer, Jr. The turntable is still in existence as is the Number 18.

At left, before a curious group of youngsters, the crew of Number 18 turns and backs the ten wheeler off the Laws turntable. [Both: Wendell Mortimer, Jr.] A few years earlier (above) Don Duke photographed the same ritual. The detailed view shows the "rollers" at the center of the Gallows turntable.

Switching Laws

Baldwin 4-6-0 Number 18 switches the Laws yards in the late 1940's. [Donald Duke.] The depot itself is seen in 1948. [Guy L. Dunscomb.] Laws, at an elevation of 4,115 feet, was tree-shaded and grass-covered, in contrast to the hot sands of Owenyo and Keeler. The 18 switches the yards (above right) south of the depot in 1953. [Wendell Mortimer, Jr.] The consist prepares to leave town in 1952 (lower right) in a Will C. Whittaker photograph.

Laws Tank
The Laws watertank, with the nearby pumphouse, oil facility and turntable, was part of the small engine servicing facility that made Laws unique. SP Number 18 takes on water on October 6, 1949, while the crew checks over the engine and train prior to heading south to Keeler. [Both photographs: Donald Duke.] On the opposite page, the 8 is ready to leave Laws on a cold winter day in 1953. [Donald Duke.] Wendell Mortimer, Jr. found the 18 and train of high cars just south of the Laws yard later the same year.

Leavin' Laws
The 18 blasts out of Laws on her southbound run to Keeler (opposite) on October 6, 1949 in a photographic study of smoke and glory. [Donald Duke.] The same train was captured on film (opposite lower), a few miles south of Monola. [Walt Thrall.] The Keeler bound train was photographed (left) from the swaying combine-caboose as she rounded a gentle curve, and (below) as the 18 smoked up the cobalt blue sky south of Laws. [Both: Donald Duke.]

HOLLYWOOD RIDES THE SPNG

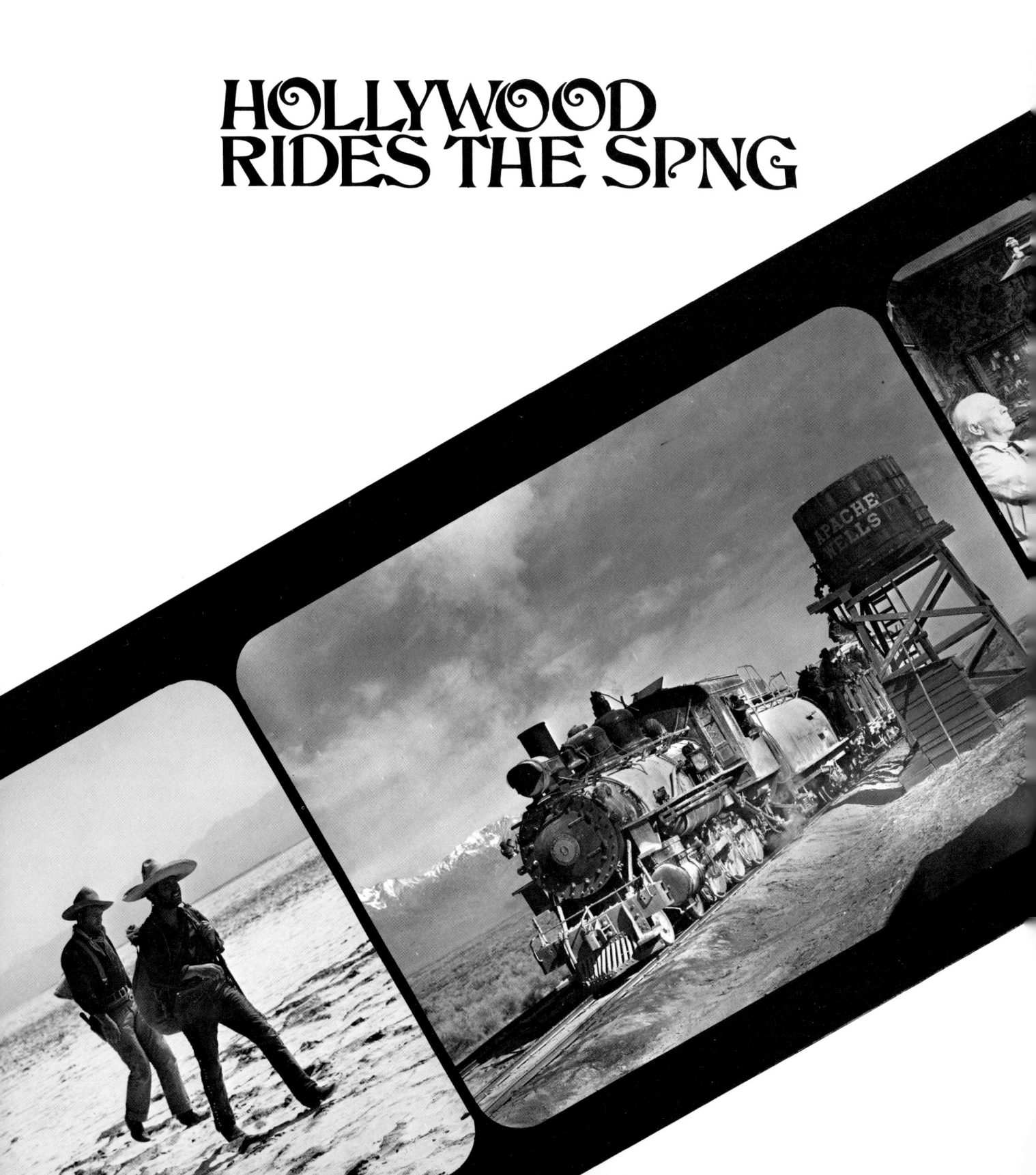

A number of feature length Hollywood films have been made in the Owens Valley, and several have included the narrow gauge. The line has appeared in "B" westerns with such stars as Gene Autry and Roy Rogers. Keeler has become "Crazy Horse, Nevada" (top) for a 1942 production. [RKO Studios.] The narrow gauge played an important role in "Three Godfathers," starring John Wayne. The movie was made in the valley (opposite lower) in 1949 and featured SP 9, flatcar 259 and combine 400. The film's train arrives at the fictional "Apache Wells, Arizona" tank. Film crews built the watertank and "weathered" the train to make it look even more dusty than usual. [Metro-Goldwyn-Mayer.] The Slim Princess was also used in the 1950's television series "Annie Oakley." "Bad Day At Black Rock" used scenes filmed on the "Jawbone line," and at Laws, while the 1965 Steve McQueen Paramount film "Nevada Smith" used Laws and the narrow gauge display train.

By 1954 steam power's days on the SP narrow gauge were numbered. A Diesel was on order and rail fans flocked to the valley to photograph and record the trains, while there was still time. Donald Duke found the 18 on a northbound "special" in February, 1954 with Mt. Whitney and the High Sierra in the background.

TWILIGHT ON THE NARROW GAUGE

The mid-1950's saw a number of changes on the Southern Pacific's narrow gauge Owens Valley line. Many older cars were taken out of service and their bodies burned or sold to valley farmers and ranchers. Locomotives 8, 9 and 18, long the mainstay of the road, were getting old. Chief Boilermaker R.R. Hovey and Carman E.E. Lyman had managed to keep the equipment in pretty good order, considering their age. Heavy repair work was handled in the Bakersfield Shops, but the cars and engines were getting old, many of them dating from the 1880's. Some cars had seen service on the Florence & Cripple Creek line in Colorado and had come to the Keeler Branch after serving on the Nevada-California-Oregon. Other rolling stock had come from the South Pacific Coast during the Tonopah gold rush, while still others had "drifted" to the valley from the Oregonian Railway and the San Joaquin & Sierra Nevada, roads long since standard gauged by the Southern Pacific.

On October 16, 1954 the steam era on the SP narrow gauge came to a formal end with the arrival in Owenyo of Diesel Number 1. Following a contest, the new engine was dubbed "Little Giant," and a "Fan Trip" was arranged to welcome the 400 horsepower machine's arrival and bid farewell to steam. Some 161 members of the Railway & Locomotive Historical Society's Southern California Chapter arrived in Owenyo aboard a special train. After a dedication of the new Diesel (she was Christened with a bottle of talc), the railfans boarded a train of open gondolas for a ride behind 4-6-0 Number 9 to Keeler and return. Fan trips on the SP narrow gauge had become quite common since the early fifties and the road had converted five gondolas into "tourist cars" with their own "his" and "hers" outhouses. The fans promptly called them "chic sales" cars. With the arrival of the Number 1 Diesel, the day to day operations seem to have lost their glamor. The tracks were still narrow, the cars archaic, but without steam, it was just not the same.

The Number 9 was retained for standby service, along with the Number 18. The Nine-spot saw occasional service each year when the Diesel was in for repairs, or when groups came to ride the slim gauge. When steam reappeared on the SP narrow gauge, so did the cameras, for now the reputation of being the last narrow gauge common carrier in the Far West was well known. The Number 9 had even been "off line" to power the three foot gauge line of the U.S. Gypsum Company out of Plaster City, California, when their Diesels were broken down in the spring of 1953. She must have been quite at home on the 26 miles of desert trackage out of Plaster City, where the temperatures are even hotter than those of the Owens Valley. She returned home in the fall of the year, for further service on the SP narrow gauge.

*Actually the construction of all five cars with "outhouses" was the result of a misunderstanding, as the order was issued to convert five cars to excursion use, one of which was to sport the "johnies." The carmen put benches on all five gondolas, but also built two of the privies on each. So, they ran that way until the late 1950's.

When the 9 was shopped at Bakersfield in the fall of 1956, she was fitted with a fake diamond stack, box headlight and was painted with gold, silver and red trim. It must have been some well meaning master mechanic's idea of what an old narrow gauge engine should look like. Nonetheless, protest soon followed from historical groups and railfans. The 4-6-0 operated until the spring of 1958 in those "gosh-awful colors", and was restored to her previous appearance of engine black, with white lettering. By this time the five "excursion cars" had been converted back to freight service in an effort to discourage excursions.

Other changes had taken place on the narrow gauge, setting the stage for an abandonment application. The classic Kearsarge Depot, long out of service, was torn down in December, 1955. The windmill powered pump at Aberdeen tank was replaced by a gas engine pump, after a windstorm blew down the windmill in 1953. The depot at Keeler was closed in August, 1957 and in February, 1959, the Laws agency closed its doors. This left only the Owenyo Depot to handle the traffic for the entire line. Despite an upturn in business, the handwriting was on the wall for SP narrow gauge.

On January 20, 1959 the Southern Pacific applied to the almighty Interstate Commerce Commission to abandon the Keeler Branch and substitute truck service by its Pacific Motor Trucking Company. July, 1959 saw the last regular use of Number 9 in freight service.

Final approval for abandonment was issued on December 30, 1959, and included permission to tear up the four miles of standard gauge trackage between Lone Pine and Owenyo. The dreams of Sharon, Yerington and Mills for their Carson & Colorado had long since been forgotten. On April 25, 1960, Diesel 1 hauled 4-6-0 Number 9 and caboose-combine 401 to Laws. The steamer and a freight train would become a part of the Laws Railroad Museum & Historical Site. This was the final movement over the northern portion of the line. Four days later the One-spot made a round trip run to Keeler and put an end to the narrow gauge. The final crew consisted of Walt Ferguson, engineer; William Graves, fireman; Conductor G.C. McGhee and brakemen Jerry Jones and Bob Olson. By September, the scrap crews were pulling up rails and selling off box and stockcars for $100 delivered to local farms. The most improbable of all short lines had come to the end of its run.

Sage Brush Rocket

Since the early days of the Carson & Colorado, excursions had been popular on the narrow gauge. As narrow gauge lines disappeared and steam motive power became less commonplace, those interested in trains came in greater numbers to see the Owens Valley line. On October 7-8, 1948 the Railway & Locomotive Historical Society sponsored a two-day excursion over the road (opposite top and center). Due to a misunderstanding by the Owenyo carmen, outhouses were installed on five "excursion cars," rather than the single car which was to have sported "johns." [Fred Stindt from Guy L. Dunscomb.] On a bright February 10, 1951 (opposite page) the 18 pulls a regular freight north of Owenyo. The extra passenger car was added for the benefit of visiting railfans. [Will C. Whittaker.]

"Little Giant" Takes Over

With the arrival of a new General Electric diesel in the fall of 1954, regular use of steam on the Slim Princess ended. Following a contest, the X-1 was named "Little Giant," and christened with a bottle of talc. A farewell excursion for steam was held on October 16, 1954, with Number 9 hauling the train on a Owenyo to Keeler roundtrip. The local band played (above), while the 18 and new diesel were displayed. The last narrow gauge common carrier in the West had gone diesel. [Three photographs: SP collection.] The 9 is turned on the Keeler wye (opposite lower) as fans and locals watch. [Wendell Mortimer, Jr.]

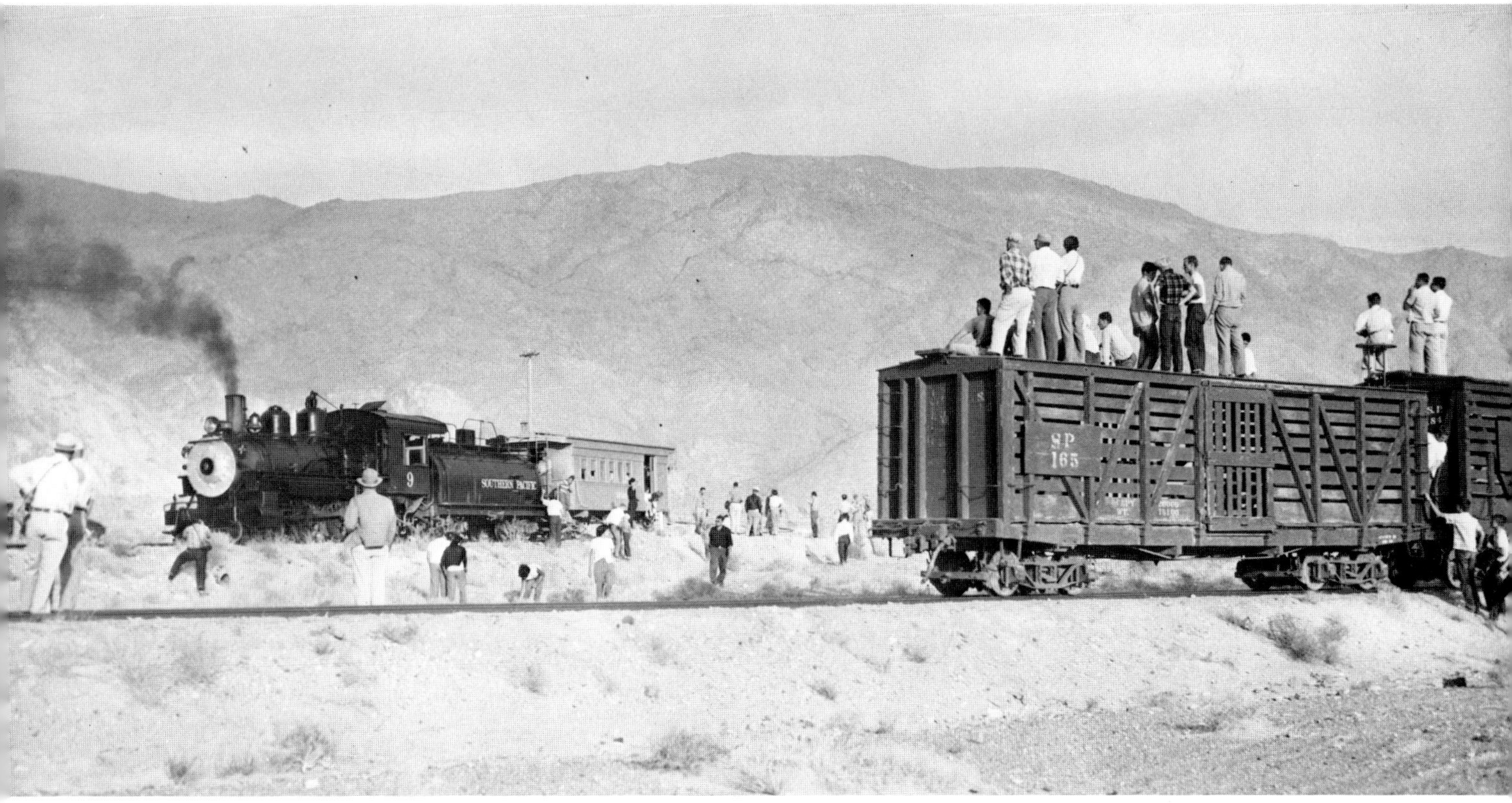

Fan Trips
Frequently during the 1950's, the spare baggage-mail car would be added to the rear of the regular freight train for the benefit of visiting railfans. Just such a consist prepares to leave Laws (above) on February 22, 1954. [Al C. Phelps.]
Following a routine trip to the Bakersfield Shops in the fall of 1956, the Number 9 emerged with a "gosh-awful" paint job and phony stack and headlight.
She operated this way until the spring of 1958, when she was restored to basic black. She is shown (below) in February, 1957. [Fred Hust.] The 9-spot operated on several excursions (opposite page) during this period.
[Both: William Kaminsky collection.]

With the arrival of the X-1 diesel, the SP narrow gauge lost some of its appeal, but was still of interest. The "Little Giant" heads a long string of cars (above) and switches a few boxcars (opposite top) shortly after arrival. [Caterpiller Tractor Co.] The diesel sets out cars at Zurich (right) in a Hugh Tolford photograph. On April 25, 1960 the diesel hauled Baldwin 9 on her final trip to Laws (opposite), as the narrow gauge prepared to quit. [Gary G. Allen.]

Last Of The Red Hot Steamers
*Following dieselization of the narrow gauge, steam still saw occasional
use when the "Little Giant" was undergoing her annual inspection or was out of
service for repairs. The 9 takes water (opposite top) at Laws on such an occasion.
[SP collection.] On March 22, 1958, the 4-6-0 powers an excursion north of Keeler.
[Fred Hust.] The Number 18 makes a caboose-hop during this twilight on the
narrow gauge. [Donald Duke.]*

The rolling stock of the Sothern Pacific's Owens Valley pike had a character all its own, caused in part by years of desert running. A string of cars has been shoved over the Owenyo turntable spur in 1946, to await the attention of carmen. Caboose 467 would not see further service, but a rebuilding and renumbering program would soon see the other cars back in service. [Guy L. Dunscomb]

6
LIKE THE LOST TRIBE...ROSTERS

The story of the rolling stock of the Carson & Colorado, Nevada & California and Southern Pacific narrow gauge is a complex one. The equipment came down through the years as a rag-tag assortment of cars that in the final analysis reminds one of the Biblical "Lost Tribe." Aside from the original roster of the C&C, which remained stable until the early 1900's, the equipment of the other former narrow gauge roads that were standardized was sent to the desert pike. These eventually included cars that had previously seen service on such roads as the South Pacific Coast; Oregonian; Florence & Cripple Creek; San Joaquin & Sierra Nevada; North Pacific Coast and the legendary Denver, South Park & Pacific.

The Carson & Colorado roster of 1883 consisted of the following cars:

    25 ore & hand cars (1-16 ore cars)
     7 passenger cars (1-7)
    30 box cars (300-329)
    83 platform cars (flats, 1-124).

The wooden, four-wheel ore cars had originally been built by the Virginia & Truckee for service on their standard gauge line between the Comstock and mills located along the Carson River. When the C&C was constructed, these cars were converted to three foot gauge by the V&T shops. The V&T had built a second series of new iron cars for the standard gauge. A group of C&C boxcars were also interesting in that they were all metal cars, a novelty in an era of iron men and wooden cars. These "tin boxcars" were ordered from an eastern carbuilder and arrived in "knocked-down" form for assembly in the V&T's huge stone shop at Carson. Henry Yerington is said to have been less than pleased with these cars. Nevertheless, they continued to see service through the turn-of-the-century, and some were still in use during the Tonopah Gold Rush in 1904-05. The "tin boxcars" even got air brakes but appear to have retained their original link and pin couplings. The body of one "tin box" remains today at Mina, Nevada. A large number of "tin flats" also appear in early C&C photographs.

By June of 1895 the Carson & Colorado reported the following cars:

    63 flats   6 oil
    17 stock   9 dump
     1 refrigerator   53 box

In addition, there were four coaches, and three baggage-mail cars, all painted "cherry red" with gold lettering. Work equipment consisted of one flat, two water cars, one flanger and one derrick.

When it was necessary to transfer narrow gauge equipment to or from the V&T's "stone fort" shops in Carson City, a special V&T flat car

Number 1 was used. This car was classed as an Engine Transfer Car, was built by W.C. Allison & Co. in 1881 and arrived on the V&T carrying C&C 4-4-0 Number 3 from Baldwin. The car was renumbered MW 54 in 1902 and later became conventional flat 182. The car is in existance today as part of the Short Line Enterprises collection. Additionally, a conventional V&T flat Number 25 was converted to Tender Transfer Car 25 in c.1897 and became MW 55 in 1902.

Tracking down the Carson & Colorado's equipment during the 1890's is compounded by the fact that the road was not even listed in the Official Railway Equipment Register, and the owning Virginia & Truckee was down to a brief entry.

Soon after the Southern Pacific purchased the Carson & Colorado from D.O. Mills, an official roster of all SP narrow gauge equipment showed the following cars:

NARROW GAUGE FREIGHT EQUIPMENT
March 1903

Road	Type	Numbers	Capty	Total
SPC	Box (even numbers)	8 to 500	20-30,000	208
C&C	Box	300-358	20,000	53
	(cars 300-329 were "tin boxes")			
SPC	Comb. Box	92, 288-336		25
NRy	Comb. Box (even numbers)	72-108	20,000	19
SPC	Flat (odd numbers)	1-909		387
NRy	Flat (odd numbers)	641-699	20,000	29
C&C	Flat	1-120		81
SPC	Hay	240-242		2
C&C	Refrigerator	344		1
C&C	Caboose	1		1
SPC	Caboose	1, 3, 46, 47, 48		5
SPC	Water	801, 817		2
C&C	Water	59, 62		2
SPC	Station	4, 5, 6, MW7-MW16		9
SPC	Derrick	8		1
SPC	Derrick Tender	9, 10		2
C&C	Derrick Tender	76		1
C&C	Oil	29-58		6
C&C	Construction	1, 2, 3, 4, 60		5
SPC	Pile Driver	1, 2		2
SPC	Pile Driver Tender	1, 2		2
C&C	Flanger	108		1
C&C	Ore Dump	4, 6, 8, 10-110		8
			Total	852

Large numbers of South Pacific Coast cars were brought in during the Tonopah Gold Rush. The SPC had been recently broad gauged and the cars were used on a per diem basis by the C&C and the three foot gauge Tonopah R. R. Following the formation of the Nevada & California Railroad in 1905, the roster consisted of the following equipment:

N&C ROSTER OF FEBRUARY 1908

Flat	2-139	20-30,000 capty	58
Gondola	3, 4, 6, 8, 75, 86	20,000 capty	6
Gondola	88, 119	20,000 capty	2
Oil	58, 66, 71, 97	20,000 capty	4
Oil	100, 101, 131	20,000 capty	3
Oil	19, 124	30,000 capty	2
Stock rack	9, 17, 72, 83, 90	30,000 capty	5
Stock rack	92, 98, 122, 133	30,000 capty	4
Box & combo.	302-454	20-40,000 capty	121
Caboose	333, 416, 455		3
Caboose	456		1
Boarding	60		1
Flanger	108		1
Derrick tender	7, 18, 347, 354		4
Water	54, 59, 61, 62, 63		5
Water	129		1

On July 1, 1907, the Nevada & California was leased to the Southern Pacific and was absorbed by the Central Pacific on March 1, 1912.

In 1917 the Southern Pacific narrow gauge roster saw an increase of some 40 cars, which were numbered 468 to 506. These may have been former Northwestern Pacific flatcars, which were sent to the Owens Valley line and used as gondola and flatcars.

During the 1920's a number of cars were lettered for the Central Pacific. These cars carried SP initials (9") with "Central Pacific" spelled out in 3" high lettering. These cars included all the boxcars, gondolas (above number 86), the "A" frame hoppers as well as tank cars and flats. A few cars continued to carry CP lettering until the 1940's. Southern Pacific purchased the property from Central Pacific Railway on October 1, 1945 in what was mainly a legal step.

In 1928-29 a large number of former Nevada-California-Oregon cars were sent to the Southern Pacific narrow gauge. These cars arrived with full size Tower (automatic knuckle) couplers. As the Southern Pacific narrow gauge used three-quarter size Sams patent couplers, the former N-C-O cars would not mate. Initially the cars were relettered and renumbered in pairs, converting them to three-quarter size MCB couplers (Master Car Builders-standard) on one end only of each pair, until the shop forces at Mina could complete the conversion.

The ex-N-C-O equipment included 15 boxcars that had been built for the Florence & Cripple Creek in Colorado (N-C-O 500-689); 22 stock cars (N-C-O 101-178); 34 gondolas (N-C-O 1-97) and 5 tank cars (N-C-O 012-021).

In 1931 a number of boxcars and combination stock and boxcars were rebuilt to haul bulk soda ash. Small doors were installed in the car sides and a horizontal sliding door was applied to one end. Some cars had the end door removed during the 1946-47 rebuilding program.

During World War II several Southern Pacific narrow gauge tank cars were sold to the U.S. Navy. Bulk oil facilities were operated by Richfield Oil; Shell Oil and Standard Oil at Laws, but privately owned tank cars were not used as on other West Coast narrow gauge roads. (N-C-O; Eureka-Nevada; Pacific Coast; Nevada County Narrow Gauge; Lake Tahoe Ry. & Transportation Co.; Nevada Central.) Tank cars that were removed from the roster during WWII, included numbers 19, 71, 168-175 (10 cars).

Just after the war, an ambitious car rebuilding and renumbering program was begun. In 1946-47 many Southern Pacific narrow gauge cars were rebuilt, repaired or simply renumbered. The Owenyo "car shop" rebuilt the cars, two at a time. The end result was that boxcars were renumbered 1-95 (**94 cars**); combination stock and box 125-139 (14 cars); stock 150-184 (35 cars); gondola 200-237 (38 cars); flats 250-259 (8 cars); "A" frame hoppers 300-340 (38 cars) and tanks 350-354 (5 cars). At this time the circular heralds were painted out and 7" high SP lettering was applied. Combination-caboose cars 400 (duckbill) and 401 (clerestory) were also renumbered.

It should be noted that for many years the freight cars were classified generally as 20,000 to 40,000 pound capacity. The only difference in the weight classification was the size of the journals. During the renumbering, the former Florence & Cripple Creek cars were the only group of freight cars to retain their previous numbers (26-40), although a few stock cars kept their old numbers. Frequently the same car would be listed as either a gondola or as a flat, depending on whether side and end boards were in place.

In the 1950's, eight 40,000 pound capacity boxcars were rebuilt with "A" frame floors and roof hatches for perlite loading. These cars had their side doors bolted shut and smaller doors cut into the sides of the car. They retained their previous numbers and were designated as "perlite cars."

By the mid-1950's, as equipment wore out, it was striken from the roster rather than be rebuilt. In July 1955, forty cars, including 16 older boxcars, were dismantled and burned. By 1960, when the line quit, there were only the following cars left in active service:

    19 stock
    74 box
     5 flat
    28 "A" frame gondola
    20 gondola
     1 caboose
     1 baggage mail
     1 water tank
     1 oil tank

The detailed rosters that follow offer a more complete picture of the rolling stock of the Southern Pacific narrow gauge during the final decades.

PASSENGER CAR ROSTER

Carson & Colorado Ry.	(1880-1905)
Nevada & California R.R.	(1905-1912)
Southern Pacific Narrow Gauge	(1912-1960)

No.	Type	Builder	Date	Notes
1	Coach	Barney & Smith, Dayton, Ohio	1880	First Class (smoker). Retired after 1929.
(2nd)1	Combine	Carter Bros., San Francisco, CA	1880	See caboose-combine 400
2	Coach	Barney & Smith	1880	Sold to NCNG No. 8, 6-11-1934. sc 1939.
3	Bag-Mail	Barney & Smith	1880	Sold to Parker Lyon, Arcadia, CA 8-14-1939, to William Harrah, Sparks, NV. Stored at Harrah's Auto Museum, Sparks, NV.
4	Bag-Mail	Barney & Smith	1880	Out of service 2-7-1939. Body used as Tool House, Keeler, CA.
5	Coach	Barney & Smith	1880	First class (smoker). To G.M. Best 3-28-1938 for Ward Kimball's Grizzly Flats R.R.
6	Bag-Mail	Barney & Smith	1880	Sold to NCNG No. 9, 6-12-1934. sc 1939.
7	Coach	Barney & Smith	1882	Rebuilt as Combine No. 7, 10-31-1931. Re-No. 17, 10-14-1940.
8	Combine	Carter Bros.	1880	Orig. SJ&SN 1009, to SPC 1009, in 1904, to N&C No. 8, 7-1-1906. To SP MW8, MW 1-B, 16, 16-B. To Caboose Service No. 401, 1947. Rebuilt with flat roof. Display at Laws, CA.
(2nd)8	Combine	Harlan & Hollinsworth, Wilmington, Delaware	1884	Former SPC 69 (coach), to N&C No. 9, 9-15-1906. Rebuilt to combine 8, 12-31-1931. Sold to Parker Lyon, Arcadia, CA, 8-14-1939. To William Harrah, Sparks, NV. Stored at Sparks, NV.
9	Coach	Harlan & Hollinsworth	1884	Orig. SPC 69, to N&C No. 9, 9-15-1906. Rebuilt to combine 8 (2nd) 12-31-1931. See (2nd) 8.
10	Officers	Central Pacific, Scaramento	1886	"Esmeralda." Car retired 1927 and set aside at Keeler, CA. To private owner in San Fernando, CA.
11	Baggage	Carter Bros.	1880	Leased to LTR&T, returned and retired 5-5-1927.
(2nd)11	Baggage	Carter Bros.	1880	Orig. SPC No. 1, to N&C No. 11, 9-26-1906. Retired, 12-23-1913. Body used at Mt. Montgomery.
12	Bag-Mail	Carter Bros.	1880	Orig. SPC No. 9 (combine), to N&C, 12, 7-1-1906. Rebuilt to Baggage Car No. 12, 11-27-1927. Used as a caboose in 1940's-1950's. To Traveltown Griffith Park, Los Angeles, CA, 1960.

No.	Type	Builder	Date	Notes
13	Coach	Carter Bros.	1879	Orig. SPC No. 22, to N&C No. 13, 7-15-1907. Sold to NCNG No. 7, 6-11-1934. sc.1939.
14	Coach	Carter Bros.		Orig. SPC 2nd class coach. Leased to LTR&T, returned 4-1927. Retired 5-5-1927.
15	Coach	Carter Bros.		Orig. SPC 2nd class coach. Leased to LTR&T, returned 12-6-1926. Sold to Hobart Estate, Hobart Mills, CA, 12-6-1926. sc.1938
16	Combine	Carter Bros.	1882	Orig. SJ&SN (coach). Became Northern Ry (SP) 1010, in 1888. To SPC 1010, 1904. To N&C No. 16, 7-17-1907. SP No. 16, 1912. Retired 12-23-1913. Used as residence at Mina, NV. Moved to Laws, CA (A flat-roofed car.)
(2nd)16	Combine	Carter Bros.	1881	See caboose combine 401.
17	Chair	Jackson & Sharp Wilmington, Del.	1879	Orig. SPC Parlor Car No. 4 "Santa Cruz." Leased to LTR&T, returned 4-1927, retired 5-5-1927. Burned at Mina, 1927.
(2nd)17	Combine	Barney & Smith	1880	See coach No. 7.
20	Business	DSP&P Denver, CO	1880	Orig. DSP&P 050, Reno. DL&G 025, sold 1894-97, to NCO "Fairport." To CP(SP) 20, 1927. Reno MW5 1-25-1944. To bunk house at San Jose, CA.
1	Caboose	V&T Shops	c1880	Body at Laws, CA (no clerestory).
5	Caboose-Coach	V&T Shops Carson City, NV	1880	Used on Tonopah R.R. 1904-05. Became the station at Millers, NV on TRR/T&G. Moved to Laws, CA 1950's clerestory roof over passenger section.
25	Combine	Carter Bros.	1880s	Orig. SPC to N&C after 2-1908. Rebuilt to caboose 467. Sold to Parker Lyon, Arcadia, CA, to William Harrah, Sparks, NV. Burned in fire, 3-1961.
400	Caboose-Combine	Carter Bros.	1880	Orig. SPC 47 (combine). To N&C 1906. To SP No. 1 caboose (1920's-1946), Renumbered SP 400, 1946. To storage shed at Keeler, CA. (Car had a "duckbill" roof.) Moved to Newark, CA 11-7-1977.
401	Caboose-Combine	Carter Bros.	1881	Orig. SJ&SN (coach), became Northern Ry (SP) 1009, in 1888. To SPC 1009, 1904. To N&C MW8 7-1-1906. To SP MW1-B, 16-B, 16, 401 (1947). Rebuilt with flat roof. (1952) Display at Laws, CA.
467	Caboose-Coach	V&T Shops (Rebuilt)	1880	Orig. No. 25. Sold to Parker Lyon, Arcadia, CA. To William Harrah, Sparks, NV. Burned in fire 3-1961.

NOTES: In 1895 the C&C listed no caboose. The 1903 C&C Roster lists one caboose (C&C #1), while the 1908 N&C Roster shows four cabooses (N&C 333, 416, 455, 456). In 1925 cabooses were listed as 1 and 467.

In the mid-1880's a combination car was used on the C&C. This car had an unusual clerestory roof line which indicates it was built by the Detroit Car Company.

The car body of a former SPC combine (similar to Owens Valley combine 25 in its original state) rests on the ground at Alturas, California. This car is 39'3" long (body) and 8'6" wide. It has one more window per side than SP narrow gauge 25 and a later style Carter Bros. roof line. This car operated as SPC 24 and also operated as 24 on the LTR&T Company line, before going to the N-C-O. It may have been used on the SP narrow gauge Owens Valley line.

BOX CARS

Number	Length	Width	Height	Capacity	Date Built	Pre-1946-47 Number	Remarks
1-14	28'0"	7'8"	9'8"	20,000	1890	359, 363, 389, 392, 403, 407, 414, 424, 430, 445, 449, 450, 451, 457	#1 to Travel Town, Los Angeles, CA. #5, #7 to Laws Railroad Museum, Laws, CA. Cars #4, #12 to William Harrah, Sparks, NV.
15-17	28'2"	7'7"	9'9"	40,000	1903	336, 337, 338	#15, #17 to Laws Railway Museum, Laws, CA Originally LTR&T 5-7, built by J. Hammond & Co. 1903. To SP 1926-27.
18-19	28'8"	7'8"	9'8"	40,000	1890	452, 453	
20	28'0"	7'8"	9'8"	20,000	1890	315	Car differs from 1-14 only by inside length, width.
21	28'2"	7'10"	9'8"	40,000	1901	332	Originally LTR&T 1, built by J. Hammond & Co. 1901. To SP 1926-27.
23	28'8"	7'8"	9'8"	40,000	1890	380	To Laws Railroad Museum (detrucked).
24	28'0"	7'8"	9'8"	30,000	1890	382	
25	30'0"	7'8"	9'8"	20,000	1890	396	Rebuilt with end door and 2 small side hatches (each side) in 1931. Car retained these doors after 1946-47 renumbering.
26-40	30'3"	7'9"	9'5"	40,000	1899-1900	26-40	Built by American Car Co., and Peninsular Car Co. (AC&F) Former F&CC, N-C-O 500-689. #26 to Universal Studios, Universal City, CA.
41-78	30'0"	7'8"	9'8"	40,000	1890	305, 306, 308, 311, 313, 331, 346, 348, 356, 360, 365, 366, 370, 371, 374, 383, 384, 391, 394, 405, 418, 420, 421, 425, 427, 428, 431, 432, 436, 437, 438, 439, 440, 441, 444, 460, 463, 464	Car 46: ex-Oregonian RR to SP (1899), to N&C 331, rebuilt to 20 ton capty. (1925), to R&LHS (1960), to Cal State RR Museum (1969). On display as SP 331. (Probably built by Carter Brothers.) 45, 47, 57, 67, 77 cars to Laws Railroad Museum (detrucked). By in-field measurements, the following cars had 28'0" long bodies: 42, 43, 44, 45, 46, 47, 48, 49, 50, 52, 54, 63, 65, 66, 67, 71, 72, 73, 74. 394 was an ex-SPC car. (59).
79-90	28'0"	7'8"	9'8"	40,000	1890	322, 364, 379, 393, 397, 402, 404, 408, 409, 412, 442, 447, 448	Cars 80, 82, 88, 89, were 30'0" long.
91	30'2"	7'8"	9'8"	30,000	1890	410	
92	28'0"	7'8"	9'8"	20,000	1890	435	Same as cars 1-14, except for inside height.
93	28'0"	7'8"	9'8"	40,000	1890	462	
94	30'2"	7'8"	9'8"	40,000	1890	465 (or 398)	
95	30'0"	7'8"	9'8"	30,000	1890	401	

NOTE: In 1950's the following box cars were rebuilt as "Perlite Cars," with "A" frame floors, roof hatches, side doors bolted shot and small doors cut into side of car: 9, 72, 73, 74, 76, 91, 92, 93. A box car numbered 1 is on display at the Kern County Museum, Bakersfield, CA.
LTR&T Box 3, built by J. Hammond & Co. 1901 went to SP Owens Valley line 1926-27 as 334. It did not survive until the 1946-47 renumbering.

COMBINATION & BOX

Number	Length	Width	Height	Capacity	Date Built	Pre-1946-47 Number	Remarks
125	28'0"	7'8"	9'8"	30,000	1890	151	Rebuilt as stock car 125
126	30'0"	7'8"	9'8"	40,000	1890	446	
127-128	28'0"	7'8"	9'8"	40,000	1890	319, 433	
129	28'2"	7'10"	9'8"	30,000	1901	333	Originally LTR&T 2, built by J. Hammond & Co. 1901. To SP 1926-27.
130	28'2"	7'7"	9'8"	40,000	1903	335	Originally LTR&T 4, built by J. Hammond & Co. 1903. To SP 1926-27.
131-132	28'0"	7'8"	9'8"	20,000	1890	350, 411	Car 132 to Laws RR Museum, Laws, CA
133	28'0"	7'8"	9'8"	30,000	1890	385	
134	30'2"	7'8"	9'8"	40,000	1890	398(?)	
135-139	30'0"	7'8"	9'8"	40,000	1890	138, 328, 372, 387, 419	Cars 135, 136 were 28'0" and 28'2" long.

NOTE: Combination stock & box cars were essentially box cars with an end door (sliding) on opposite end from brake wheel.

STOCK CARS

Number	Length	Width	Height	Capacity	Date Built	Pre-1946-47 Number	Remarks
125	28'0"	7'8"	9'8"	30,000	1890	151	Former combination box, rebuilt as stock car.
150	28'0"	7'8"	9'8"	30,000	1890	150	
151	35'4"	8'5"	10'4"	40,000	1890	63	Ex-N-C-O
152	30'0"	—	10'0"	40,000	1890	152	
153-156	28'0"	7'8"	9'8"	30,000	1890	153, 154, 157, 156	
157	27'10"	7'8"	9'8"	20,000	1890	155	To Ward Kimball, San Gabriel, CA
158-159	28'0"	7'8"	9'8"	20,000	1890	158, 159	Car 159 to William Harrah, Sparks, NV
160	30'0"	7'10"	9'8"	40,000	1890	160	
161-165	30'0"	7'10"	9'8"	20,000	1890	161-165	Car 161-165 originally C&C flat cars. Car 163 to Traveltown, Los Angeles, CA. Car 162 to William Harrah, Sparks, NV.
166	30'0"	7'10"	9'8"	20,000	1890	166	Originally a C&C flat car. To Laws RR Museum, Laws, CA.
167-169	30'0"	8'5"	10'4"	40,000	1909 1901 1900	58 60 62	Ex-N-C-O
170-171	30'0"	8'5"	10'4"	40,000	1901	59, 61	Ex-N-C-O. Car 171 to Y.M.&S.P., Fish Camp, CA.
172	30'10"	8'5"	10'4"	40,000	1911	64	Faint lettering: Central Pacific (1960). Ex-N-C-O
173-175	30'4"	8'5"	10'4"	40,000	1912	65, 66, 67	Ex-N-C-O
176	32'0"	8'5"	13'1"	40,000	1911	542	Ex-N-C-O
177-183	31'6"	8'5"	13'1"	40,000	1914 1913 1909 1913 1912 1900 1911	544 545 547 550 551 552 553	Ex-N-C-O. Car 180 (550) was Ex-N-C-O 177.

stock cars (cont)

Number	Length	Width	Height	Capacity	Date Built	Pre-1946-47 Number
184	38'4"	8'5"	13'1"	40,000	1900	549

NOTE: Former N-C-O cars 543, 546, 548 (L-31'6", W-8'5", H-13'1") not renumbered as they were off roster by 1941. N-C-O stock cars originally 101-178. One former N-C-O to Tropicana Gold Mine, Rosemead, CA.

GONDOLA

Number	Length	Width	Height	Capacity	Date Built	Pre-1946-47 Number	Remarks
200	30'0"	7'8"	5'9"	20,000	1890	8	Rebuilt by Bakersfield Shops as a 30'0" steel flat in c.1949. Wt. 17,770; 40,000 capty. Theilson trucks, "K" brakes.
201-206	30'0"	7'8"	3'3"	40,000	1890	10	Cars 203, 204 to M-C RR Mt. Pleasant, Iowa 1960.
					1892	107	
					1892	112	
					1890	132	
					1917	468	
					1917	483	
207	28'0"	7'8"	5'9"	30,000	1890	11	Used as spare wheel car.
208	28'0"	7'8"	3'3"	20,000	1890	78	
209-210	30'0"	7'8"	5'9"	40,000	1890	87, 103	
211	28'0"	7'8"	5'9"	20,000	1890	88	
212	30'0"	7'8"	5'9"	20,000	1890	119	
213	28'0"	7'8"	5'9"	40,000	1890	130	
214	30'0"	7'8"	5'9"	30,000	1890	141	A flat car in later years.
215-216	30'0"	7'8"	5'9"	40,000	1890	142, 144	Car 216 to Tropicana Gold Mine, Rosemead, CA.
217-218	30'0"	7'8"	8'9"	40,000	1890	188, 190	Cars fitted with coke rack and small doors, used to carry coke until 1952-53. Used as open top stock cars (sheep) in later years.
					1917		
219-220	28'0"	7'8"	8'9"	40,000	1890	196, 198	Cars fitted with coke rack and small doors, used to carry coke until 1952-53. Used as open top stock cars (sheep) in later years.
221	29'11"	7'3"	5'9"	40,000	1917	474	
222	30'0"	7'2"	5'3"	40,000	1917	475	To M-C RR, Mt. Pleasant, Iowa 1960.
223	32'0"	7'2"	5'1"	40,000	1917	476	To Ward Kimball, San Gabriel, CA.
224	29'11"	7'2"	5'3"	40,000	1917	478	
225	28'0"	7'2"	5'10"	40,000	1917	479	To William Harrah, Sparks, NV.
226	28'0"	7'2"	5'9"	40,000	1917	480	
227	39'0"	7'2"	5'3"	40,000	1917	484	
228-235	29'11"	7'2"	5'3"	40,000	1917	489, 490, 494, 497, 502, 503, 504, 506	
236	30'0"	7'2"	5'3"	40,000	1917	492	A flat car at end of operations. 1960.
237	29'11"	7'2"	5'3"	40,000	1917	496	

NOTE: Gondola cars were frequently listed as flat cars, when side and end boards were removed.

FLAT CARS

Number	Length	Width	Height	Capacity	Date Built	Pre-1946-47 Number	Remarks
250	30'0"	7'8"	3'3"	40,000	1892	106	
251	28'0"	7'8"	3'3"	40,000	1890	109	Used as gondola and tourist car.
253	30'0"	7'8"	3'3"	40,000	1890	123	Used as gondola and tourist car.
254-257	30'0"	7'8"	3'3"	40,000	1890	471, 472, 491, 493	
258-259	30'0"	7'8"	3'3"	40,000	1890	477, 481	259 to William Harrah, Sparks, NV. 258 used as gondola. To Traveltown, Los Angeles, CA.
209	30'0"	7'8"	—	40,000	1890 (circa 1949)	8	Rebuilt by Bakersfield Shops as a steel flat in c1949, from gondola car. Wt. 17,770, Theilson Trucks, "K" brakes. To M-C RR, Mt. Pleasant, Iowa. 1960.

NOTE: Two flat cars, formerly owned by Dale Gentry, are on RC&BT, Felton, CA, while others are in service as excursion cars on the M-C, Mt. Pleasant, Iowa.

"A" FRAME HOPPER (GONDOLA)

Number	Length	Width	Height	Capacity	Date Built	Pre-1946-47 Number	Remarks
300-302	30'0"	7'6"	6'8"	40,000	1890	2, 43, 45	
303-304	30'0"	7'8"	6'8"	40,000	1890	7, 15	
305	30'0"	7'5"	6'6"	40,000	1890	86	
307-312	30'0"	7'6"	6'5"	40,000	1917	187	
					1917	189	
					1917	191	
					1917	194	
					1917	195	
					1890	200	
313	28'0"	7'6"	6'5"	40,000	1890	197	
314	37'2"	8'5"	6'7"	40,000	1928	508	
315-321	37'0"	8'2"	6'6"	40,000	1927	510-517	Car 321 to R.C.&B.T., Felton, CA.
322	34'5"	8'2"	6'6"	40,000	1927	518	
323	37'0"	8'5"	6'7"	40,000	1928	519	
324-340	37'0"	8'4"	6'6"	40,000	1928	520-529, 531, 533-541	Car 333 to R.C.&B.T. Felton, CA. Car 339 to Laws RR Museum, Laws, CA. Car 340 built 1929. Car 337 rebuilt 4-1951. Cars 336, 337, 338, 339, 340 were 35'0" long.

NOTE: Cars 314-340 former N-C-O flatcars. Six cars of 314-340 series used to build excursion cars, caboose for RC&BT, Felton, CA. 1961.

TANK CARS

Number	Length	Width	Height	Capacity	Date Built	Pre-1946-47 Number	Remarks
350	30'0"	7'10"	—	40,000	1890	101	Aux. water tank. Capty. 3,300 gal.

351	30'0"	7'8"	–	40,000	1890	135	Tank is ex-SPC, car body from former C&C flat. Capty. 3,300 gal. (oil).
352	30'0"	8'0"	–	40,000	1890	145	Capty. 3,300 gal. (oil) to Cal. State RR Museum.
353	29'7"	8'5"	–	40,000	1928	178	Ex-N-C-O. Capty. 5,297 gal. Sc. 1960.
354	26'4"	8'4"	–	40,000	–	179	Ex-N-C-O. Capty. 5,110 gal.
54	30'0"	8'5"	–	–	1899	54	Water car 3,300 gal.
–	28'0"	8'0"	7'7"	40,000	–	59	Water car (wood, square tank) 3,200 gal.
–	28'0"	8'0"	7'7"	40,000	–	60	Water car (wood, square tank) 3,200 gal.
MW61	26'0"	8'5"	3'5"	–	1908	61	Water car, ex-N-C-O. Retired 5/1950, Sc. 8/10/1950. Capty. 5,055 gal.
–	28'0"	7'8"	–	40,000	–	19	Off roster during WWII. (See text.)
–	28'0"	7'8"	–	40,000	–	71	Off roster during WWII. (See text.)
–	30'0"	6'10"	–	40,000	–	168-175	Off roster during WWII. (See text.)
–	31'2"	8'10"	–	5,956 gal.	–	176	Ex-N-C-O. Off roster during WWII.
–	30'10"	8'11"	–	4,867 gal.	–	177	Ex-N-C-O. Off roster during WWII.

WORK EQUIPMENT

Number	Service	Remarks
1	Derrick	
1-A	Wheel	Car wheel service (flat car with sides) .29'11", 10 ton capacity.
1-B	Combine	Original SJ&SN coach, N. Ry 1009 (1888) to SPC 1009 (1904); N&C MW 8 (1906) to SP MW 1-B, later renumbered 16B; 401 (1948). Rebuilt with flat roof, to Laws Museum.
1-C	Box-Tool Car	Former derrick tender 354. To William Harrah, Sparks, NV.
1-D	Crew Car	Open platforms, with steps.
54	Water	3,300 gal. tank car, wooden frame.
108	Flanger	22' long car, ex-C&C

NOTE: Construction dates, where shown, are from Southern Pacific engineering records and appear in some cases to be the date acquired by the SP system.

Abbreviations:

CP . . . . Central Pacific
C&C . . . . Carson & Colorado
N&C . . . . Nevada & California
N-C-O . . . . Nevada-California-Oregon
NWP . . . . Northwestern Pacific
N Ry . . . . Northern Railway (SP)
LTR&T . . . . Lake Tahoe Ry & Trans.

SPC . . . . South Pacific Coast
SJ&SN . . . . San Joaquin & Sierra Nevada
F&CC . . . . Florence & Cripple Creek
AC&F . . . . American Car & Foundry Co.
RC&BT . . . . Roaring Camp & Big Trees
YM&SP . . . . Yosemite Mountain & Sugar Pine
M-C . . . . Midwest Central

In 1960, car bodies were offered to valley ranchers and farmers by the scrappers for $100 to $140 delivered. Additional Southern Pacific narrow gauge equipment can be found preserved at the California State Railroad Museum, Sacramento; Traveltown, Los Angeles; Laws Railroad Museum, Laws, California; Harrah's Automobile Collection, and Sparks Railroad Park, Sparks, Nevada; Universal Studios, Universal City, California; Eastern California Museum, Independence, California and in several private collections.

A number of car bodies remain along the former narrow gauge and elsewhere, used as sheds and farm buildings in many cases. The following is a listing of such car bodies as sold by the SP and the scrappers in 1960-1961. Many of the car sales were handled by Inyo Builders of Lone Pine.

Additionally, other car bodies are scattered at various locations, as follows:

Combine 24 at Alturas, CA. This car is ex-SPC, N-C-O and is the sister car to SP Combine 25.

Baggage-Mail-Express 4, plus other car bodies at Keeler, CA.

Business Car "Esmeralda" 10, at San Fernando, CA. Partially restored by private owner.

Caboose-Combine 401 at Newark, CA. Restoration is planned by a group interested in the SPC.

Caboose-Coach 5 at Laws, CA. Car has clerestory over passenger section and was used on Tonopah RR and as station at Millers, NV.

Caboose 1 at Laws, CA. A flat roofed car.

Combine 16 formerly at Mina, NV and moved to Laws, CA.

Box Car 306, the last remaining "Tin Box" at Mina, NV.

Box Car 443 at Bevilacqua Moving Co., Reno, NV. This 28'0" long car was off roster by 1928.

Box Car 474 at Montgomery Pass station (site). A former SPC car.

Box	Car Body To	Length
5	At Laws Railroad Museum, Laws, CA	27'11"
15	At Laws Railroad Museum, Laws, CA	28'2"
23	At Laws Railroad Museum, Laws, CA	28'7"
45	At Laws Railroad Museum, Laws, CA	28'1"
47	At Laws Railroad Museum, Laws, CA	28'0"
57	At Laws Railroad Museum, Laws, CA	30'0"
67	At Laws Railroad Museum, Laws, CA	28'1"
77	At Laws Railroad Museum, Laws, CA	30'0"
6	Sold to Lone Pine Recreation Club, Lone Pine, CA	28'½"
21	Sold to Lone Pine Recreation Club, Lone Pine, CA (at Lone Pine Rodeo Grounds)	28'2"
9	Sold to Richard Joseph, Lone Pine, CA	28'2"
13	Sold to Charles Mates, Lone Pine, CA	28'2"
16	Sold to Ben Randolph, Lone Pine, CA	28'2"
53	Sold to Ben Randolph, Lone Pine, CA	30'1"
93	Sold to Ben Randolph, Lone Pine, CA	28'0"
18	Sold to F.H. Arcularius, Bishop, CA	28'0"

44	Sold to F.H. Arcularius, Bishop, CA	28'0''
19	Sold to Chris Carrasco, Lone Pine, CA	28'8''
25	Sold to Mr. Malley, Lone Pine, CA	30'0''
42	Sold to Ben Baker, Lone Pine, CA	28'0''
55	Sold to Ben Baker, Lone Pine, CA	30'0''
58	Sold to Ben Baker, Lone Pine, CA	30'½''
71	Sold to Ben Baker, Lone Pine, CA	28'8''
46	To Railway & Locomotive Historical Society (complete)	28'0''
49	Sold to Maggie Wilson, Lone Pine, CA	28'0''
50	Sold to Edward Butterworth, Olancha, CA	28'1''
52	Sold to James Cashbough, Laws, CA	28'7½''
54	Sold to White Cap Mining Co., Lone Pine, CA	28'5''
61	Sold to Paul Hunter, Independence, CA	30'1''
65	Sold to Ed Kivett, Lone Pine, CA (at Dolomite)	28'2''
139	Sold to Ed Kivett, Lone Pine, CA (at Dolomite)	29'11''
68	Sold to Harold Yeates, Lone Pine, CA	30'1''
70	Sold to Andy Garcia, Lone Pine, CA	30'0''
72	Sold to William Poole, Independence, CA	28'0''
73	Sold to Les Stewart, Laws, CA	28'1''
74	Sold to John Walker, Bishop, CA	28'0''
76	Sold to John Walker, Bishop, CA (at Benton)	30'2''
75	Sold to Bob White, Bishop, CA	30'0''
78	Sold to Matt Perez, Lone Pine, CA	30'2''
79	Sold to Dr. Smart, Lone Pine, CA	28'0''
90	Sold to Dr. Smart, Lone Pine, CA	28'0''
80	Sold to George Hancock, Lone Pine, CA (at Lone Pine)	30'1''
81	Sold to Bobbie Miller, Lone Pine, CA	28'0''
82	Sold to Ken Highfield, June Lake, CA	30'2''
83	Sold to Henry Olivis, Lone Pine, CA (on farm)	28'0''
84	Sold to William J. Reed, Bishop, CA	28'0''
135	Sold to Ken Smalley, Lone Pine, CA	28'0''
86	Sold to Elmer Humphrey, Lone Pine, CA	28'2''
88	Sold to Clarence Dixon, Lone Pine, CA	30'1''
92	Sold to Silvas Ness, Olancha, CA	28'1''
95	Sold to C.O. Bowles, Lone Pine, CA	30'1''
134	Sold to Ken Smalley, Lone Pine, CA	30'2''
136	Sold to Malcolm Simmons, Lone Pine, CA	28'2''
137	Sold to Foster Smith, Lone Pine, CA	30'2''

Stock

160	Sold to Pete Olivis, Lone Pine, CA (on farm)	30'1''
174	At service station, Olancha, CA	30'3''
176	At Lone Pine Gas, Lone Pine, CA	30'8''
177	Sold to E.C. Butler, Lone Pine, CA (on farm)	30'3''
184	At gravel pit, Lone Pine, CA	36'11''

Lengths shown are actual measurements from existing car bodies and do not in all cases agree with official SP records. SP records indicate car length over endsills or coupler pocket.

NOTE: Roster information comes from a number of sources, but special credit is due to Dale Darney and Herman Darr for their help. Additional information came from Robert W. Richardson; Gerald M. Best; Thomas Armstrong; Kyle Wyatt, Robert Sloan, Paul Martineau, Bob Bader, Stephen Drew, and Bill McClung.

Combine-caboose 401 in 1951. [Wendell Mortimer, Jr.]

Combine-caboose 12 was painted "sunburn red." [Wendell Mortimer, Jr.]

SP Combine/Caboose 400

Plan by Al E. Barker

The little duckbill combine turned caboose that trailed trains through the Owens Valley for many years began life on the South Pacific Coast as Number 47. The car was built by Carter Brothers and came to the desert narrow gauge in 1906. She operated as caboose 1 until 1946, when she was renumbered 400. The car continued in regular service until wornout in the late 1940's. The car is being preserved in the Bay Area by a group which plans to rebuild her. [Drawing by Al E. Barker.]

Donald Duke

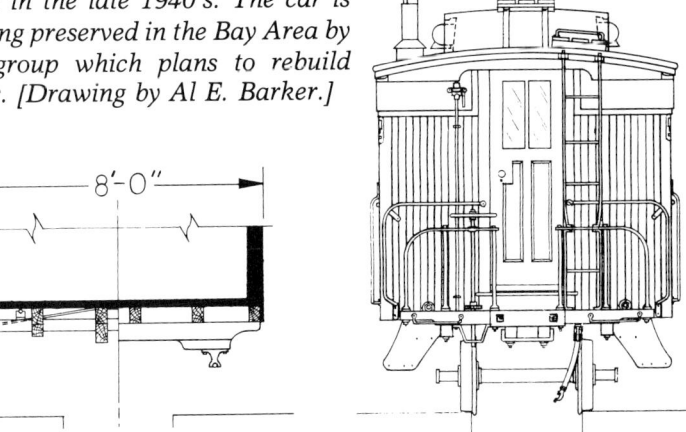

SCALE 3/16" = 1'0" (Full Size SN3)

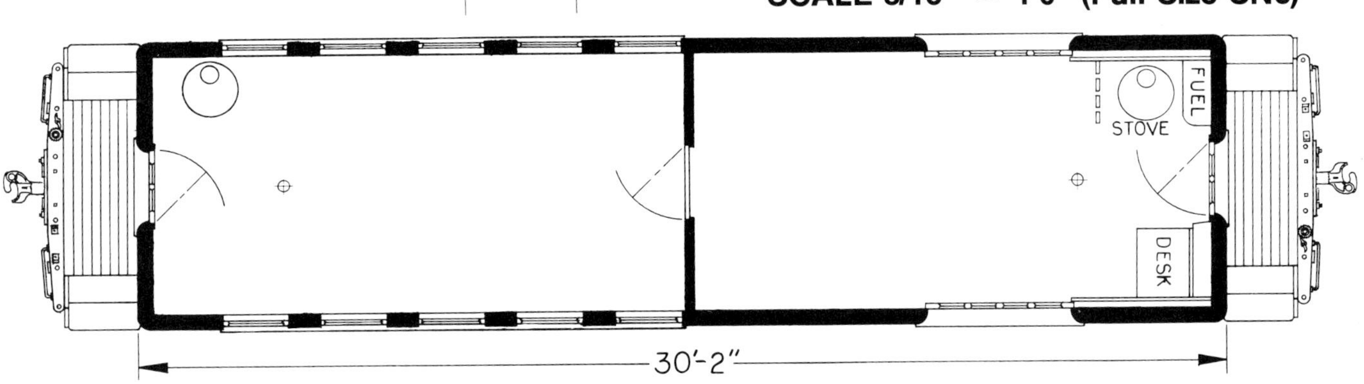

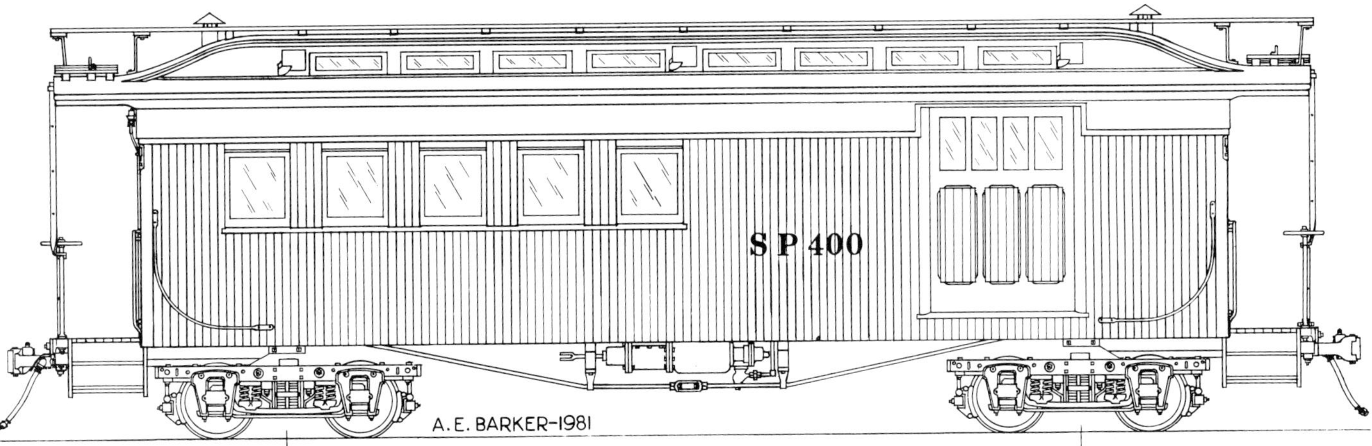

Bert Ward.

THIS SCALE PLAN MAY NOT BE REPRODUCED IN PART OR IN WHOLE TO BE USED IN CONJUNCTION WITH ANY COMMERCIAL HOBBY OR MANUFACTURING ENDEAVOR WITHOUT EXPLICIT WRITTEN CONSENT OF A. E. BARKER.

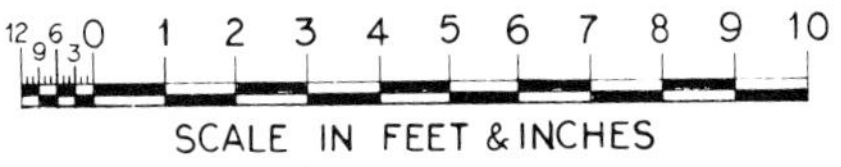

SCALE IN FEET & INCHES

Combine-Caboose 401
Combine-Caboose 401 was built by Carter Brothers as a coach for the San Joaquin & Sierra-Nevada and came to the Owens Valley in 1904. Used in work train service (top), the car was photographed at Owenyo in July, 1946 with trucks proclaiming "V&T Carson." [Bert Ward.] The car was rebuilt as a caboose 401 and is seen at Keeler in March 1948. [Garrie Tufford Col.] In 1952 the car was again rebuilt and had lost its passenger trucks and acquired a flat roof. [Photograph by Richard F. Thomas.] The car is now on display at Laws, California.

Caboose 467
Caboose 467 was a beautiful car, with a lot of class (above) when found at Keeler in 1940. [Donald Duke Co.] The car was worn-out by the end of World War II at Owenyo in 1946. [Bert Ward.] The car was later purchased by William Harrah of Sparks, Nevada (right), but was badly damaged by a fire in 1961. [Dale Darney.]

SP Baggage-Mail-Caboose 12

Carter Brothers-built Baggage-Mail 12 had a long and varied history after coming to the desert narrow gauge from the South Pacific Coast as a combination car during the Tonopah Gold Rush. Rebuilt as a baggage-mail car in 1927, the car served as a caboose and even was taken out of service to serve as quarters for Keeler crewmen. Later, equipped with Theilson freight trucks, the car became the spare caboose and on occasion served as a passenger car. The plan by Al E. Barker, reproduced full size HO scale, depicts the two styles of trucks used on car 12. At left, the original 5'0" WB passenger type, and right, the replacement Theilson freight type trucks used on the car during its last years of service.

Baggage-Mail 12 was found at Keeler in 1940, still on pasenger trucks. [Donald Duke Collection.]

Serving as a caboose, the 12 was photographed at Owenyo in 1952 with Theilson trucks. [Richard F. Thomas.]

SCALE 3:5mm = 1'0" (Full Size HON3)

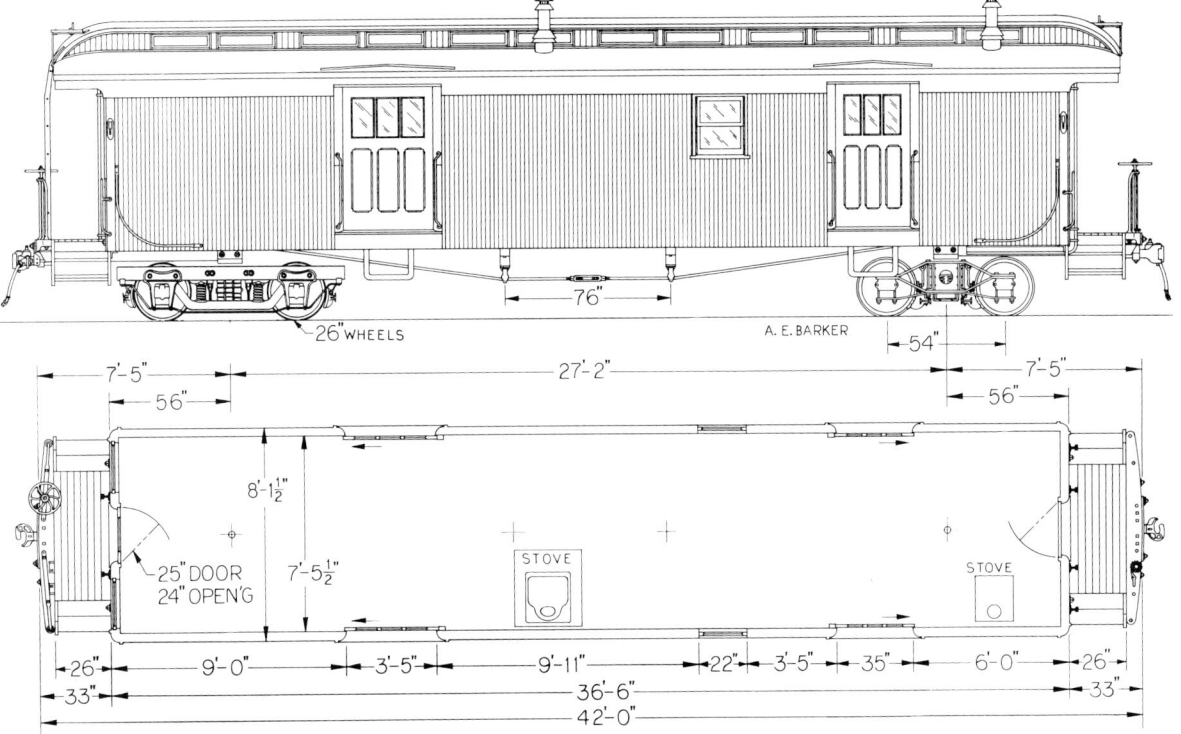

THIS SCALE PLAN MAY NOT BE REPRODUCED IN PART OR IN WHOLE TO BE USED IN CONJUNCTION WITH ANY COMMERCIAL HOBBY OR MANUFACTURING ENDEAVOR WITHOUT EXPLICIT WRITTEN CONSENT OF A. E. BARKER.

PASSENGER EQUIPMENT

The Carson & Colorado Railway's original passenger train equipment was constructed in 1880 by the Dayton, Ohio carbuilding firm of Barney & Smith. The order for seven cars was made by Henry Yerington of the Virginia & Truckee and called for the cars to be finished in "Cherry Red" paint with gold lettering for the new C&C. Cars 1, 2, 5 and 7 were coaches, while the baggage-mail-express cars were numbered 3, 4 and 6. These cars served the Carson & Colorado throughout its corporate lifetime. Additionally, caboose-coaches were used on mixed trains and in 1886, the office car "Esmeralda" was added to the roster.

On May 11, 1905 the C&C's original seven passenger cars, along with the "Esmeralda" and a 30 foot long caboose were transferred to the new Nevada & California Railroad, along with the C&C's freight equipment and other physical assets.

The Tonopah Gold Rush saw an influx of rolling stock on the N&C. Additional passenger equipment came to the desert narrow gauge from the South Pacific Coast and the San Joaquin & Sierra Nevada lines, which had been standard gauged by the Southern Pacific Lines. The N&C was merged into the Central Pacific (SP) in 1912.

In 1928-29 the Nevada-California-Oregon Railway, which ran north out of Reno, was standard gauged by the Southern Pacific. While a large number of freight cars were moved to the Mina-Keeler narrow gauge, only one piece of passenger equipment, Business Car 20, came south. The Southern Pacific narrow gauge did receive a number of spare parts from the N-C-O, including passenger car trucks built by the St. Charles works of the American Car & Foundry Company. Following the purchase of the Carson & Colorado by the Southern Pacific Lines, passenger equipment was painted Pullman Green. Equipment transferred to work or caboose service was painted a Tuscan Red, when painting was necessary, but there were many years in which both green and red former passenger cars were seen on the road.

By the late 1940's, the only former varnish remaining on the Southern Pacific narrow gauge were caboose-combines 400, 401 and baggage-mail-express car 12. After caboose 467 wore out during World War II, the three former passenger cars served alternately as cabooses. The 400 wore out in 1949 and was retired.

Despite the ravages of narrow gauge operations by the C&C, N&C and SP, nine of the passenger cars survive today in various states of repair and restoration.

S.P. 4 at Mina in 1936 was one of the original Carson & Colorado cars. [Jim Wight from G.M. Best.]

Baggage-Mail 12 was lettered for Central Pacific in the 1930's. [Bert H. Ward.]

Original Carson & Colorado coach 5 at Mina in 1937 was built by Barney & Smith. [Ted G. Wurm from Bert Ward.]

Originally a C&C coach, Number 7 was rebuilt as a combine in 1931. [Jim Wight.]

S.P. 17 was renumbered from Number 7 in 1940 and was found by Ken Kidder at Owenyo in 1942. [Will C. Whittaker.]

Business Car 20 was a former N-C-O car with a long history dating back to the Denver, South Park & Pacific. Gerald M. Best found the car at Mina in 1936.

FREIGHT EQUIPMENT...A Garland of Desert Nomads

Southern Pacific narrow gauge freight cars line the Owenyo "car shop" track in August, 1939. It was here in the open air that the equipment was repaired, rebuilt and maintained. [Al C. Phelps Photograph.]

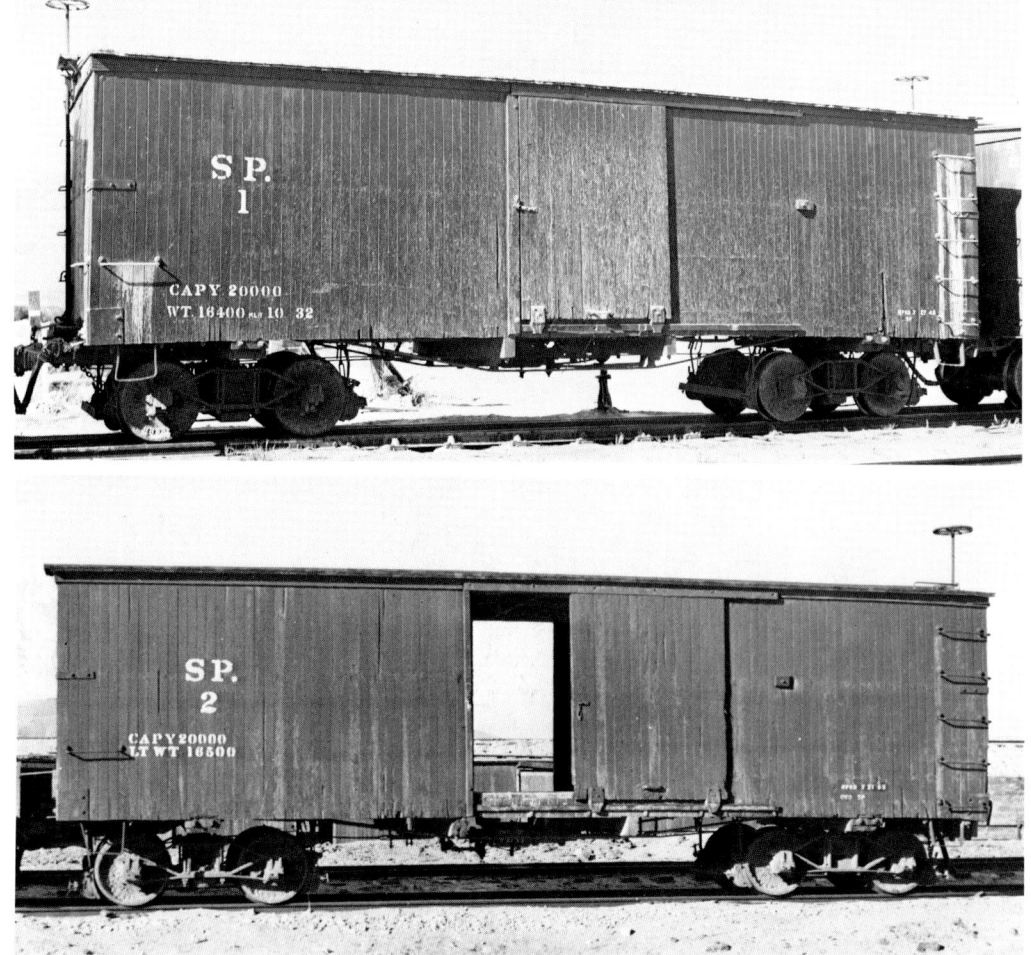

Box Cars

Upon close inspection, no two Southern Pacific narrow gauge cars were identical, making them each unique. After rebuildings and years of desert operation, the cars became rolling historical examples of the car builders' art of mating wooden bodies with metal hardware, trucks and couplers. SP Number 1 was photographed in 1948. [Bert Ward.] The two-spot was found in 1954 by Will C. Whittaker. Box 8 had been freshly painted and renumbered in February, 1946. [Bert Ward.] Cars 13 and 63 were photographed at Owenyo in the 1950's. [Robert W. Brown.]

Boxcar Variations
Southern Pacific narrow gauge boxcars came in assorted sizes, style and shapes. By the 1950's they were a rag-tag assortment of individuals. The photo shows that even body height varied from car to car, as the former F&CC box 36 was coupled to box 48 at Keeler. [Richard F. Thomas.] The plan (opposite lower) shows box 72, as rebuilt in the 1950's to haul perlite. The cars had "A" frame floors, roof hatches, small doors cut in the sides and the sliding doors bolted shut.

Desert Nomads
The boxcars on these pages were built by the American Car & Foundry Company in 1899-1900 for the Florence & Cripple Creek, and ran on the Nevada-California-Oregon before coming to the Southern Pacific in 1928-29 as numbers 26-40. They retained their numbers during the 1946-47 renumbering and rebuilding. Bert Ward photographed box 26 at Laws in 1946 and the 37 at Keeler the same year. The detailed photographs of car 26 are by Richard F. Thomas.

SP Box Car 72

Plan by Herman Darr

Paint: box car red, white lettering
Air brakes: 8" × 12" Westinghouse KC
Converted from box car in late 1950's. A-frame floor similar to hopper car allowed gravity unloading of crushed perlite. Cars converted, nos. 9, 72, 73, 74, 76, 91, 92, 93

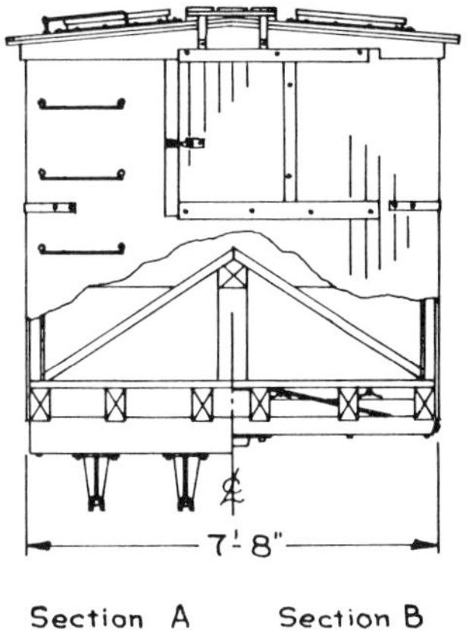

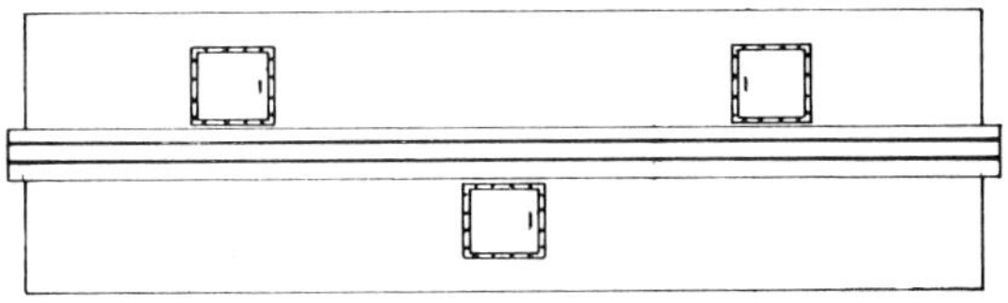

Top view showing roof hatch locations

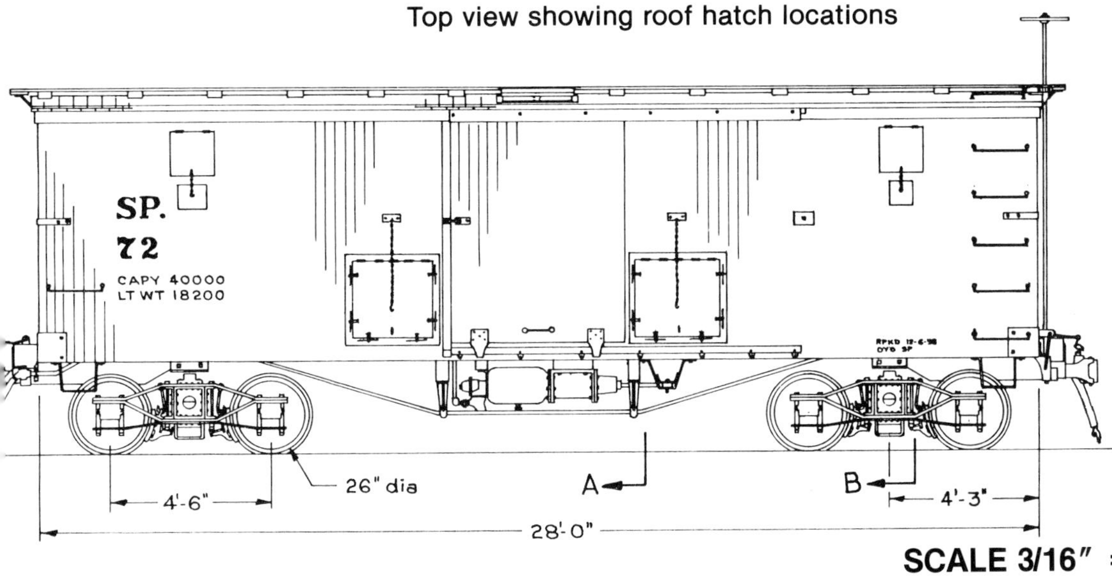

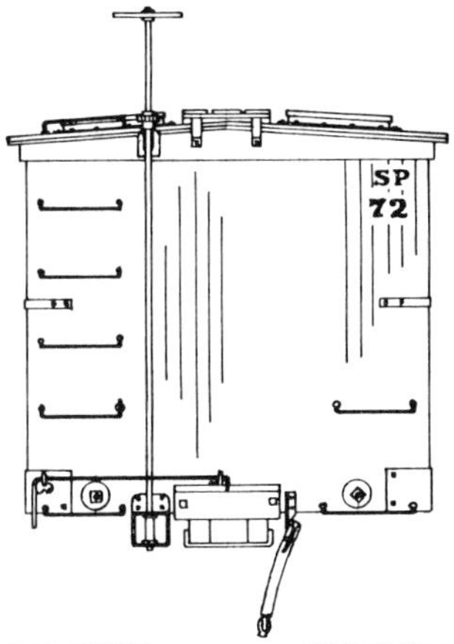

Section A Section B

SCALE 3/16" = 1'0" (Full Size SN3)

Flanger 108 saw little use in the Owens Valley. [Wendell Mortimer, Jr.]

Stock 177 was former N-C-O car. [Wendell Mortimer, Jr.]

Freshly painted box 2 at Keeler. [Wendell Mortimer, Jr.]

End view of former F&CC box 36. [Lawrie Brown.]

S.P. narrow gauge box 36 at Laws. [Lawrie Brown.]

Box 88 was a 30'-0 long car. [Lawrie Brown.]

Detail of truck on gondola. [Wendell Mortimer, Jr.]

In 1931 a number of boxcars were rebuilt to haul bulk soda ash and other products like talc. These cars had small doors installed in each side, plus an end door. Box 49 (above) is an example of the series as shown in Herman Darr's scale drawing. [Photo by Richard F. Thomas.]

Detail of Theilson truck under box 132. [Author.]

SP Box Car 74
Plan by Herman Darr

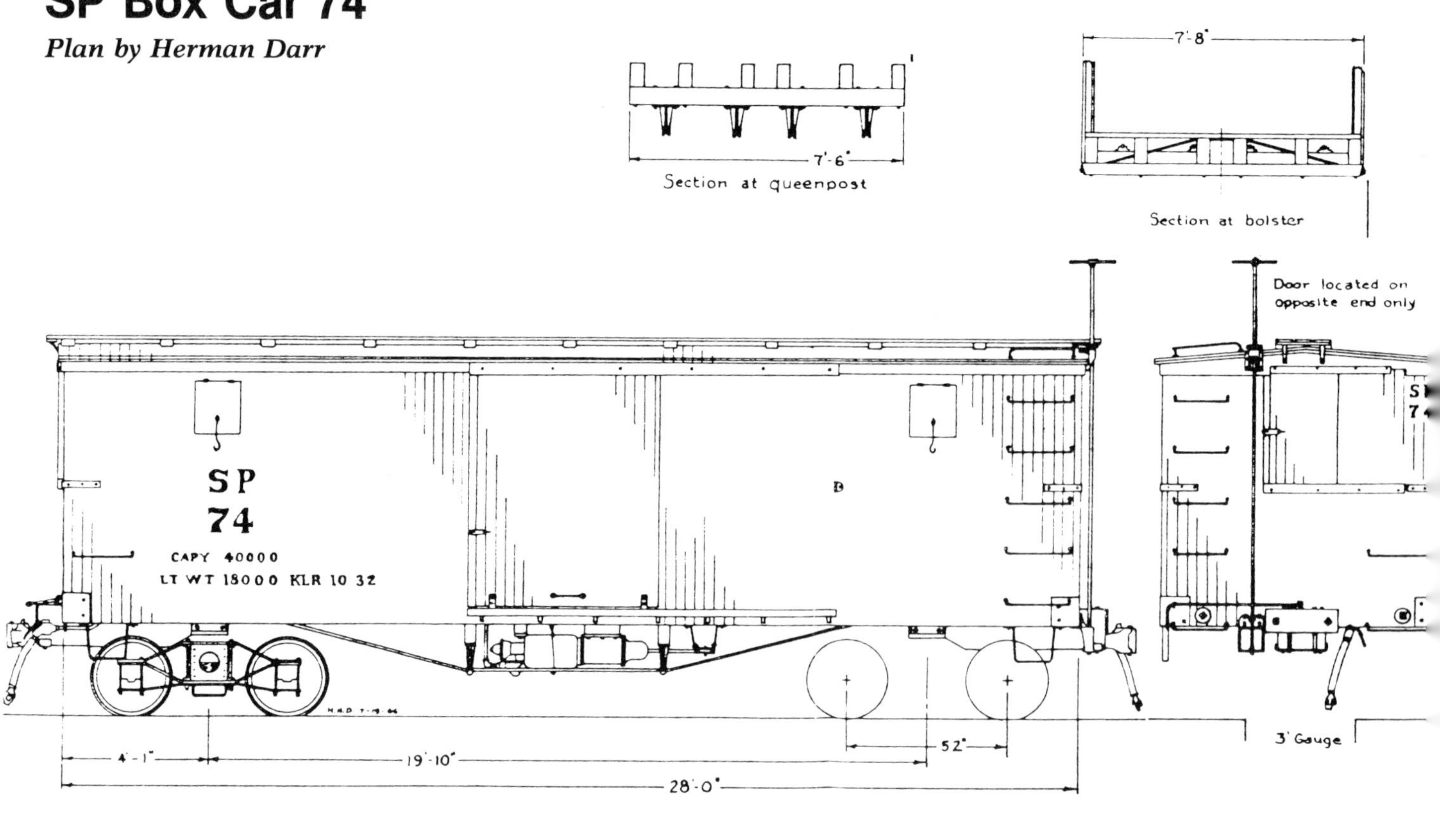

SCALE 3/16" = 1'0" (Full Size SN3)

SP Coke Rack Car *Plan by Ken Pruitt*   SCALE 3/16" = 1'0" (Full Size SN3)

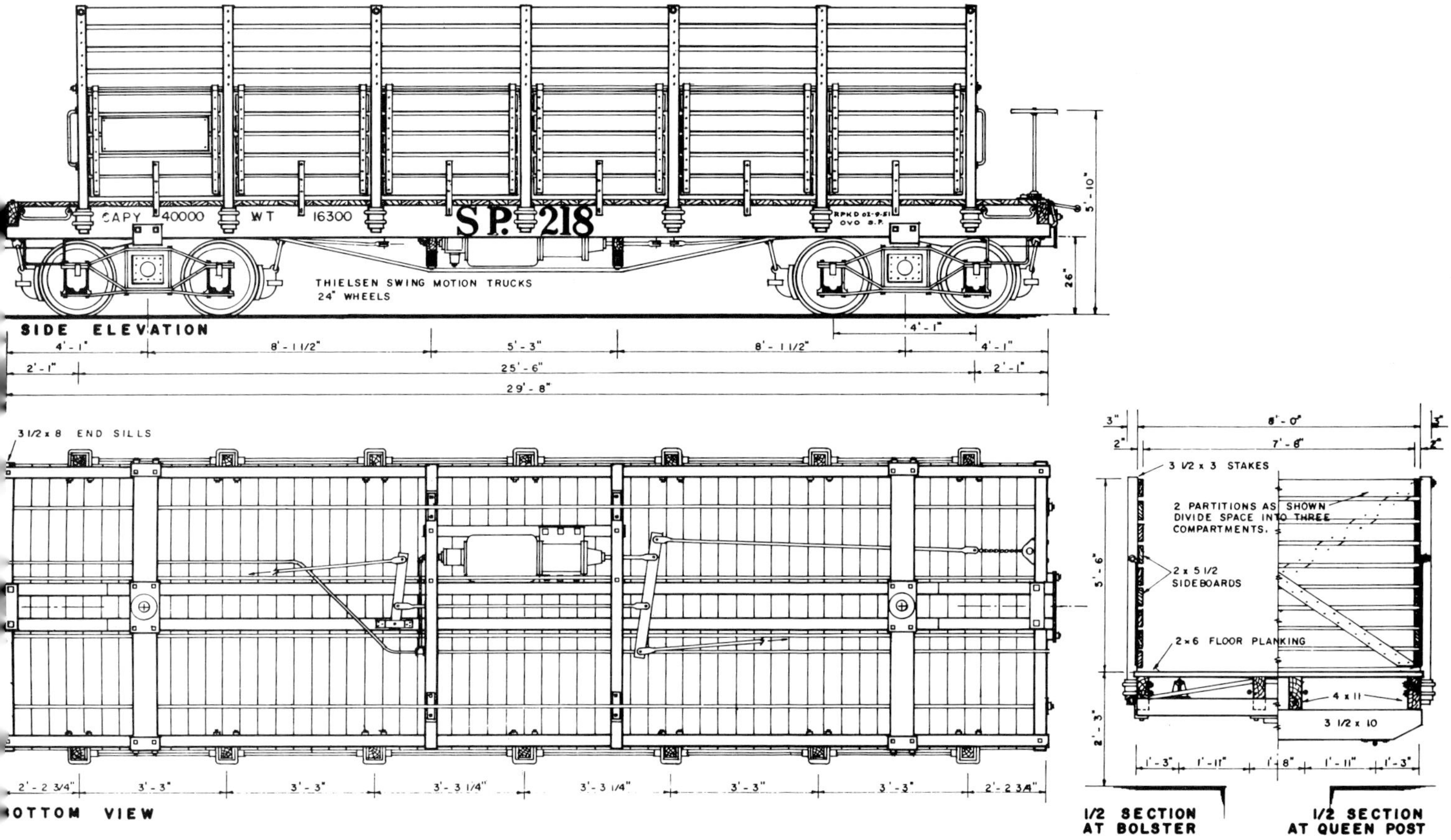

Several gondolas were fitted with high sides and became coke rack cars. The soda kilns at Keeler were fired by coke and these cars were used in this service until the Natural Soda Products plant closed in 1952. The coke cars (217-220) were also used as open top stock cars on occasions. S.P. 218 is shown in a Richard F. Thomas photograph and in Ken Ruitt's scale drawing. The 190, later renumbered 218, was found near the Laws stock pens with a string of stock cars in August, 1939. [Al Phelps.] The 219 was photographed in 1953 by Robert W. Brown.

SP Stock Car 153

Plans by Hermann Darr

SCALE 3/16" = 1'0" (Full Size SN3)

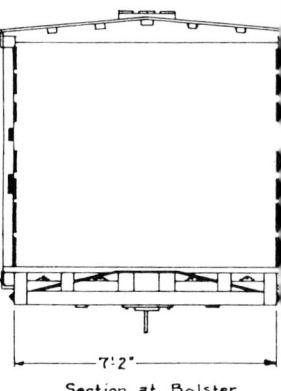

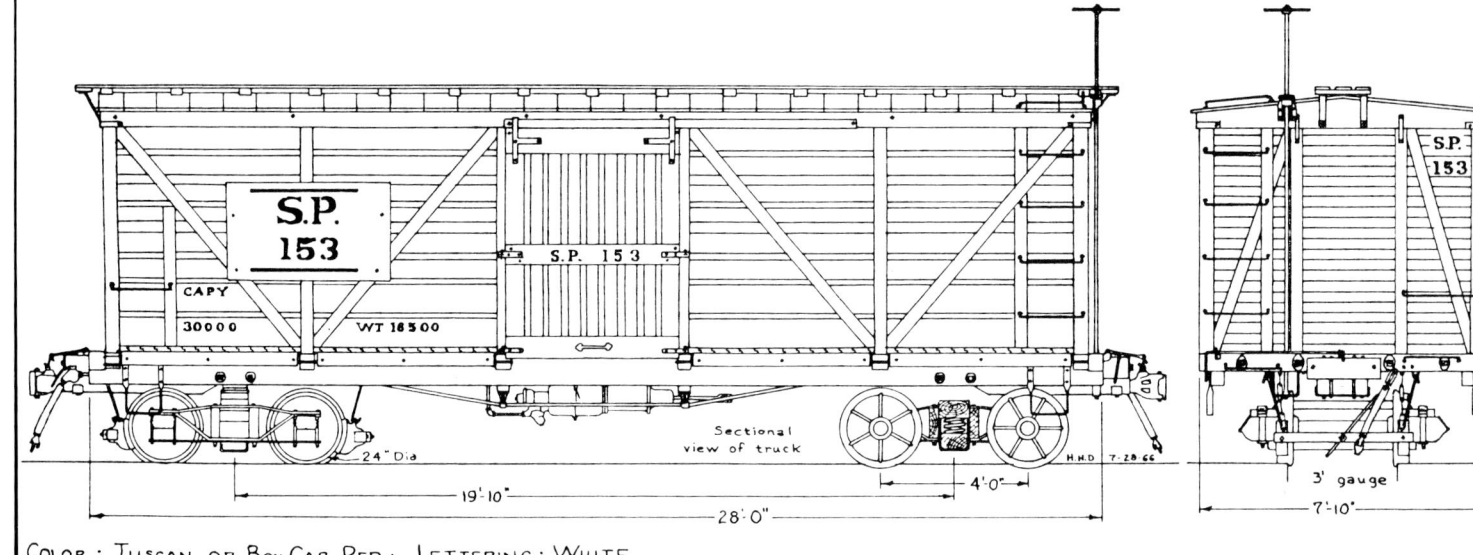

COLOR: TUSCAN OR BOX CAR RED; LETTERING: WHITE

Most S.P. narrow gauge stock cars were "one of a kind," even within the same class. Car 152 was a 30'-0" car with Theilson trucks. [M. D. McCarter.] The plan by Herman Darr shows car 153, while the second photo shows car 166, which began life as a Carson & Colorado flat car. [Author.] Stock car 161 was another former C&C flat, as was car #160, shown in the plan by Herman Darr.

SP Stock Car 160

Plan by Herman Darr

Paint: box car red, white lettering
Air brakes: 8" × 12" Westinghouse KC
Dimensions from car body 6-24-78
Details from photographs

SCALE 3/16" = 1'0" (Full Size SN3)

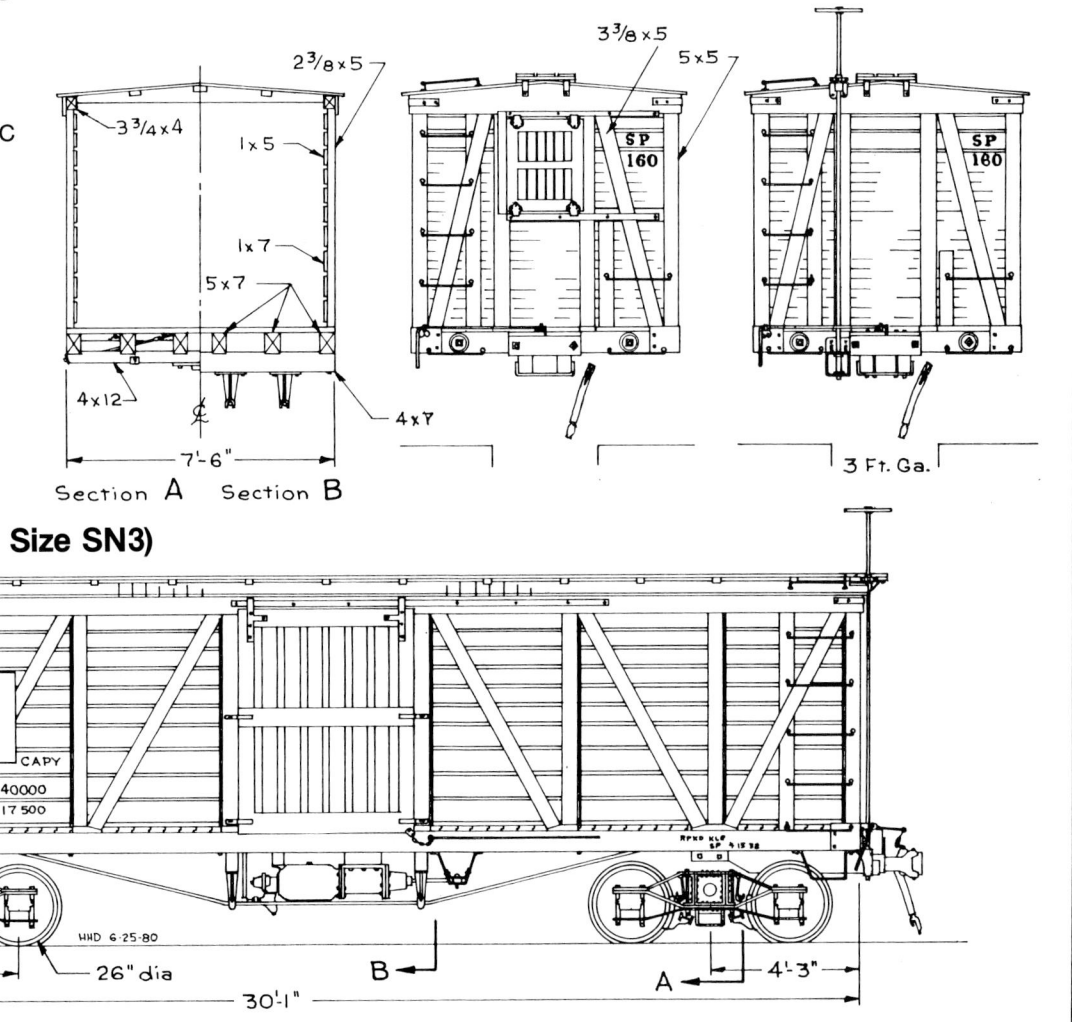

231

SP Stock Car 184
Plan by Herman Darr

Car built by Nevada California Oregon RR as a flat car in early 1900's. Rebuilt to stock car by 1916. Transfered to SP in 1928, numbered 549. Renumbered to 184 in 1946. Scrapped 1960. Car body measured 18 July 1979.
Paint: Box car red with white lettering
Air brakes: Westinghouse 6" × 8" KC

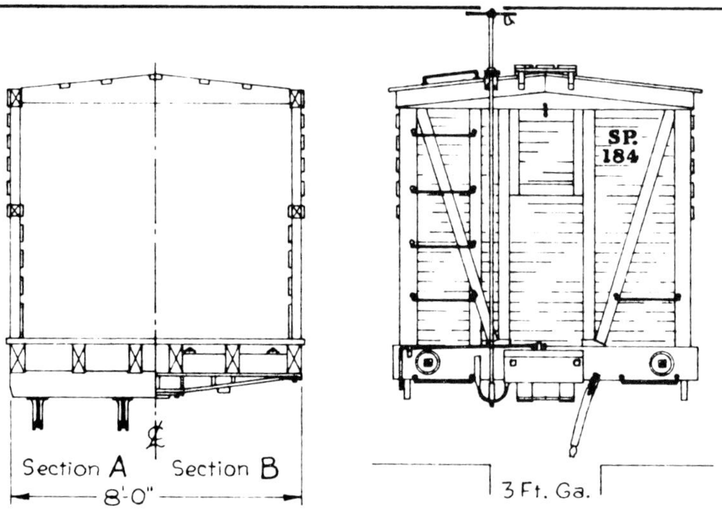

SCALE 3/16" = 1'0" (Full Size SN3)

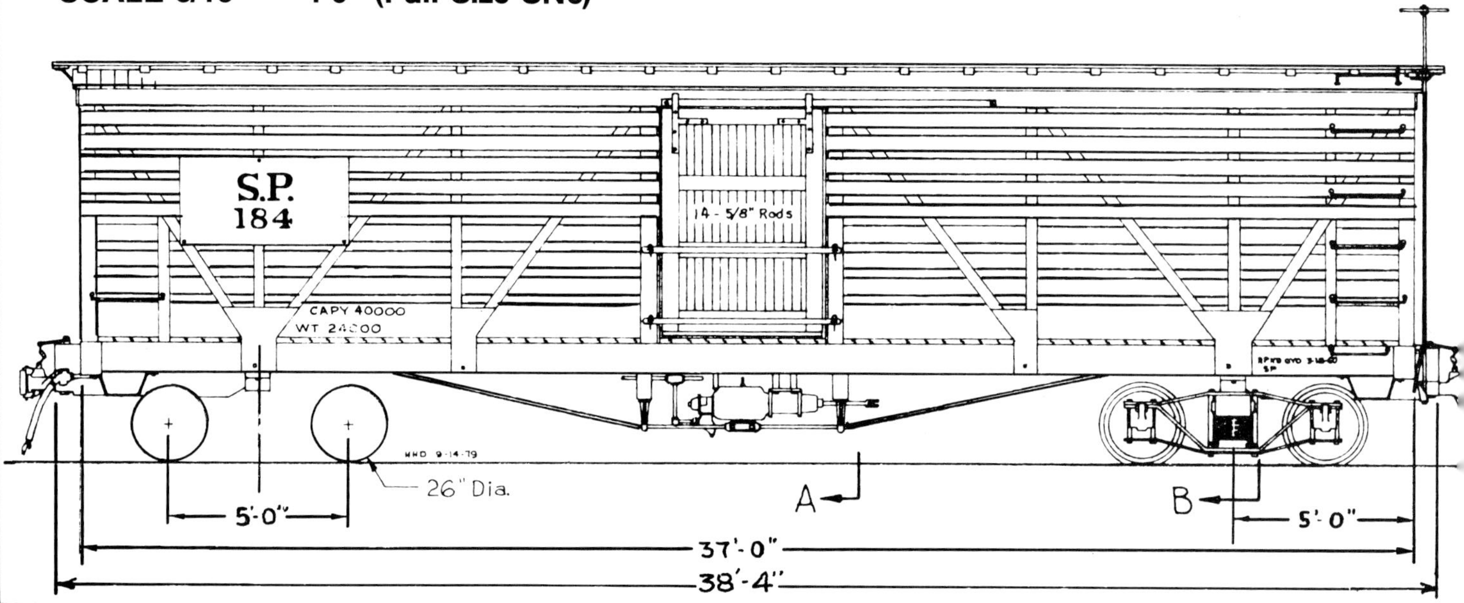

Former N-C-O Stock Cars
Even the former Nevada-California-Oregon stock cars were different. They varied in length from the short 182 (31'-6") to the long (38'-4") number 184. The 182 was photographed at Alico in 1954. [Author.]

Gondolas by the simple expedient of adding side boards. Flatcar 259 is shown on this page in a photograph by Richard F. Thomas and in the plan by Herman Darr.

SP Flat Car 259

Plan by Herman Darr

Paint scheme: box car red, white lettering
Air brakes: 8" × 12" Westinghouse KC

SCALE 3/16" = 1'0" (Full Size SN3)

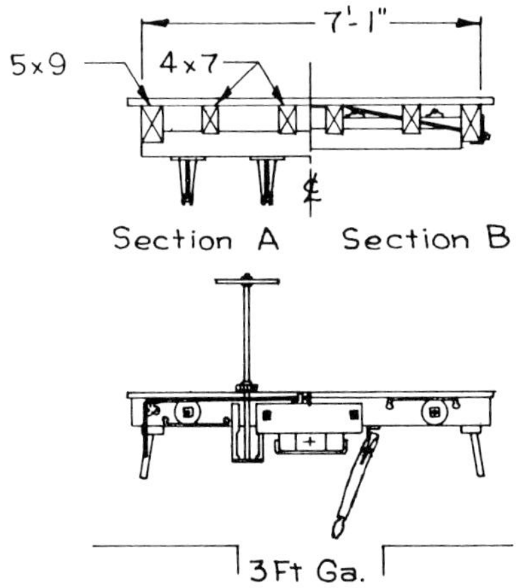

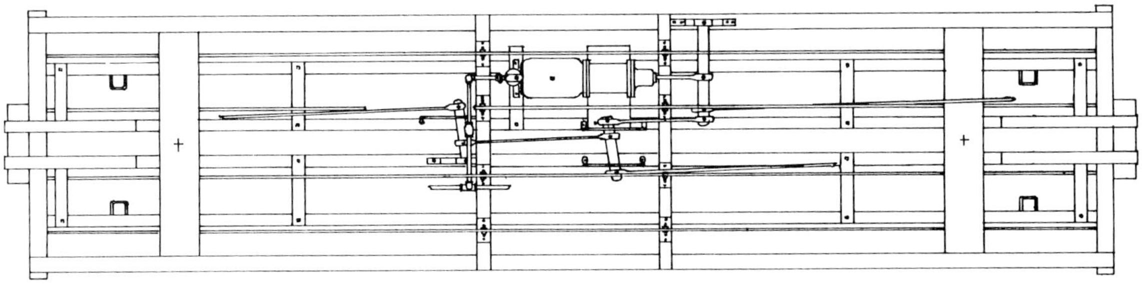

Bottom View showing brake rigging

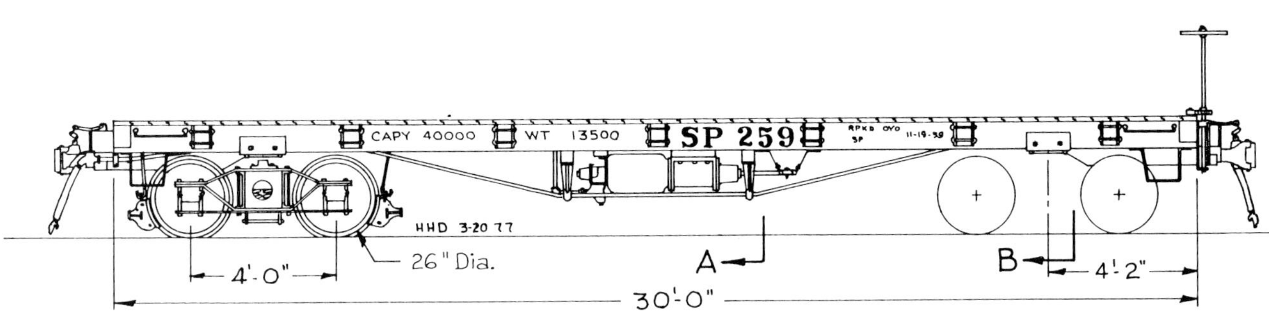

Flats, Gons, Etc.
Gondolas on the SPng were used to haul a wide variety of minerals and were rebuilt into flatcars, coke racks and back to gondolas as the traffic demanded. S.P. 504 is shown with a load of soapstone in 1946. This car was renumbered 234 later that year. [Bert Ward.] Gondola 202 was found at Owenyo in 1954 by the author, while the underside of gon 11 was photographed by Richard F. Thomas, and shows the wood beam swing-bolster Carter Brothers truck.

SP Gondola 225 Pre-1948 and Post-1948)

Plans by Herman Darr

Air brakes: 8" × 12" Westinghouse KC
Dimensions from existing car and photographs

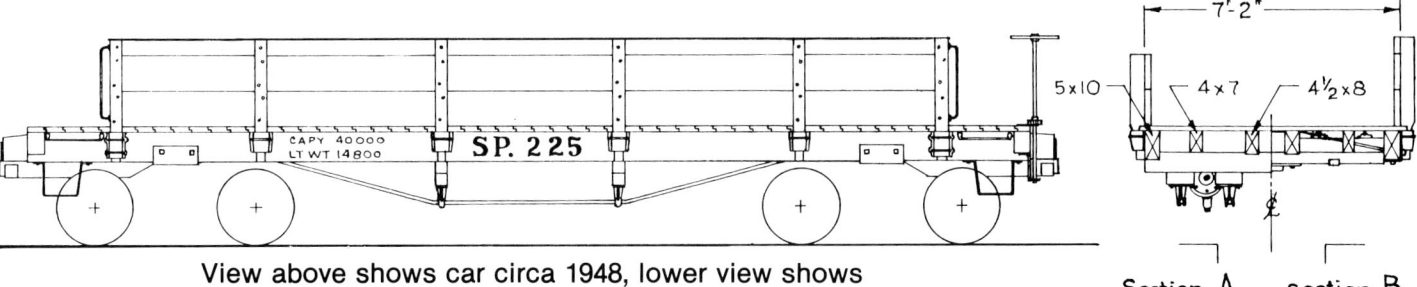

View above shows car circa 1948, lower view shows rebuilding in early 1950's. Door on one side only, sides lowered from 30" to 24". Sheet metal lining inside.

SCALE 3/16" = 1'0" (Full Size SN3)

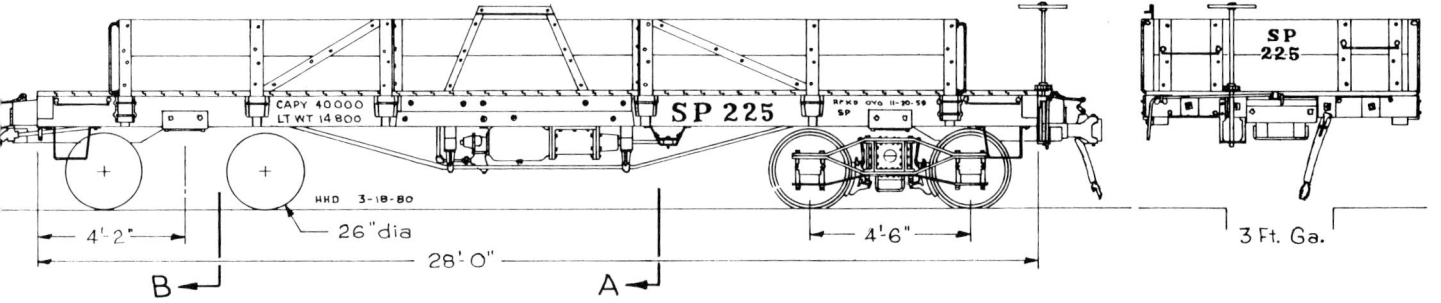

It was difficult to find a "standard" gondola in the Owens Valley. Essentially the cars were two or three side boards high, while lengths varied. During the rebuilding and renumbering program following World War II, some cars had sheet metal linings put inside and in the early 1950's many cars had a removable side section on one side only to facilitate loading and unloading of mineral traffic. Car 215, shown at Owenyo in 1952, retained the original sides as shown in the plan. The 228 is shown at Owenyo as rebuilt with removable door. The plan shows S.P. 225 "before" and "after" and is by Herman Darr.
[Photographs by Richard F. Thomas.]

A broadside view of gon 232 taken at Owenyo in 1953 by Richard Thomas. The lower view shows former flat 253 as a "tourist car" with twin outhouses. [Guy L. Dunscomb Collection.]

"Heading for Laws" painting by Jan Rons

SP "A" Frame Hoppers

Plan by Al E. Barker

This scale plan may not be reproduced in part or in whole to be used in conjunction with any commercial hobby or manufacturing endeavor without explicit written consent of A. E. Barker.

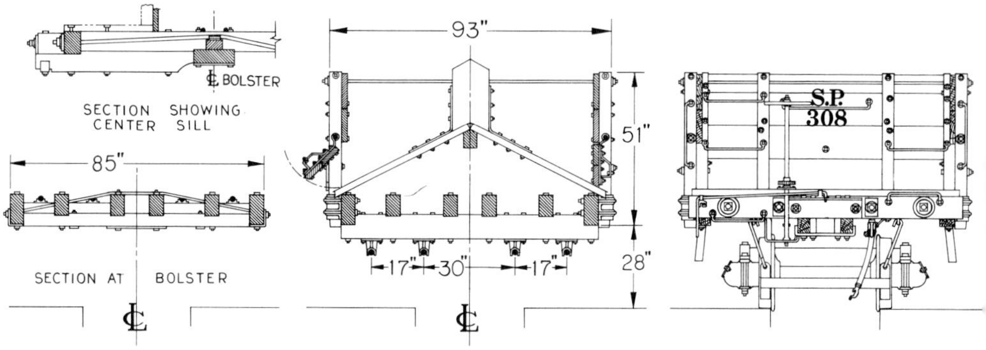

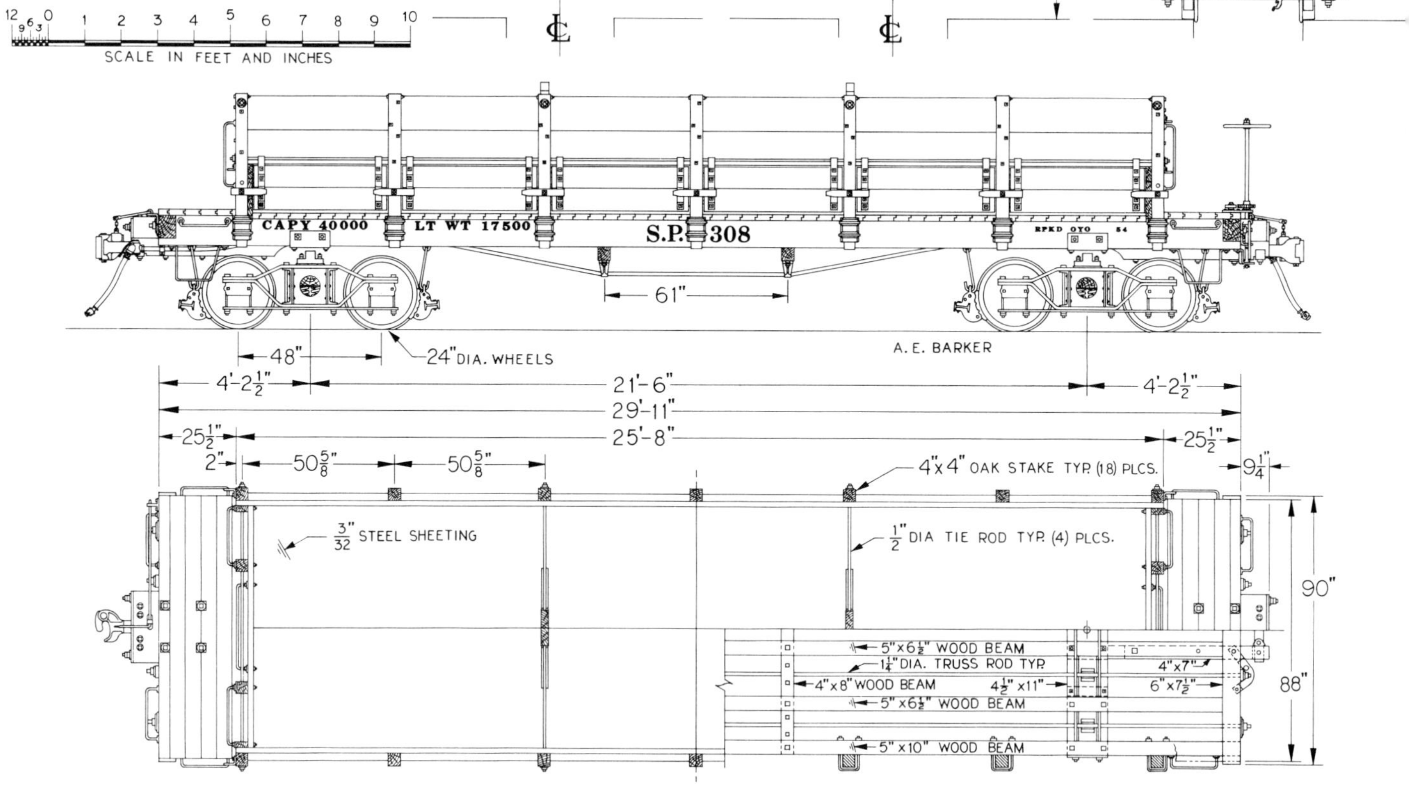

SCALE 3/16" = 1'0" (Full Size SN3)

The "A" Frame hoppers on the S.P. narrow gauge were used for bulk mineral products that had to be transferred to standard gauge cars on the transfer trestle. Many of these cars were former N-C-O flat cars that were rebuilt by the S.P. The cars on these pages are former N-C-O flats. Number 332 was at Owenyo in 1954 while 339 is shown in two views. [Author and Richard F. Thomas.]

SP Oil Tank Car 353
Plan by Herman Darr

Car built by Nevada California Oregon RR in early 1900's. Transfered to SP 1928. Renumbered from 178 to 353 about 1946. Scrapped by 1960.
Paint: Black with white lettering
Air brakes: Westinghouse 6"×8"KC

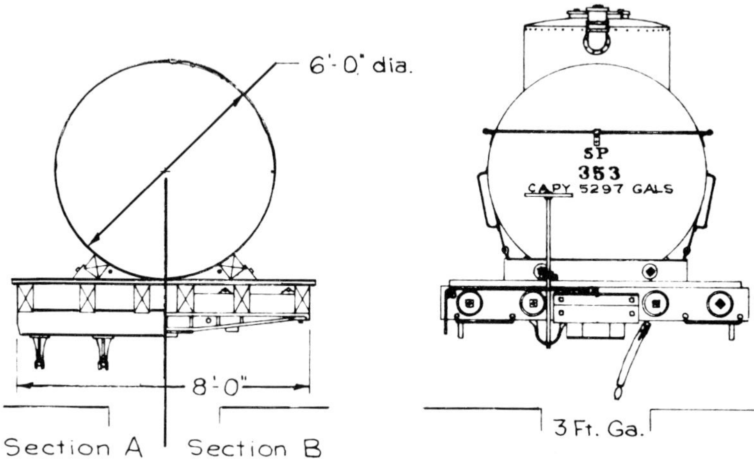

SCALE 3/16" = 1'0" (Full Size SN3)

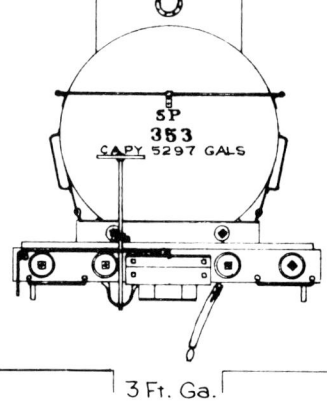

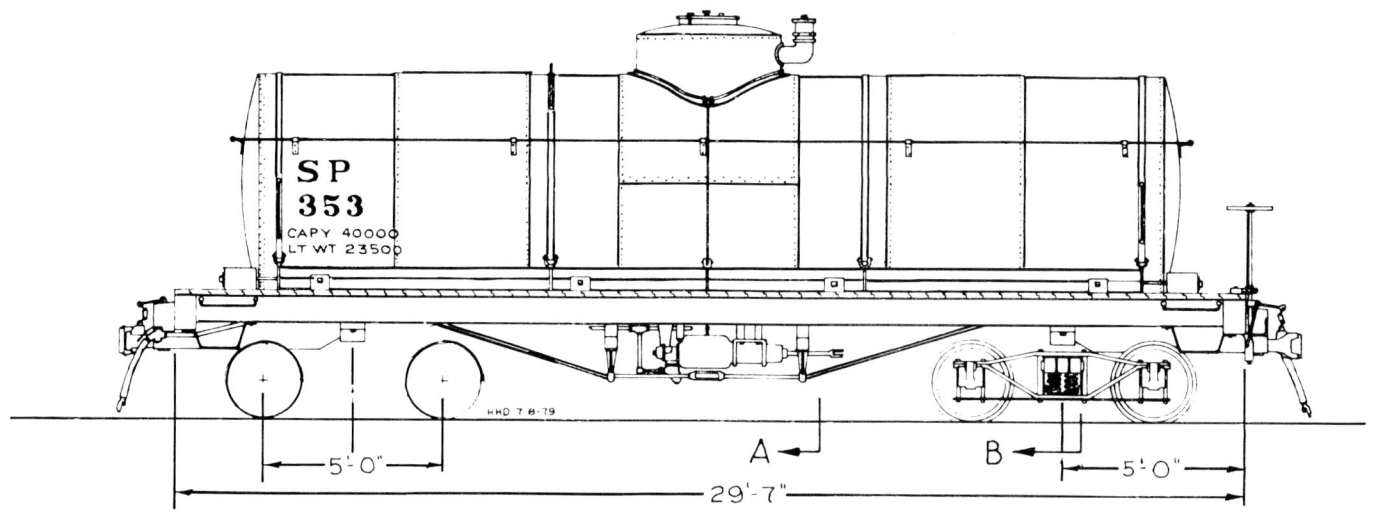

Tank Cars
Early water cars had wood tanks. Gerald M. Best photographed the 59 at Mina in 1935. The 350 was photographed at Owenyo in 1954. [Author.] Photographer Richard F. Thomas found the 351 at Owenyo in 1952. She carried oil and was painted black. Oil tank 353 was a former N-C-O car. [Richard F. Thomas.]

S.P. 54 was found on a siding at Owenyo in 1954. [Author.]
The car was painted tuscan red.

SP Water Tank Car 54
Plan by Ken Pruitt

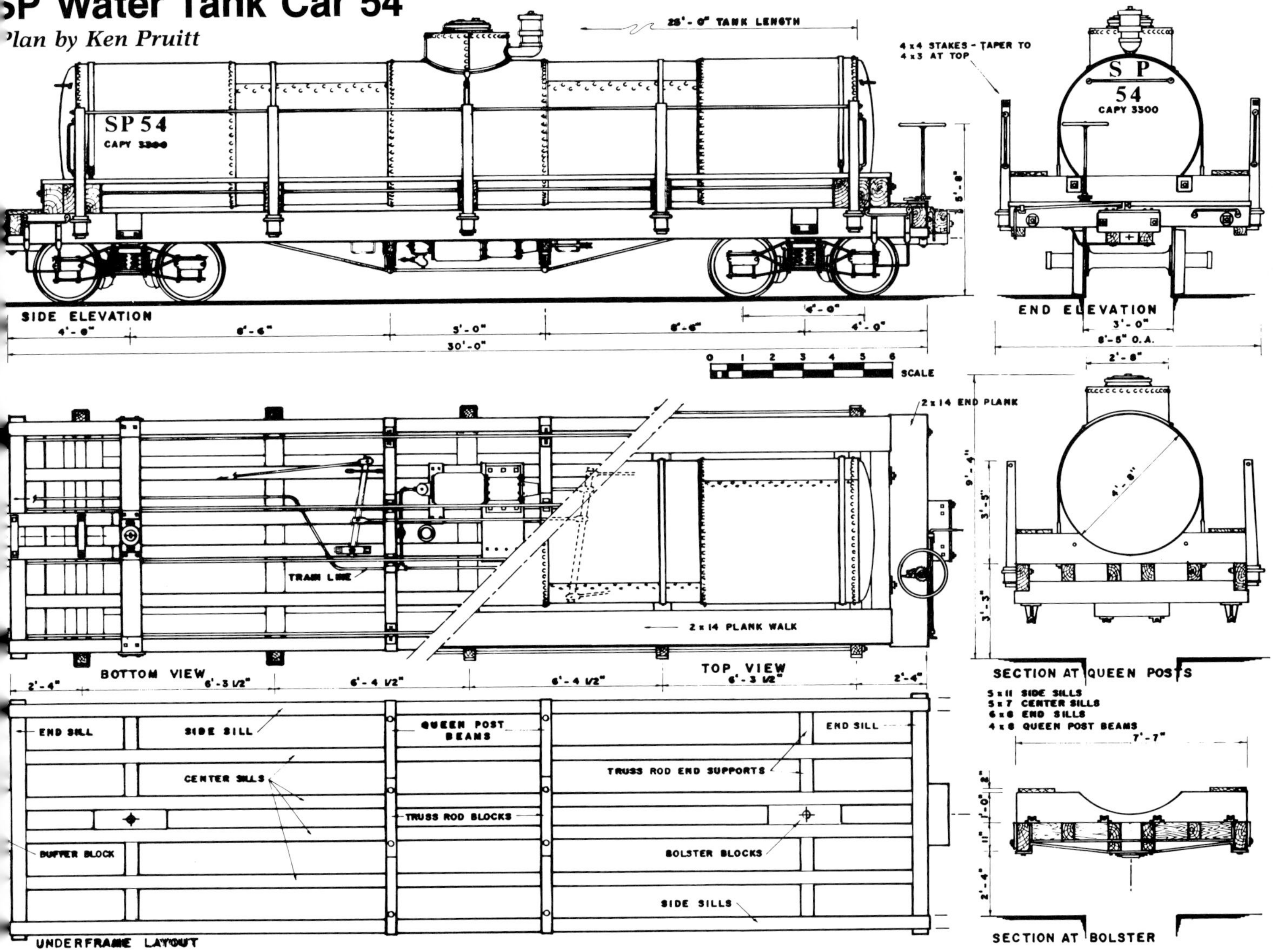

SCALE 3/16" = 1'0" (Full Size SN3)

SP Water Tank Car 61

Plan by Herman Darr

SCALE 3/16" = 1'0" (Full Size SN3)

Car built by Nevada California Oregon RR after 1900
Transfered to SP June 1928. Retired 5-50, sc
8-10-50. Paint: Black with white lettering
Air brakes: Westinghouse 6" × 8" KC

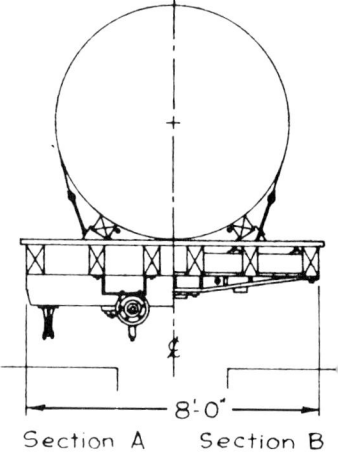

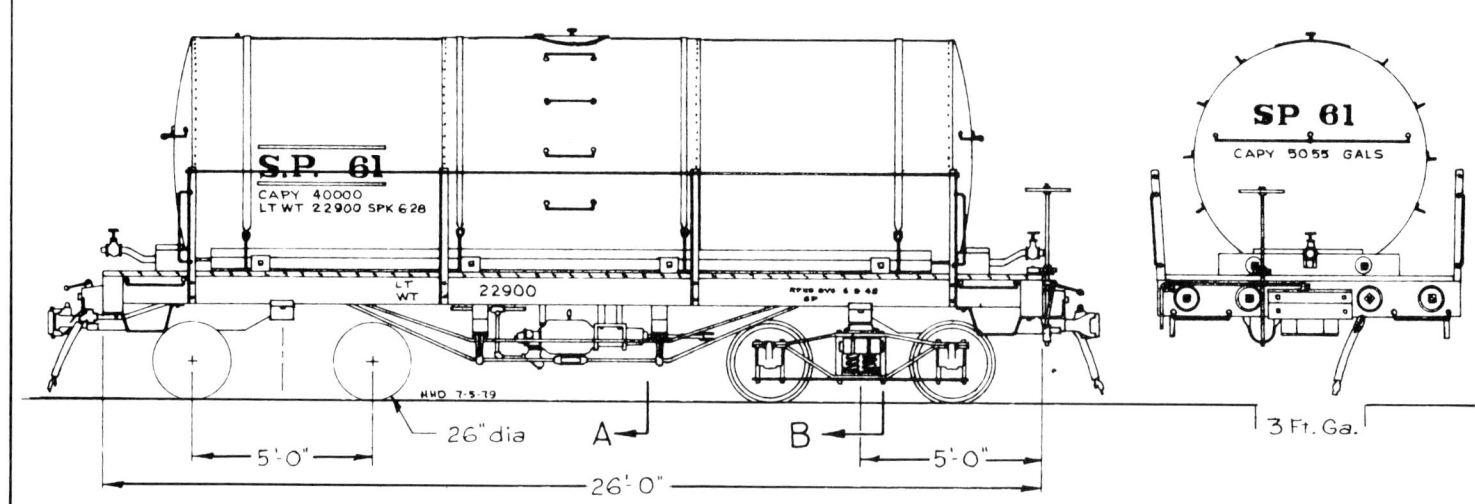

Domeless tank 61 was a former N-C-O car that saw water service duty on the S.P. narrow gauge. The car was photographed at Keeler in 1946 and was later relettered MW61. [Bert Ward.] The car was painted black with white lettering.

Crew car 1-D at Mina in 1936. [G. M. Best.]

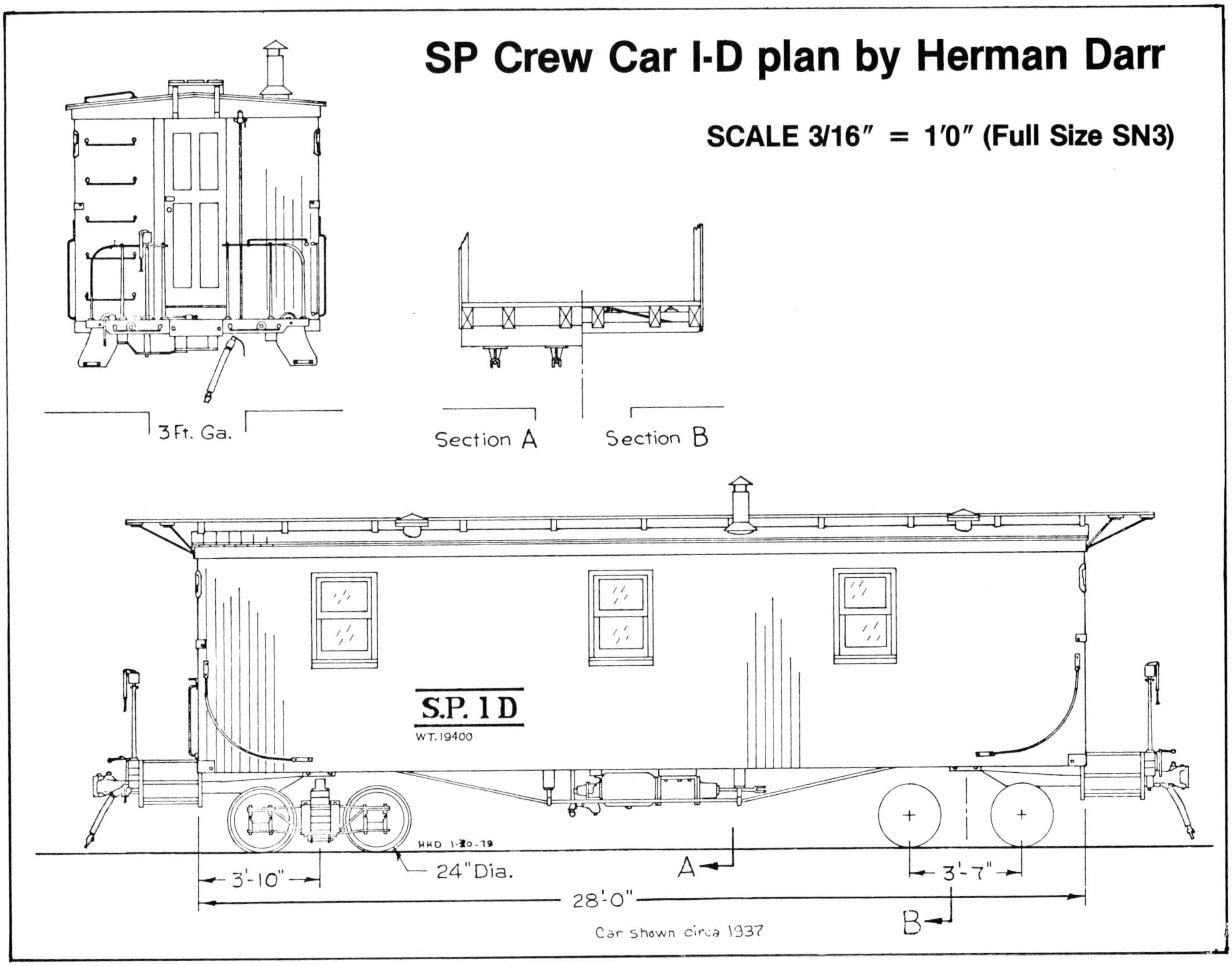

WORK CARS

S.P. 1 Derrick at Mina in 1936. [G. M. Best.]

S.P. 1-A was wheel car. [G. M. Best.]

Combine 1-B housed wrecking crew. [G. M. Best.]

Water tank car 350 often served as an auxiliary tender behind steam engines. In work service the car was painted red with white lettering. [Richard F. Thomas.]

During the late 1940's, former Baggage car 12 was set aside at Keeler for a crew quarters, but was placed back on the active roster as the spare caboose a few years later. She is shown at Keeler in March, 1946. [Guy Dunscomb.]

S.P. Flanger 108 dated from Carson & Colorado days and was only 22' long. Following abandonment of the line to Nevada, the car was brought south to the Owens Valley, but saw little service. The car still sported her Carter Brothers trucks when photographed in November, 1940 at Laws. [Donald Duke Collection.]

LOCOMOTIVE ROSTER
Carson & Colorado Ry. (1880-1905)
Nevada & California R.R. (1905-1912)
Southern Pacific (CP) (1912-1960)

THREE FOOT GAUGE

No.	Type	Builder	Date	Const. Number	Cylinders	Drivers	Weight	Remarks
1	4-4-0	Baldwin	9/1880	5285	14x18	41	48,000	"Candelaria." Relettered N&C 1 on 3-17-1906. Sold to Eureka & Palisade 9, 4-20-1907 ($2,500.00).
1 (2nd)	2-8-0	Baldwin	4/1914	41300	17x20	40	94,000	Orig. N-C-O 14, to SP 5-11-1928. To N.C.N.G. 9, 12-31-1933. To US Navy No. 17, Pearl Harbor in 1942. Sold for service in Libya, North Africa, $10,823.00 FOB Phil.
2	4-4-0	Baldwin	12/1880	5430	14x18	41	48,000	"Bodie." Scrapped 7-20-1907.
3	4-4-0	Baldwin	12/1880	5428	14x18	41	48,000	"Colorado." Relettered N&C 2 on 3-24-1906. Scrapped 9-23-1908.
4	4-4-0	Baldwin	8/1881	5782	14x18	44	48,000	"Churchill." Relettered N&C 4 on 4-4-1906. Sold to Nevada County Narrow Gauge R.R. 7, 6-6-1929. Scrapped 1-1937.
5	4-4-0	Baldwin	3/1882	6089	14x18	44	48,000	"Belleville." Relettered N&C 5 on 3-31-1906. Out of service 1-31-1921, Sparks. Scrapped 1-20-1932, Sacramento.
6	4-4-0	Baldwin	3/1882	6090	14x18	44	48,000	"Hawthorne." Scrapped 7-31-1907.
6 (2nd)	4-4-0	Baldwin	12/1877	4223	12x18	44	45,500	Orig. SPC 6. Leased to San Bernardino & Redlands R.R. (SP) 1906–1-1917. To SP 6 and placed in service at Mina 11-1-1917. Out of service 11-30-1921. Scrapped 5-4-1926.
7	4-4-0	Baldwin	4/1883	6687	14x18	44	48,000	"Benton." Relettered N&C 7 on 4-12-1906. Out of service 1-31-1929, Sparks. Scrapped 1-20-1932, Sacramento.
8	4-4-0	Baldwin	4/1883	6689	14x18	44	48,000	"Darwin." Relettered N&C 8 on 3-21-1906. Out of service 1-31-1929, Sparks. Scrapped 2-10-1932, Sacramento.
8 (2nd)	4-6-0	Baldwin	8/1907	31445	16x20	44	87,150	Orig. N-C-O 8, to SP in 1928, to state of Nevada, Carson City, NV 5-9-1955. Moved to Sparks Railroad Park, Sparks, NV 1977.
9	4-4-0	Baldwin	6/1885	7604	15x18	48	52,000	Orig. SPC 16. Sold to N&C 9, 8-2-1906. ($2,614.00) Scrapped 2-10-1933, Sacramento.
9 (2nd)	4-6-0	Baldwin	11/1909	34035	16x20	44	87,150	Orig. N-C-O 9, to SP 9 9-1-1929. Rebuilt Sparks 2-31-1930. Held for standby service after 10-1954. Donated to city of Bishiop, Inyo County 4-30-1960. Display at Laws R.R. Museum.
10	4-4-0	Baldwin	6/1885	7605	15x18	48	52,000	Orig. SPC 17, sold to N&C 10, 8-2-1906 ($2,614.50). Scrapped 4-20-1933.
11	2-6-0 (4-6-0)	Baldwin	5/1881	5649	14x18 (15x18)	44 (43)	49,900 (73,600)	Orig. SPC 11. Sold to N&C 11, 7-11-1906 ($2,240.00). Rebuilt as 4-6-0 1-19-1924. Out of service 5-31-1932, Mina. Scrapped 7-6-1934, Sacramento.
12	2-6-0 (4-6-0)	Baldwin	5/1881	5650	14x18 (15x18)	44 (43)	49,900 (73,700)	Orig. SPC 12. Sold to N&C 12, 7-9-1906 ($2,240.00). Rebuilt as 4-6-0 12-31-1921. Out of service 5-31-1932, Mina. Scrapped 6-21-1934, Sacramento.

No.	Type	Builder	Date	Const. Number	Cylinders	Drivers	Weight	Remarks
13	2-8-0	Baldwin	4/1882	6157	15x18	36	57,100	Orig. SPC 13. Sold N&C 13, 10-21-1906 ($5,060.00). Out of service 12-1909. Leased to LTRy&T 13 4-1915 to 4-1927. Scrapped 11-9-1927, Sacramento.
14	4-6-0	Baldwin	6/1886	7939	16x20	48	74,000	Orig. SPC 18. Sold to N&C 14, 7-1-1906, ($3,069.00). To stationary boiler service, Colfax, CA 12-10-1945. Scrapped 10-18-1951. Engine weight 83,900 in final service.
15	4-6-0	Baldwin	6/1889	9929	16x20	48	74,000	Orig. SPC 22. Sold to N&C 15 7-1-1906, ($3,487.50). Out of service 1-1-1934, Mina. Scrapped 12-21-1935, Sacramento.
16	4-6-0	Baldwin	6/1886	7941	16x20	48	74,000	Orig. SPC 19. Sold to N&C 16 8-1-1907 ($2,500.00). Out of service 10-31-1921, Sparks. Retired 1-31-1934, Mina. Scrapped 12-27-1935, Sacramento. Engine weight 83,900 in final service.
17	4-6-0	Baldwin	6/1887	8487	16x20	48	74,000	Orig. SPC 21. Sold to N&C 17 8-1-1907, ($4,500.00). To stationary boiler service Salem, OR 12-10-1945. Scrapped 4-10-1952. Final engine weight 83,900.
18	4-6-0	Baldwin	12/1911	37395	16x20	44	87,150	Orig. N-C-O 12. Sold to SP 18 5-11-1928 To Eastern California Museum, Independence, CA 5-13-1955 (display). Final engine weight 88,900.
22	4-6-0	Schenectady	1/1900	5399	16x20	45	89,400	Orig. F&CC 22 "Vindicator." To N-C-O 22 5-1915. Rebuilt by SP Sparks shop 5-1-1925 for N-C-O. To SP 9-1-1929. Driver size increased to 45" 5-20-1937 (Ogden shops). To steam service Bayshore shops (San Francisco) 1942. Scrapped 3-28-1949.
1 (3rd)	Diesel B-B	General Electric	10/1954	32226	Caterpillar Diesel 450 h.p.			New. Sold to Pan American Engineering Co., Dallas, TX (dealer) 4-17-1961. Sold to Cananea Mining Co. (Compania Minera de Cananea), Cananea, Sonora, Mexico. Engine named "Little Giant" on SP, the result of a contest.

NOTES: Air brakes were added to C&C locomotives in 1897. Conversion from wood to oil was accomplished between September 1900 and October 1901 by the V&T's Carson City shops. The change saw diamond stacks replaced by straight stacks with firebox grates and tenders modified to burn oil. Link and pin couplers were removed and three quarter size Sams Patent (automatic) couplers installed in 1903-04 on all equipment.

The Tonopah Gold Rush saw in increased demand for motive power on the hard-pressed C&C in 1900-1907. During this period nine former SPC locomotives were purchased. The bonanza also saw the use of several engines from the San Joaquin & Sierra Nevada. The SJ&SN had been taken over by the SP (Bracks-Valley Springs, CA) and was standard gauged in 1904. Former SJ&SN engines were not placed on the C&C's roster and were sold as soon as the larger ex-SPC engines became available. The SJ&SN engines were:

1024 2-6-0 H.K. Porter 1882. Original SJ&SN 2, used on C&C 1904-1906. Scrapped 1907, Sacramento.

1025 2-6-0 Pittsburg 1880 - #430. Original Oregon Ry 4 "Brownsville," Oregonian Ry 4. To SP 1025 (2nd) 12-28-1903. Used on SJ&SN, C&C. Sold to C.D. Bunker 8-8-1906 (scrap).

1026 4-4-0 Baldwin 1880 - #5478. Original Oregonian Ry. 8 "C.N. Scott." Sold to SP 1026 12-28-1903 (SJ&SN). Used on C&C 1904-06. Sold to McKenzie Shipyard, Oakland, CA 9-29-1906 (hoisting engine).

Following the SP take-over of the N-C-O Ry and standard gauging (1927-28), former N-C-O locomotives 8, 9, 14, 12 and 22 were sent to the Mina-Keeler branch. Five other former N-C-O locomotives (3, 4, 5, 6, 7) were transferred from the N-C-O in 1928, but these engines were held at Sparks and there is no record of their use on the SP. They were all scrapped in 1934.

Abbreviations: CP Central Pacific E&P Eureka & Palisade N-C-O Nevada-California-Oregon NCNG Nevada County Narrow Gauge
SPC South Pacific Coast LTRy&T Lake Tahoe Railway & Transportation Company F&CC Florence & Cripple Creek
V&T Virginia & Truckee SJ&SN San Joaquin & Sierra Nevada

S.P. Number 1 pauses at Mina, Nevada in the early 1930's. [Bert Ward.]

Southern Pacific 5, one of the original C&C 4-4-0's, prepares to depart Mina, Nevada. The "Belleville" has been modernized greatly but retains some of her 1882 charm. [Guy Duscomb Collection.]

South Pacific Coast 6 was the oldest engine on the S.P. narrow gauge when she arrived in 1917. Baldwin built the little 4-4-0 in 1877 and she operated in Southern California before going to the deserts of Nevada and California. [Author.]

Southern Pacific 7, the former "Benton," was out of service at Mina by the mid-1920's. [Bill Pennington from Bert Ward.]

The Eight Spot

Ten-wheeler 8 was one of a trio of former Nevada-California-Oregon 4-6-0's that held down the Espee's Owens Valley run during the last decades. She became one of the best remembered and most photographed engine on the road. The photographs on this page represent several stages in the life of number 8. Above, the locomotive is shown at Keeler, in a photograph taken in 1946 by Bert Ward. Just a year later (center), also at Keeler, the 8 is unchanged except for a white painted smokebox front — a feature common to S.P. engines after WWII. [Robert M. Hanft, Collection of Guy Dunscomb.] By 1951 (below), several changes were evident. A Pyle-National "winged" headlight has been added and the 8 has lost her original steam dome and valve covers. [W. C. Whittaker Collection.] The 8 is preserved today at Sparks, Nevada.

Number Nine

Former Nevada-California-Oregon 9 was the last steam engine to operate on the Espee narrow gauge. Looking the worse for wear, she is seen (above) at Keeler in March, 1948. [Robert M. Hanft.] In contrast, looking fresh and clean, the 9 waited at Keeler in 1940. [Author's Collection.] The lower view shows the rear of the tender at Keeler in 1952. [Richard F. Thomas.]

Southern Pacific 10 served as the "snowplow engine" and was photographed beside the Mina enginehouse in the 1920's. [Bill Pennington from Bert Ward.]

Ten-wheeler 11 began life as a Mogul and was rebuilt into a 4-6-0 in 1924. She was out of service at Mina by the early 1930's. [Guy Dunscomb Collection.]

Former South Pacific Coast 12 also began life as a 4-6-0 in 1881, but was rebuilt by the S.P. in 1921. The 4-6-0 is pictured here by the Mina enginehouse in about 1930. [Guy Dunscomb Collection.]

Baldwin Number 13 was built for the South Pacific Coast in 1882 and was sold to the Nevada & California in 1906. She was leased to the Lake Tahoe Railway & Transportation Co. from 1915-1927 and is seen here at Truckee, CA in 1924. [Author's Collection.]

Espee 14 provided years of service for the Owens Valley narrow gauge and was found (above) at Keeler at the start of WWII. [Donald Duke.] In 1945 the 14 was taken to Colfax, CA to provide stationary boiler service (below) and was scrapped in 1951. [Author's Collection.]

Ten-wheeler 15 came from the South Pacific Coast in 1906 and was on the Mina "dead line" (top) in 1934. [Bert Ward Collection.] The 15 was shipped to Sacramento (lower) and scrapped in December, 1935. [Guy Dunscomb.] Someone had written "My work is done" on her air tank.

Southern Pacific 16 awaits the scrappers torch at the Sacramento Shops on December 15, 1935; by years' end she would be gone. The 16 had seen happier days as she headed-up a three engine stock extra at Mina. [Both: Guy Dunscomb.]

The 17 arrived on the Nevada & California in 1907 and is seen (top) at Mina in January, 1938. [G. M. Best.] Later the same year, L. C. Rowe found her at Keeler on the ready track. [Bert Ward Collection.]

Number 18 still sported a slotted knuckle coupler for use with link and pin equipment, when found by Richard F. Thomas at Keeler in 1952. She shows the "weathering" of desert railroading, too.

Seldom photographed, but of importance to scale model builders, is the rear and top of the tender. The 18 is on the Keeler ready track. [Richard F. Thomas.]

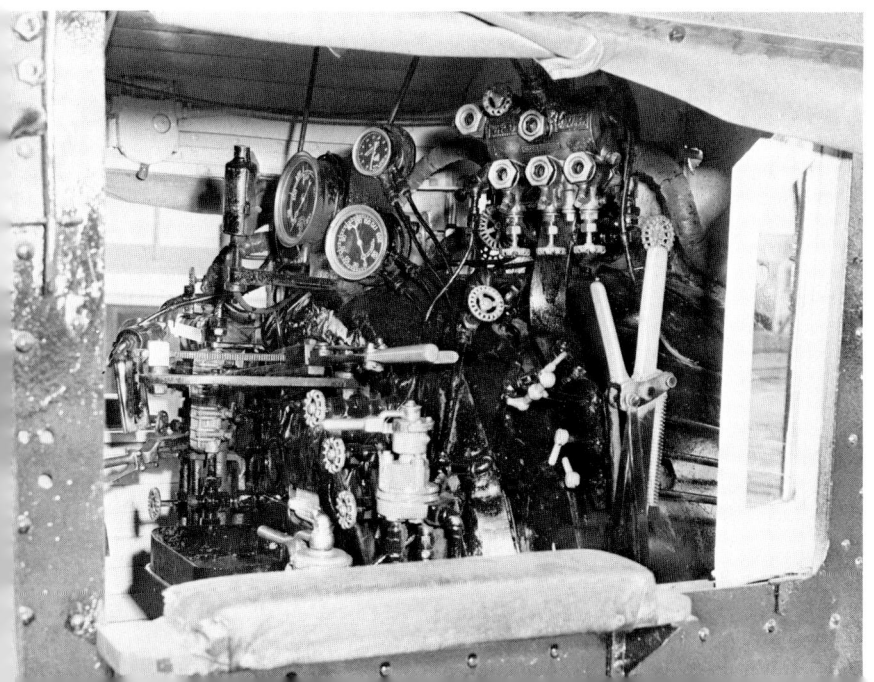

A view of the engineer's side of 4-6-0 Number 18, shows the fully "detailed" backhead. [S.P. Collection.]

The classic 18 has stopped in the desert near Owenyo, while the crew tends to a "hotbox." Photographer Bert Ward took advantage of the opportunity to record this view.

Number 18 had a lot of character! From her tall stack to her alkali-dust covered 44" drivers, she was a trim machine, perhaps the most graceful of all the latterday engines on the road. She posed at Keeler in March, 1948 for Robert M. Hanft. [Guy Dunscomb Collection.]

The 18 in her final configuration, around 1954. Very little has changed except for the addition of the Pyle-National visored headlight, and odd cone-shaped steam dome cover. For some strange reason, all three locomotives, 8, 9 and 18, had their graceful Baldwin steam dome covers replaced during their final years on the road. [William H. Radcliffe.]

"Desert Run" watercolor (18x24) by Mike Pearsall. [Collection of Robert Dezelin.]

During the Tonopah Gold Rush of 1900-1907, the Carson & Colorado Railway was hardpressed to meet the influx of traffic and the owning Southern Pacific sent narrow gauge equipment from other lines, many of which were being standard gauged. The South Pacific Coast 22 was one of a group of engines that were sold to the newly renamed Nevada & California Railway in 1906, becoming the Number 15. She is shown at Alameda, CA in about 1900. [Dale Darney Collection.]

Colorado Boomer

The only non-Baldwin steamer on the Espee narrow gauge was the former "Vindicator" of the Florence & Cripple Creek. The 22 was built by Schenectady in 1900 and was sold to the Nevada-California-Oregon Railway in 1915, after the Colorado line was wiped out by a flood. The 22 came to the Owens Valley line in 1929 and was a popular engine. She is seen (above) at Mina in 1936. [Guy Dunscomb.] In 1942 she was sent to the Bayshore shops near San Francisco to provide steam service. Will C. Whittaker found her there in 1946 (left). The 22 was a sister engine to Rio Grande Southern 20, which is preserved at the Colorado Railroad Museum, Golden, CO.

FACILITIES...

At Keeler, a former Carson & Colorado baggage-mail car 4 provided storage space for tools, along with a boxcar and several sheds. Most of the repair work was done outside, under a cobalt-blue sky with summertime temperatures frequently over 100 degrees. [Richard F. Thomas.]

The Tool Shed at Keeler began as an 1880 baggage-mail car and was placed on the ground here in 1939. [Richard F. Thomas.]

The Laws servicing area was a tidy layout, with tanks for water, fuel oil and an 1883 Gallows turntable. The back side of the tanks are seen in a Richard F. Thomas view from 1953 (above). In the lower view is the Laws table. [Richard F. Thomas.] Fortunately the trackage, tanks, and turntable have been preserved as part of the Laws Railroad Museum.

259

At Owenyo, the facilities were equally simple. The car repair "shop" area was outdoors. [Richard F. Thomas.] The Owenyo turntable was an 1883 Gallows type that originally saw service at Keeler. The turntable stub was often used as a storage track for rolling stock that required extensive rebuilding, and is show in 1939. [Al Phelps.]

DEPOTS

Keeler, at the southern end of the narrow gauge, had a huge depot with a two-story addition that also housed the agent and his family. A number of "railfans" have come to visit in the fall of 1948 and the Cerro Gordo Tramway Terminal can be seen in the distance. [Fred Stindt from Guy Dunscomb.]

The Owenyo depot was a much simpler structure dating from 1910. It was the operating headquarters of the last few decades. A northbound train is given the "highball" as Agent Tommer and a retired "rail" look on in March, 1954. [S.P. Collection.]

The Kearsarge depot was an original Carson & Colorado structure, shown here in the summer of 1939. The 20' × 50' building was painted in the standard "depot buff" yellow, with brown trim and was torn down in 1955. [Al Phelps.]

The Laws depot has been preserved as a part of the Laws Railroad Museum. It is seen here with Diesel 1 in April, 1960. [Gary G. Allen.] This frame depot along with those at Dayton, NV. and Keeler, CA. still stand.

The original 20' × 40' Laws depot was expanded on both ends over the years and today serves as a museum devoted to narrow gauge days. [Author.]

The 18 takes water at Laws in 1953. [Wendell Mortimer, Jr.]

SOUTHERN PACIFIC NARROW GAUGE AT A GLANCE—1950

Southern Pacific's Narrow Gauge Owens Valley Line

TRACKAGE: Laws to Keeler, California 70.4 miles. Three Foot gauge.

STATIONS: Laws (MP 506.8) Frame Depot. (Originally 20'x40' and later added to on each end.) Closed 2/1959. Elevation: 4,115.

Kearsarge (MP 550.1) Frame Depot (20'x50'). Torn down 12/1955. Elevation: 3,925.

Owenyo (MP 559.8) Frame Building. Closed 4/1960. Elevation: 3,690

Keeler (MP 576.5) Frame Depot. Closed 8/1957. Elevation: 3,610.

Former Station Names:
Laws, formerly Bishop Creek
Zurich, formerly Alvord
Aberdeen, formerly Tibbets
Kearsarge, formerly Independence, then Citrus Keeler, formerly Hawley.

TURNTABLES: Laws: Gallows type, built 1883.

Owenyo: Gallows type, moved here from Keeler in 1910. Dismantled 1948.

Keeler: Gallows type, built 1883 and moved to Owenyo 1910.

ENGINEHOUSE: Keeler, single stall. Burned 1946. With advent of diesel (1954) servicing was done at Owenyo.

WATER TANKS: Laws: originally windmill powered.
Aberdeen: windmill powered until 1953.
Kearsarge
Owenyo: used standard gauge water supply via pipe.
Keeler

FUEL OIL: Laws
Owenyo

TRANSFERS: Owenyo:
Trestle: with narrow gauge above standard gauge.
Gantry: (Queen Truss) Hand powered gears.
Dock: Manual labor used to transfer materials.

PRODUCTS HAULED: Cattle, sheep, soda, pumice, talc, clay, soapstone, dolomite, slate, pyrophylite (crop dusting), lead, melatenterite, aluminum silcate, silver ore, potatoes, hay and farm products, sugar beets.

LOCOMOTIVES: Three Baldwin 4-6-0's. Number 8, 9, 18.

ROLLING STOCK: Box—91; Combination Box/Stock—14; Stock—35; Flat—8; Gondola—36; Ballast—38; Tank—4; Caboose—1; Baggage & Express—1; Work—4.

INDEX

Page numbers in bold type denote photographs.

A

Aberdeen 10, 74, water tank 101, 192, **160-165**
Agler, Jas. (Manager, C&C Ry.) 60
Allen, Jim 32
Allison, W.C. & Co. 204
American Car & Foundry 220
Argentum Mines 25, 28

B

Baggage Car #12 **117, 120, 216,** plan 219, **220, 245,** roster **207-208**
Bakersfield (Ca.) 75, shops (SP) 191-192
Baldwin Locomotive Works 60, 97
Barney & Smith (Car builders) 220
Barstow, Jn. (Agent at Candelaria) 24
Basalt water tank **91**
Beckes, Clyde 99
Beebe, Lucius 9, **12 (with Charles Clegg),** 27
Belleville 24, 26-27, mills, 28, **44-45**
Bender, D.A. (Gen. freight & Pass. agent, C&C Ry.) 19, 25, 28
Belmont 59
Benton 17, 75, 97
Big Pine Creek 17
Bishop Creek (later Bishop) 17, 27
Bishop, Samuel 17
Bliss, Duane C. 19, 28, 31-32
Bodie 19, 22, 24-25
Bodie Consolidated Mining 25
"Bodie & Candelaria Express" 24
"Bodie & Hawley Express" **25**
Bodie Ry. & Lumber Co. 25
Bodey, William J. 17
Box cars **222-227,** roster 209, plan #72, **225,** plan #74 **228**
Brennan, J.A. "Jim" (Conductor) 99-100, **118, 122**
Bristlecone Pine 17
Business Cars **84-85, 221**
  See also roster 207-208
Butler, Jim (DA Nye County, Nev.) 23

C

California Car Works 60
California Gold Rush 17
Candelaria 9, 24-25, 27-28, **47,** depot 24, **48-49, 50-51,** mountains 24, water works 24, mining co. 25
Carson City 19, 23, 203
Carson River 9, 19, 22, 27

Carson & Colorado 9, map 18, 19, 21-28, 32, 59, 69, 75, 98, 203, roster of cars (1903) 204, 220
Carson & Tahoe Lumber & Fluming Co. 19
Central Pacific 26, 73, 205
Cerro Gordo (mine) 9, 17, 19, 26, 28, 63, 74, 98, **117**
Churchill Canyon 23
Coke Rack Car **229,** plan 229
  See also roster 211
Cole, Josephine "Jo," 100, **141,**
Colorado River 9
Combine-Cabooses #467 **103,** 208, **218;** #401 192-**193,** 208, **216, 218,** 220; #400 plan 217, 220
  See also rosters 207-208
Comstock (ore strikes) 17, 59
Consolidated Virginia Mining Co. **29**
Cottonwood Branch 32, 60

D

Darwin (silver strike) 17
Dayton 22, 24, **36-37,** 70
Death Valley 10, 17, 19, 26, 63, 97
  Railway 26
Denver & Rio Grande 60
Denver South Park & Pacific 74, 203
Desert Club Bar (Keeler) 98
Dogtown 17
Dolomite 10, 74, 99, **125**
Donner Pass 97

E

"Esmeralda"—private car 74, **85,** 220
  See also roster 207-208
Excelsior Flat Valley 24

F

"Fairport" (former N-C-O business car) 74, **85**
  See also roster 207-208
Fallberg, Carl 9, cartoon 14-15
Fan Trips , **196-197**
Ferguson, W.C. "Walt" 99-100, **107,** 192
Finnell, Jim (painting) 161
Flanger #108 **90, 226, 245**
  See also rosters 213
Flat Cars **233-234,** plan #259 233
  See also rosters 212
Florence & Cripple Creek 9, 74, 97, 191, 203, 205

Fogg, Howard 10
Forbes, John 28
Fort Churchill 19, 22, 60-61, 73
Fort Tejon 17
Fremont, John C. 17

G

Genoa 19
Glenbrook 19
Goldfield 60, 73
Gondola Cars **235-236** plan #225 235
  See also roster 211
Graves, William 192
Great Basin 19
Great Depression 74
Greenfield (former Pizen Switch) 22

H

Hanson, Carl 99
Harp Switchstands 98
Harte, Bret 25
Hawley (later Keeler) 26-28
Hawthorne 22-24, 27, depot 28, **40-43**
  map 42, 61-62
"Hawthorne" locomotive **42, 55**
  See also rosters 246-247
Hawthorne, W.A. 22
Hazen (Nv.) 62, 73
Hoppers "A" frame **238-239**, plan #308 238
  See also roster 212
Hovey, R.R. (chief boilermaker) 191
Huntington, Collis P. 59
Huntley Industrial Minerals Co. 101, **176, 182**

I

Independence (Ca.) 27
Interstate Commerce Commission 192
Inyo County 10, 75
Inyo Development Co. **56-57**, 74
Inyo Mountains 28, 63, 74, 99

J

Japan 97
"Jawbone" branch (SP) 63, 73, 98-99, 101, **148**
Jenks General Store 22

K

Keeler (Ca.) 9-10, 61-62, 73-74, 97-101, 191-102
  terminal **107-109**, "Downtown" **112-113**
  depot **114-115, 121, 261**, 118-120, map 124,
  water tank **121**, facilities **258**
Keeler, James M. 28
Keersarge 10, 17, 100, depot **158, 160, 262**
  water tank **160**, 192
Kruttschnitt, J. (GM of C&C Ry.) 60
Kneiss, Gilbert 27

L

Lake Tahoe Narrow Gauge 30-31
Laws (Ca.) 9-10, 26, 73, 75, 97, 100-101, **156**
  map 174, yards **174-185**, 192, depot **176, 182, 263**, facilities **259**
Laws Museum & Historical Site 192
Laws, Robert C. (Superintendent) 22, 24, 26, 28, 32, 60
Locomotives: C&C #3 "Colorado" **58**
  C&C "Hawthorne" **42, 55** SP #1 **248**
  SP #5 **248** SP #6 **248** SP #7 **248**
  SP #8 **13, 72, 79, 82, 86, 97, 106, 156-157, 167, 172-173, 185, 193, 249** SP #9 8, 75, **81, 94-95**, 97, **121, 123, 132, 139-140, 145-147, 151-155, 159**, 191-192, **195-197, 200, 250** SP #10 **251** SP #11 **251**
  SP #12 **88-89, 251** SP #13 **251** SP #14 **72**, 75, **79, 83, 86, 95, 252** SP #15 **252**
  SP #16 **88-89, 253** SP #17 **83, 93-94, 253**
  SP #18 **title p., 11, 72, 75, 86, 88-89, 92, 94-95, 97, 99-100, 106-107, 115, 118-119, 125-131, 133-134, 147, 149-150, 152, 158, 160, 163-166, 168-171, 175, 176-187, 190, 191, 193-196, 200, 254-255** SP #22 **90, 96, 102-105, 257**
  (Also former SPC #22 **257**) Diesel #1
  "Little Giant" 191-192, **194-195, 198-199**
  See also Locomotive rosters 246-247

Lombardy Poplars (trees) 100
Lone Pine (Ca.) 26-27, 100, 192
Los Angeles (Ca.) 9, 60, 63, 73, 100
Luce, Israel (Inyo Marble Works) 32
Lyman, E.E. (carman) 191

M

Mammoth 17
Manzanar 10
Mason Valley 19
Maxwell, John W.C. 32
Milbrae 22
Mills Darius 19, 27, 32, 59-60, 63, 74, 192, 204
Mina (Nv.) 61-62, 73-75, **78-79**, depot **79**, facilities **80-83**, map 80-81, last train **95**, 97, 101, 203
Mojave 25, 32, 62, 73

267

Mono County 25
Mono Lake 17
Monola 75-76, 100
Moore, Lt. Tredwell 17
Mound House (Nv.) 9, 19, 21-24, 26-28, **33,** depot **34-35, 38,** 59-61, 74
Mount Diablo Mines 25, 28, **46**
Mount Montgomery Pass 9-10, 25, 27, **52-53,** 75, **92-93,** map 87
Mount Whitney 10, 97, 101
Mount Whitney Siding **11, 128**
Movies (made on SPng) **188-189**
Murry, George (fireman) 99

Mc

McGhee, G.C. 192

N

Naileigh Copper Mine 23
National Reclamation Service 60
National Soda Products Co. 74
Nevada & California R.R. 62-63, 73, **76-77,** Engine #17 **77,** 203
See also roster of cars (1908) 204, 220
Nevada-California-Oregon Ry. 9, 60, 74, 97, 191, 205, 220
Nevada Copper Belt R.R. 22
New York 59
Northern Belle Mining Co. 25, 28, **46**
North Pacific Coast R.R. 203

O

Oliver, James T. 26
Olson, Bob 192
O'Nan, Harry (conductor) **192**
Oregonian Ry. 191, 203
Owens Lake 26-28, 74
Owens River 74, 100, **166-167**
Owens, Lt. Richard 17
Owens Valley 9, early explorations 17, 25-27, 60, 63, 73, 98, 191
Owenyo (Ca.) 9-10, 63, 73, 98-101, hotel 101, **134-135,** 191-192, transfer trestle **136-137, 138-147, 149,** map **142, 143,** facilities **142, 143, 152, 260,** depot **262**

P

Pacific Motor Trucking Co. 192
Panamints (mountains) 10, 19
Parrish, J.S. (agent at Laws) 100

Passenger Cars #4 **220,** #5 **220,** #7 **221,** #17 **221,** #20 (business car) **221**
See also roster 207-208
Pearsall, Mike (paintings) 110-111, 256
Piutes (Indians) 17, 22-23, 99
Plaster City (Ca.) 191

R

Railway & Locomotive Historical Society 191, fan trips **192**
Randol, W.M. 32
Passenger Cars #4 **220,** #5 **220,** #7 **221,** #17 **221,** #20 (business car) **221**
See also roster 207-208
Pearsall, Mike (paintings) 110-111, 256
Piutes (Indians) 17, 22-23, 99
Plaster City (Ca.) 191

R

Railway & Locomotive Historical Society 191, fan trips **192**
Randol, W.M. 32
Reno (Nv.) 59
Rio Grande Southern 97
Richardson, G.F. (Supt. of Trans.-C&C Ry.) 60
Rons, Jan (painting) 237
Rosters:
C&C (cars) 204; N&C (cars) 205, passenger cars 207-208, boxcars 209, Combo-Box 210, Stock Cars 210, Gondolas 211, Flat Cars 212, "A" frame Hoppers 212, Tank Cars 212, Work Cars 213, Car Bodies sold 214-215, Locomotives 246-247

S

Saline Valley Salt Marsh 74
San Antonio Mountains 59
San Francisco 25, 32, Newspaper "Call" 59, 101
"San Francisco & Virginia Express" 24
San Joaquin Division (SP) 75, 99
San Joaquin & Sierra Nevada R.R. 191, 203, 220
Santa Cruz (Ca.) 60
Schurz 22, 61
Sharon, William 19, 27, 31, 59, 192
Sheffield, England (rail for C&C) 24, 98
Short Line Enterprises 204
Sierra Nevada (mountains) 9, 17, 60, 97
Sierra Talc Co. 98

Silver Panic of 1893 32
Smith, Francis, Marion "Borax" 26
Smith, Jedediah Strong 17
Smith, S.P. 28
"Snow on the Narrow Gauge" **90-91**
Soda Springs Valley 24
Sodaville, 24, 28, 59-61, **61**, 62, 75, mill 25
Southern Pacific R.R. 9, 25, 59, 60-62, 73, 75, 191-192, 204, 220, Locomotives (standard gauge) #702 **148**, #4332 **148**, –605 **148**, #3203 **147**, Alco diesel switcher #5297 **147**
South Pacific Coast R.R. 9, 60, 191, 203, 220
"SPNG at a glance—1950" 265
Sparks (Nv.) 98
Spooner Summit 19
Standard Consolidated Mine 25
Stewart, Bob 62
Stock Cars **230-232**, plan #153 230, #160 231, #184 232
 See also roster 210
Stock Trains **72**, 75, **86, 88-89**
Sutro's, Adolph 32
Sutter's Mill 17

T

Tank Cars **240-242**, plan #353 240, #54 241, #61 242
 See also roster 212
Teels Marsh 26
Tevis, Lloyd 28
"Tin" Box Cars (C&C) 270
Tinemaha Reservoir 74, 100, **168**
Tobey, W.D. 28
Tommer, W.F. 99-100, **168**
Tonopah (Nv.) 9, 24, 59-60, **64, 67**, 73, 75, 191, railroad 61-62, **68-69**, 75, Engine #1 **66**, 204, Junction 61-62, 97

U

U.S. Gypsum Co. 191
U.S. Vanadium Co. (Laws) 97

V

Vining, Leroy 17
Virginia City (Nv.) 9, 17, 19, 23, 26
Virginia & Truckee R.R. 9, 19, 21-24, 28, 59-60, 73-74, 203; Locomotive "Reno" **29**, 32; Engine #11, **23**

W

Wabuska (Nv.) 22, **38-39,** 60-61
Walker, Joseph Reddeford 17
Walker Lake 19, 22
Walker River 22
Wall St. (stock market crash) 74
Wayne, John **189**
Wellington 19
Wells Fargo 60
White, A.J. 22
White's (Mrs.) Broading House 22
White Mountains 25
Whitell, George 32
Wood, W.S. 32
Work Cars Crew Car #1D **243**, plan 243, Derrick #1 **244**, Wheel Car #1-A **244**, Wrecking Car #1-B **244**, Water Tank Car #350 **244**, Box #452 **245**, Baggage #12 (in work service) **245**, Flanger #108 **91, 226, 245**
Wrinkle, L. F. S. 74
Wrinkle, Noel 74

Y

Yerington, Henry 9, 19, 21-22, 27-28, 63, 192, 203, 220
Yuma 25

Z

Zurich (Ca.) 97, 100-101, **170**

269

One final and rare item...C&C Tin Box Cars

In July of 1880, the Carson & Colorado RR ordered 30 box cars of the LaMothe patent. These cars were ordered through Jesup, Paton & Company of New York and were equiped with trucks supplied by Allison & Son of Philadelphia, PA. The order of box cars was unusual in that the cars were of the pipe frame design and were received in "kit" form. These cars began arriving in December 1880 and delivery was completed by January 1881. The cars were assembled during March-July 1881 and comprised the line's original 300 series of box cars. (Numbers 300-329.)

The C&C also ordered 30-40 LaMothe "metal" flat cars, which were assembled and placed in service by February 1881. The "tin cars" proved to be a plumbers nightmare during assembly. Parts were found to be missing and once in service, the cars tended to shake themselves loose. Henry Yerington was most dissatisfied with them. The cars were fitted with air brakes in the 1890's, but do not appear to have been converted to knuckle couplers during the 1903-04 period. The remains of one "tin box car" still exists at Mina, NV and has provided the data for Herman Darr's scale drawings. Additional data and patent papers on the LaMothe Metal Car were provided by Stephen Drew of the California State Railroad Museum. Photographs of these cars appear elsewhere in this book.

C&C TIN BOX CAR
Plan By Herman Darr

LaMothe patent metal covered box car, assembled at Mound House, NV in March-July 1881 from "kits." Cars came with trucks from Allison & Son. Converted to automatic air brakes c.1897-98 and out of service by 1910. Cars were painted red with white lettering.

Note A: This style truck on some cars
Note B: This truck used on cars 306 & 307

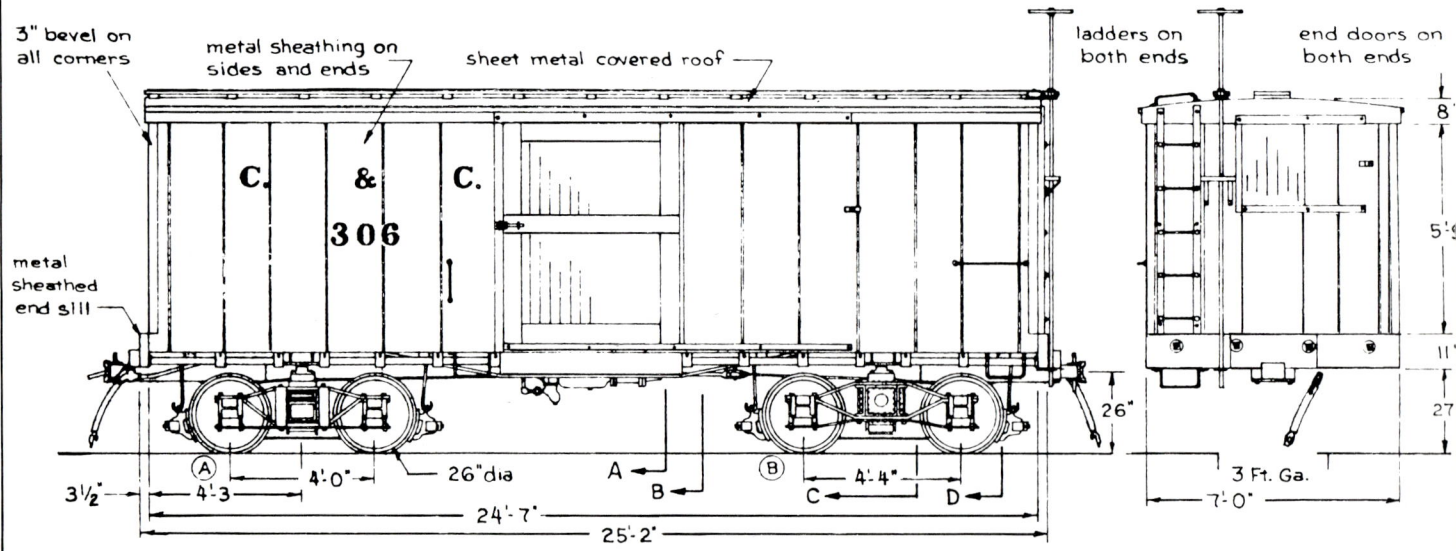

BIBLIOGRAPHY

BOOKS

The Slim Princess, John B. Hungerford, The Hungerford Press, CA, 1956.
Steamcars To The Comstock, Lucius Beebe and Charles M. Clegg, Howell-North Books, Berkeley, CA, 1957.
Southern Pacific Steam Locomotives, Donald Duke, Golden West Books, San Marino, CA, 1965.
Nevada County Narrow Gauge, Gerald M. Best, Howell-North Books, Berkeley, CA, 1965.
Narrow Gauge Nostalgia, George Turner, Trans-Anglo Books, Los Angeles, CA, 1965.
Slim Rails Through The Sand, George Turner, Trans-Anglo Books, Los Angeles, CA, 1964.
A Century of Southern Pacific Steam Locomotives, Guy L. Dunscomb, Modesto, CA, 1967.
Bonanza Railroads, Gilbert H. Kneiss, Stanford University Press, Stanford, CA, 1941.
Mixed Train Daily, Lucius Beebe, E.P. Dutton, New York, N.Y., 1947.
Central Pacific & Southern Pacific Railroad, The, Lucius Beebe, Howell-North Books, Berkeley, CA, 1963.
South Pacific Coast, Bruce MacGregor, Howell-North Books, Berkeley, CA, 1968.
Narrow Gauge Portrait-SPC, Bruce MacGregor, Glenwood Publishers, Felton, CA, 1975.
Railroads of Nevada & Eastern California, David Myrick, Howell-North Books, Berkeley, CA, 1962, '63 (Vol I & Vol. II).
Age of Steam, Lucius Beebe and Charles Clegg, Rinehart & Co., New York, N.Y., 1957.
Story of Inyo, The, W.A. Chalfant, Stanford University Press, Stanford, CA, 1922 (1933).
Big Bonanza, The, C.B. Glasscock, Bobbs-Merrill Pub., New York, N.Y., 1931.
City Makers, Remi Nadeau, Doubleday Books, New York, N.Y., 1948.
Water Seekers, Remi Nadeau, Doubleday Books, New York, N.Y., 1950.
Illustrated Sketches of Death Valley, John R. Spears, Rand-McNally Pub., Co., 1954.
Nevada Ghost Towns & Mining Camps, Stanley W. Paher, Howell-North Books, Berkeley, CA, 1970.
Pioneer Nevada, Harolds Club, Reno, NV, 1951.

OTHER PUBLICATIONS AND MATERIALS

Interstate Commerce Commission, Valuation Report No. 45 p. 404-410 Washington, D.C. ICC, 1933.
Interstate Commerce Commission, Central Pacific Ry. Co. et al Abandondment, 175 ICC 580 (1931); 199 ICC 225 (1934), 224 ICC 191 (1937), 567 ICC 246 (1960).
Official Railway Equipment Register, 1895, 1897, 1917, 1926, 1931, 1934, 1937, 1941, 1948, 1951 (Colorado Railroad Museum, Golden, CO Library).
Narrow Gauge News, No. 57, August 1955, Alamosa, CO (edited by R.W. Richardson).
Poors Manual, 1880-1901, Henry V. Poor, New York, N.Y. (annual editions).
Southern Pacific Company, San Francisco, CA. Files of the Public Relations and Engineering Departments.
Romantic Heritage of Inyo-Moho, California Interstate Telephone Co., Bishop, CA (n.d.) c.1955.
Carson & Colorado R.R., Construction Book 1880- (Author's collection).
C&C, V&T Record books, files (author's collection).

MAGAZINES

Western Railroader: Vol. 22, No. 7 (Issue 235) "Carson & Colorado RR" John F. Due, May 1959; Vol. 19, No. 8 (Issue 200) June 1956; Vol. 24, No. 3 (Issue 255) March 1961. Booklets: "The Nevada-California-Oregon" by David Myrick (1955).
Rail Classics: Sept. 1976.
Railroad Stories: Feb. 1935, p. 36 and following.
Railroad: Aug. 1941 p. 24-26; Jan. 1943 p. 81 and following; Sept. 1943 p. 153; May 1945 p. 85; July 1947 p. 28-29; July 1954 p. 10; Oct. 1955 p. 40 and following; Feb. 1959 p. 26-29.
Desert Magazine, Vol. 37, No. 7 July 1969 p. 35-37.
Nevada Magazine, Jan. 1946.
R&LHS Bulletin: No. 45, Jan. 1938 (V&T); No. 94, March 1956.
Slim Gauge News: Vol. 2, No. 1 p. 10-31; Vol. 3, No. 4 p. 34-49; Vol. 4, No. 1 p. 34-48; Vol. 4, No. 2 p. 54..
NMRA Bulletin, April 1972.
"S" Gauge Herald, May 1970.
Narrow Gauge & Short Line Gazette, complete files.
Pacific News, complete files.
Trains: Sept. 1945; March 1947; Jan. 1948; Sept. 1960.
Model Railroader: Aug. 1964; Sept. 1965; Sept. 1970.
Railroad Model Craftsman: Aug. 1955; Dec. 1955; Sept. 1959; Dec. 1959; Jan. 1960; Feb. 1960; March 1960; Apr. 1960; May 1960; Aug. 1960; Sept. 1960; June 1961; Feb. 1962; March 1962; June 1962; May 1964.
Finelines: Jan. 1970; July 1970; Aug. 1970.
Southern Pacific Bulletin, Nov. 1954 p. 3, 5-7.
Kaiser Builder, Sept. 1960 p. 6-10.
Pacific Railroad Journal, Vol. 1, No. 2 June-July 1954.

NEWSPAPERS

Virginia City Evening Chronicle, 1880-1883, (Bancroft Library, University of California, Berkeley, CA).
Candelaria True Fissue, 1880-1883, (Bancroft Library, University of California, Berkeley, CA).
Bodie Daily Free Press, various, (Bancroft Library, University of California, Berkeley, CA).
Virginia City Enterprise, (Nevada State Library, Colorado).
Inyo Independent, Sept. 23, 1955.
Nevada State Journal: Sept. 18, 1955; Sept. 20, 1955.
Territorial Enterprise, Feb. 13, 1959.
Mojave News, Jan. 29, 1959.
Inyo Register: Oct. 14, 1954; Feb. 12, 1959; Jan. 14, 1960.
Los Angeles Times: Oct. 25, 1954; Jan. 11, 1959; Jan. 27, 1959.
San Francisco Chronicle: Jan. 27, 1959; June 1, 1950; May 31, 1950; June 25, 1934.
Carson City Appeal, Aug. 28, 1947.
San Francisco Call Bulletin, July 28, 1938.

*. . . sand, sagebrush and time have reclaimed their own.
[Mallory Hope Ferrell.]*

figura 7 figura 8

usando la cuenta de grapa

Para comprimir con alicates de punta encadenada, sencillamente apriete la cuenta de grapa aplanándola lo más posible, asegurándose de que los alambres no estén cruzados dentro de la grapa.

La compresión con alicates de grapas tiene dos pasos. Es buena idea colocar una cuenta entre la cuenta de grapa y el broche para aliviar la tensión en el alambre en el punto donde esté puesta la cuenta de grapa. Asegúrese de poder pasar el alambre por esta cuenta dos veces.

Figura 7: Ensarte una cuenta de grapa en uno de los extremos del alambre flexible y luego ensarte una cuenta de agujero grande. Pase por uno de los extremos del broche. Vuelva a pasar el alambre por la cuenta y la cuenta de grapa dejando una cola de 3 pulgadas (7.6cm). Acerque bien la cuenta y la cuenta de grapa al broche dejando un espacio corto. Comprima la cuenta de grapa con fuerza en la ranura que esté más cerca del mango, la se parece a una media luna. Mantenga apartados los alambres de modo que uno de los filamentos esté a cada lado de la abolladura honda.

Figura 8: Ponga la cuenta de grapa abollada en el agujero de frente de los alicates levantados sobre su extremo, y comprímala con toda la fuerza que tenga. Esto dobla la cuenta de grapa y convirtiéndola en cilindro.

figura 9 figura 10

puntada cuadrada

Figura 9: Ensarte el número de cuentas requeridas para la primera fila. Luego ensarte la primera cuenta de la segunda fila y pase por la última cuenta de la primera fila y la primera cuenta de la segunda fila en la misma dirección. La nueva cuenta se asienta encima de la cuenta, y los agujeros están paralelas.

Figura 10: Ensarte la segunda cuenta de la fila 2, y pase por la penúltima cuenta de la fila 1. Continúe por la nueva cuenta de la fila 2. Repita este paso para la fila entera.

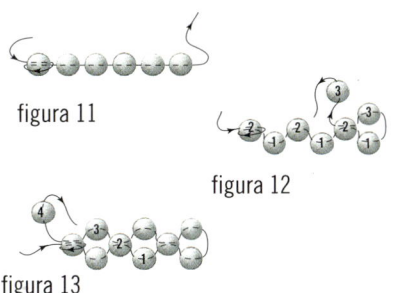

figura 11

figura 12

figura 13

puntada de peyote plano (números pares)

Figura 11: Ensarte una cuenta y vuelva a pasar el hilo por la cuenta en la misma dirección, dejando una cola de 3–4 pulgadas (8–10cm). Ensarte más cuentas para llegar a un número par. Estas cuentas comprenden las primeras dos filas. (Quite el lazo de sobra y entreteja la cola en el tejido de cuentas más tarde.)

Figura 12: Cada dos cuentas de la **figura 11** cae medio espacio para formar la fila 1. Para la fila 3 (las filas se cuentan diagonalmente), levante una cuenta y pase el hilo por la segunda cuenta desde el extremo. Levante una cuenta y pase por la cuarta cuenta desde el extremo. Siga trabajando de esta manera. Termine al pasar por la primera cuenta que ensartó.

Figura 13: Para empezar la fila 4 y todas las otras filas, levante una cuenta y pase por la última que añadió a la fila previa.

Termine los hilos zigzagueándolos por el tejido. Empiece un hilo de la misma manera, saliendo de la última cuenta añadida en la misma dirección para empezar de nuevo.

tejido en ángulo recto

Figura 14: Par empezar la primera fila, ensarte cuatro cuentas y átelas en un círculo bien cerrado. Vuelva a pasar la aguja por las tres primeras cuentas.

Figura 15: Levante tres cuentas (#5, 6, y 7) y cosa en la dirección opuesta, pasando por la última cuenta del círculo previo y las #5 y #6.

Figura 16: Levante tres cuentas y cosa en la dirección opuesta pasando por la #6 y las primeras dos nuevas cuentas. Continúe a añadir tres cuentas para cada punto hasta que la primera fila tenga el largo deseado. Está cosiendo círculos en forma de 8 y alternando la dirección con cada punto.

Figura 17: Para empezar la fila 2, pase

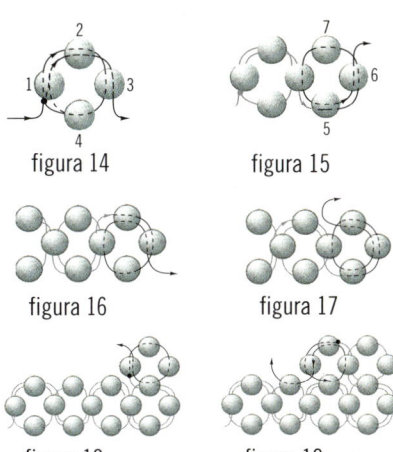

figura 14 figura 15

figura 16 figura 17

figura 18 figura 19

la aguja por las tres últimas cuentas del último punto de la fila 1, saliendo de la cuenta al borde de un de los lados largos.

Figure 18: Levante tres cuentas y pase la aguja por la cuenta de la que salió en la **figura 17** (la primera cuenta "superior" de la fila 1) y la primera cuenta nueva.

Figura 19: Levante dos cuentas y pase la aguja por la siguiente cuenta superior de la fila inferior y la última cuenta del punto previo. Siga cosiendo por las nuevas cuentas y por la siguiente cuenta superior de la fila inferior.

Siga moviendo el hilo en forma de 8. Levante dos cuentas para el reso de los puntos de la fila. No cosa líneas rectas entre los puntos.

figura 20 figura 21

nudo cuadrado

Figura 20: Cruce la cuerda izquierda por encime de la derecha y alrededor del ella.

Figura 21: Ponga la cuerda derecha por encima de la izquierda y pásela por el lazo.

nudo de medio enganche

Figura 22: Salga de una cuenta y forme un lazo perpendicular al hilo entre las cuentas. Pase el aguja por debajo del hilo y en sentido opuesto del lazo. Vaya después por encima del hilo y por el lazo. Tire suavemente de modo que el nudo no se estire antes de tiempo.

figura 22

Los fabulosos años 50

Inspirada por un brazalete clásico de los años 50, usé el tejido de red para crear un brazalete de última moda. La técnica que se usa en esta pieza es más fácil de lo que parece, y se hace muy rápidamente cuando que aprenda el patrón.

❶ Enhebre una aguja en 3 yardas (2.7m) de Fireline. Ensarte dos veces un triángulo 10º para que sirva de cuenta de pare, y deja una cola de 5 pulgadas (12.7cm). Ensarte* una redonda pulida al fuego (PF) de 6mm y tres triángulos, repitiendo del * hasta que llegue al largo deseado de su brazalete.

Acaba de crear la sarta central de cuentas. El resto del brazalete se elaborará en el uno y el otro lado de ella.

❷ Ensarte la mitad del broche de palanca y tres triángulos. Vuelva a pasar por la última PF que se ensartó (**figura 1**).

❸ Volviendo hacia el punto de partida, ensarte tres triángulos entre cada PF a lo largo del brazalete.

❹ Ensarte tres triángulos, la otra mitad del broche, y tres triángulos. Vuelva a pasar por la primera PF y los primeros dos triángulos de la siguiente serie de tres (**figura 2, a–b**). Revise el largo y quite la cuenta de pare.

❺ Ensarte siete triángulos y vuelva por el segundo triángulo de la próxima serie de tres (**figura 2, b–c**). Ensarte siete cuentas de triángulo entre cada segundo triángulo a lo largo del brazalete.

❻ Pase por los cuatro triángulos finales que sujetan el broche (**figura 3, a–b**), entonces ensarte todos los lazos formados por los siete triángulos al otro lado del brazalete (**figura 3, b–c**).

❼ Pase por los cuatro triángulos finales que sujetan la otra mitad del broche, ensarte el lazo de siete triángulos que falta en el primer lado, y pase por las cuatro primeras cuentas del lazo siguiente (**figura 4**).

❽ Ensarte un triángulo, una PF, y un triángulo. Entonces pase por el cuarto triángulo del siguiente lazo de siete triángulos (**figura 5**).

Siga añadiendo un triángulo, una PF, y un triángulo entre cada lazo en el primer lado del brazalete.

❾ Después del cuarto triángulo del primer lado, pase por 12 triángulos para traer el hilo al cuarto triángulo de otro lado.

Ensarte un triángulo, una PF, y un triángulo. Luego pase por el cuarto triángulo del siguiente lazo de siete triángulos.

Añada un triángulo, una PF, y un triángulo entre cada cuarto triángulo de los lazos de siete triángulos en el segundo lado del brazalete.

❿ Pase por los 12 triángulos de este extremo del brazalete y ensarte la serie final de un triángulo, una PF, y un triángulo (**figura 6, a–b**).

⓫ Pase por la siguiente serie de un triángulo, PF, y un triángulo (**figura 6, b–c**). Ensarte tres triángulos y pase por la siguiente serie de un triángulo, una PF, y un triángulo (**figura 6, c–d**). Continúe este patrón alrededor de ambos lados del brazalete.

⓬ Entreteja las colas, haga varios nudos de medio enganche entre algunas de las cuentas del brazalete (vea "Fundamentos," p. 2), y corte los cabos. ● – *Glenda Payseno*

materiales

- 6 gramos de mostacillas triangulares (triángulos) de tamaño 11º
- 37 cuentas redondas pulidas al fuego de 6mm
- hilo para pescar Fireline a prueba de 6 libras
- broche de palanca
- agujas para cuentas, #12

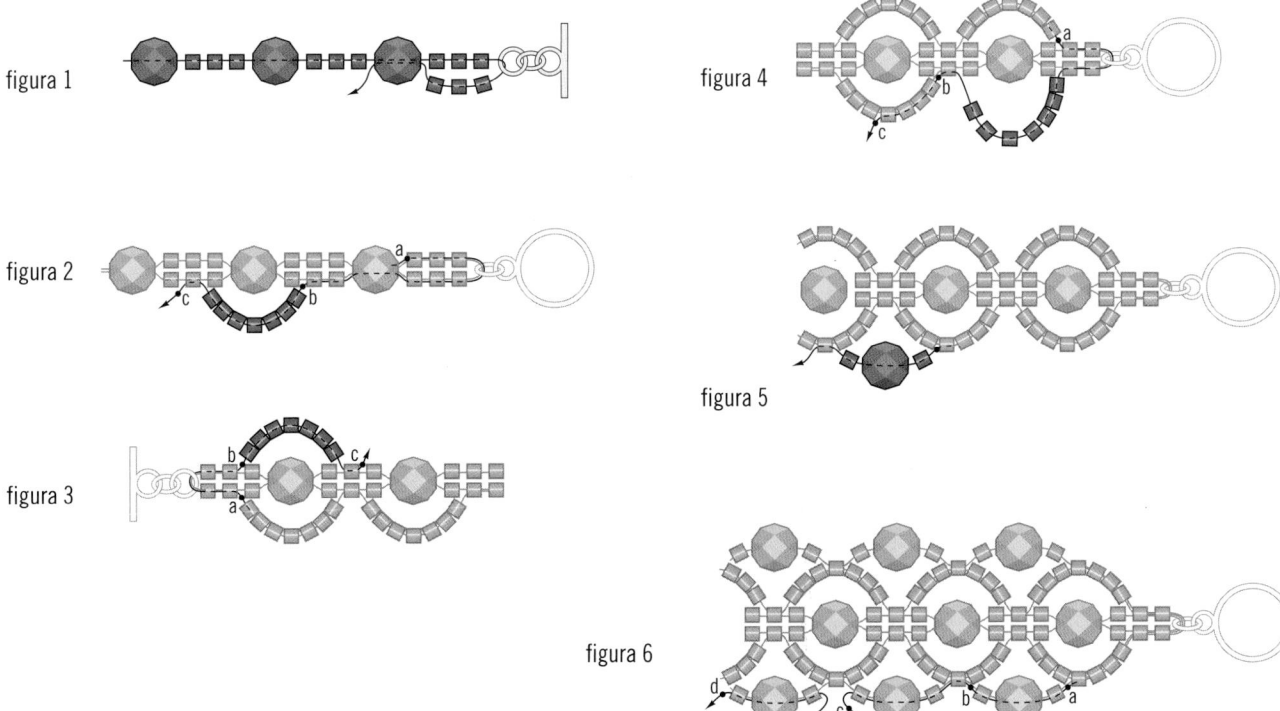

figura 1

figura 2

figura 3

figura 4

figura 5

figura 6

Cinta de flores y flecos

Contraste las mostacillas mates y brillantes sobre una base plana de puntada herringbone.

empiece la base

❶ Empiece con 3 yardas (2.7m) de hilo. Use una escalera de cuentas para la base (vea "Fundamentos," p. 2 y **figures 1–3**). Ensarte dos mostacillas del tamaño 8°. Deje una cola de 10 pulgadas (25cm). Vuelva cosando por la primera cuenta en el extremo de la cola. Entonces, cosa por la segunda cuenta (**figura 1**).

❷ Continúe hacer una escalera de cuentas para un total de cuatro cuentas (**figuras 2 y 3**).

❸ Vuelva zigzagueando a la primera cuenta, de modo que el hilo operante y la cola del hilo salgan de lados opuestos. El hilo operante sale por la parte superior de la cuenta y está a la izquierda. Tejerá de la izquierda hacia la derecha (o dé vuelta el trabajo y teja de la derecha a la izquierda si usted es zurdo).

❹ Ahora empiece al puntada herringbone. Ensarte dos 8°s. Baje por la segunda cuenta y suba por la tercera cuenta de la fila previa (**figura 4**).

❺ Ensarte dos 8ºs. Baje por la cuarta cuenta de la fila previa (**figura 5**).

❻ Ensarte un triángulo para doblar la esquina. Suba la última cuenta ensartada de la fila previa (**figura 6**). Voltee el trabajo de modo que la aguja esté a la izquierda. Repita del paso 4 hasta que el brazalete se acomode confortablemente alrededor de la muñeca. Deje el resto del hilo para hacer un lazo para el broche.

cree el broche

❶ Teja la cola de 10 pulgadas hacia arriba pasando por tres filas antes del borde para salir de una cuenta de una de las dos columnas en medio, de modo que la flor o el botón quede alineado con la primera fila (**figura 7, a–b**). Ensarte una mostacilla de tamaño 11º, la flor, y una 11º. Vuelva a pasar por la flor y la primera 11º. Vuelva a coser por la otra columna en medio (**figura 7, b–c**). Repita el camino del hilo para reforzar la flor. Ate la cola con nudos de medio enganche (vea "Fundamentos") y corte.

❷ Para el lazo al otro lado del brazalete, saque la aguja de la segunda cuenta de la última fila (**figura 8, a–b**). Haga un lazo de tamaño 11ºs de largo suficiente para contener el broche de flor (mío tienen un largo de 24 cuentas). Baje por la tercera cuenta de la última fila para completar el lazo (**figura 8, b–c**). Vuelva a pasar por el lazo para reforzarlo.

❸ Pase la aguja por las primeras dos o tres mostacillas del lazo (**figura 8, c–d**).

haga los flecos

Alterne flecos lisos con flecos divididos cada pocas mostacillas del lazo.

❶ Flecos lisos: Alterne dos cuentas de tamaño 11º con una de cristal tres veces. Termine con tres 11ºs. Omita las últimas tres 11ºs y vuelva a pasar por todas las cuentas que acaba de añadir (**figura 8, d–e**). Pase por unas de las cuentas siguientes del lazo.

❷ Flecos divididos: Ensarte tres 11ºs, una 8º, tres 11ºs, una cuenta de cristal, y tres 11ºs.

Omita las tres últimas 11ºs y vuelva a pasar por la cuenta de cristal y tres 11ºs (**figura 8, e–f**).

Añada tres 11ºs, una cuenta de cristal, y tres 11ºs, y vuelva a pasar por la cuenta de cristal, tres 11ºs, una 8º, y las tres primeras 11ºs (**figura 8, f–g**). Pase por unas cuentas siguientes del lazo.

❸ Siga haciendo flecos alrededor del lazo. Ate la cola como el otro lado y corte. ● – *Anna Nehs*

materiales

- 10 gramos de mostacillas de tamaño 8º, para el brazalete y los flecos
- 6 gramos de cuentas triangulares (triángulos), de tamaño 10º, para el brazalete
- 2 gramos de mostacillas de tamaño 11º para los flecos
- 40 (aproximadamente) cuentas de cristal o cuentas facetadas pulidas al fuego
- hilo para cuentas Silamide o hilo para pescar Fireline a prueba de 6 libras
- agujas para cuentas, #12
- cuenta de flor plana para el broche (de la Eclectica, www.eclecticabeads.com), o use un botón de dos agujeros

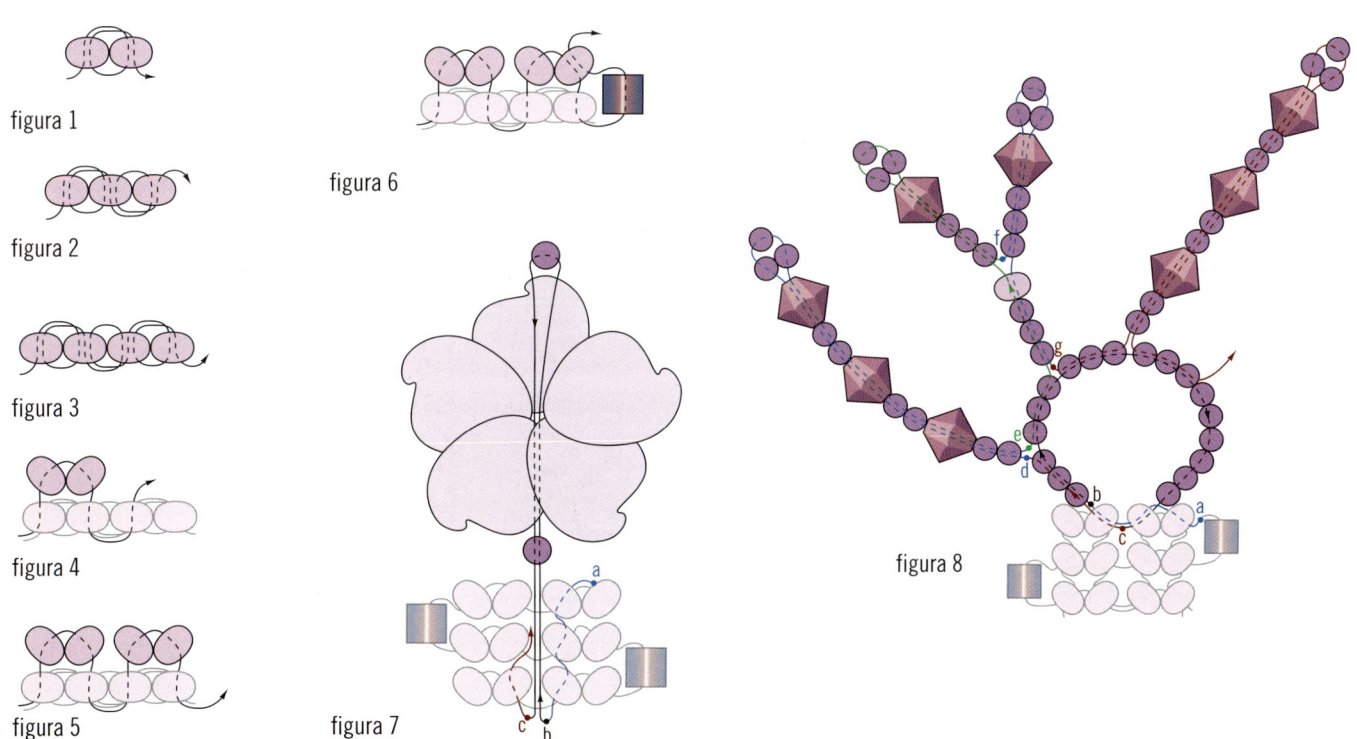

figura 1
figura 2
figura 3
figura 4
figura 5
figura 6
figura 7
figura 8

⑤ Pase por dos cristales de modo que el hilo salga del lado opuesto enfrente del punto de partida (**foto c**). Mantenga tirantes los círculos.
⑥ Repita los pasos 4 y 5 hasta llegar al largo deseado.

broche

Cuando llegue al largo deseado, cosa la mitad del broche a ese extremo. Teja abrazos por encima de los cristales, y entonces cosa la otra mitad del broche al otro extremo del brazalete.

Para añadir la primera parte del broche, salga del último cristal, ensarte nueve cuentas cilíndricas CA y el broche, y pase por el lado opuesto del último cristal (**foto d**). Refuerce al pasar dos veces por las cuentas añadidas. Termine al salir del último cristal.

besos

① Ensarte dos cilíndricas CP, uno CA, y dos CP. Pase a través del círculo y cose por el cristal perpendicular (horizontal) y enfrente del punto de que salga el hilo, orientando la aguja hacia el broche (**foto e**).
② Ensarte dos cilíndricas CP y pase por el cristal CA del paso 1. Ensarte dos cristales CP y pase por el siguiente cristal vertical (**foto f**).
③ Repita los pasos 1–2 para hacer besos por encima de los cristales hasta que llegue al otro extremo del brazalete. Entonces añada la otra parte del broche como la primera.
④ Entreteja las colas, ate con nudos de medio enganche (vea "Fundamentos"), y corte. ● – *Rachel Zash*

Brazalete de abrazos y besos

Este brazalete comienza con círculos de cristal tejidos en ángulo recto: los abrazos (vea "Fundamentos," p. 2 y **fotos a–c**). Entonces teje las X—besos—de mostacillas por encima de los abrazos.

Cuando uno usa cualquier tipo de hilo con cristales, debe siempre pasarlo directamente por el cristal, no contra el borde, lo cual es a veces agudo.

abrazos

① Enhebre la aguja con 3 yardas (2.7m) de Fireline.
② Ensarte cuatro cristales y muévalos hasta el final del hilo, dejando una cola de 10 pulgadas (25cm).
③ Haga un nudo cuadrado (vea "Fundamentos") de modo que los cristales formen un círculo tirante (**foto a**). Luego vuelva a pasar por los dos cristales siguientes.
④ Ensarte tres cristales y pase por el lado opuesto del cristal de que sale el hilo (**foto b**).

materiales

- **100** (aproximadamente) cristales de biconos para un brazalete de 8 pulgadas (20cm)
- 3 gramos de cuentas cilíndricas (Delicas) de color principal (CP)
- 1 gramo de cuentas cilíndricas de color de acento (CA)
- broche de pinza de langosta con **2** anillas soldadas or dividas
- hilo para pescar Fireline, a prueba de 6 libras, o Silamide
- agujas para cuentas, #12

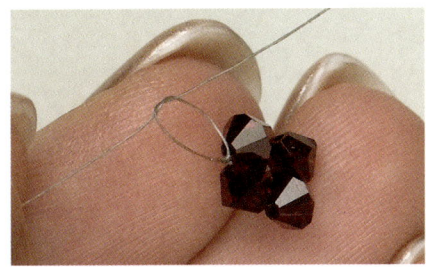

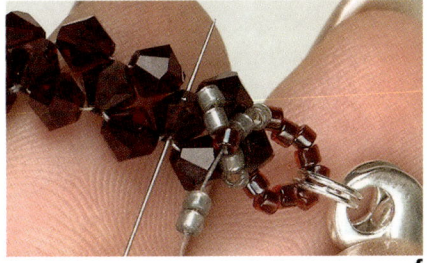

Diamantes amontonados

Teja estos pendientes del centro hacia los extremos mientras aprenda a aumentar y disminuir puntada ladrillo (vea "Fundamentos," p. 2). El patrón de las filas y de los colores se muestra en la ilustración en la p. 10.

filas de disminución

❶ Enhebre la aguja con una yarda (.9m) de Nymo D. Haga una escalera de cuentas (vea "Fundamentos," p. 2) por la primera fila de cinco cuentas, alternando una CA y una CP. Deje una cola de 16 pulgadas (41cm).

❷ Para la fila 2, ensarte una CA y una CP, y trabaje como en "Fundamentos," **figura 4**. Luego, ensarte una CP, pase por debajo del hilo entre las dos cuentas siguientes de la fila 1, y suba por la nueva CP ("Fundamentos," **figura 5**). Repita con una CA.

❸ Haga la fila 3 como la 2, añadiendo tres cuentas y siguiendo el patrón de colores de la **figura** en la p. 10.

❹ Haga la fila 4 como el comienzo de la fila 2 con dos cuentas CP.

filas de aumento

❶ Para la fila 5, ensarte una CP y una CA, pase por debajo del hilo entre las dos cuentas de la fila 4, y suba por la nueva CA. Ensarte una CP, vaya por debajo del mismo hilo de la fila 4, y vuelva a subir por la nueva CP.

❷ En la fila 6, ensarte una CP y una CA, pase por debajo de hilo entre las primeras dos cuentas de la fila 5, y suba por la nueva CA. Ensarte una CA y trabaje como en la **figura 5** de "Fundamentos." Termine la fila con una CP añadida al mismo lazo.

❸ Empiece la fila 7 como la 6, con una CP y una CA. Luego, ensarte una CP, pase por debajo del hilo entre las dos cuentas siguientes de la fila 6, y vuelva a subir por la nueva CP. Ensarte una CA, pase por debajo del hilo entre las dos últimas cuentas, y vuelva a subir por la nueva CA. Termine la fila con una CP añadido al mismo lazo.

Sigue en la página siguiente

materiales
- **78** mostacillas o cuentas cilíndricas (Delicas) de color principal (CP) de tamaño 11º
- **60** mostacillas o cuentas cilíndricas (Delicas) de color de acento (CA) de tamaño 11º
- **4** cuentas cristales de 4mm
- **2** anillas soldadas de 4mm
- **2** alambritos de pendiente
- hilo para cuentas Nymo D
- agujas para cuentas, #12

Puño de herringbone sin fin

siga amontonando

❶ Continúe a tejer usando las instrucciones de disminución para las filas 8–10 y siguiendo el patrón de colores mostrado adelante. Salga de la última CP añadida.

❷ Ensarte una CP, un cristal, una CP, y un anilla. Vuelva a bajar por la CP, cristal, y CP (**figura, a–b**). Teja el hilo por el diamante que acaba de completar. Ate el hilo con nudos de medio enganche (vea "Fundamentos") y corte la cola.

❸ Dé vuelta del trabajo para repetir las filas 2–10 al otro lado de la fila 1, usando la cola de partida.

❹ Termine con una CP, un cristal, y tres CPs. Vuelva a pasar por el cristal y la primera CP (**figura, c–d**).

❺ Termine esta cola como en el paso 2. ● – *Anna Nehs*

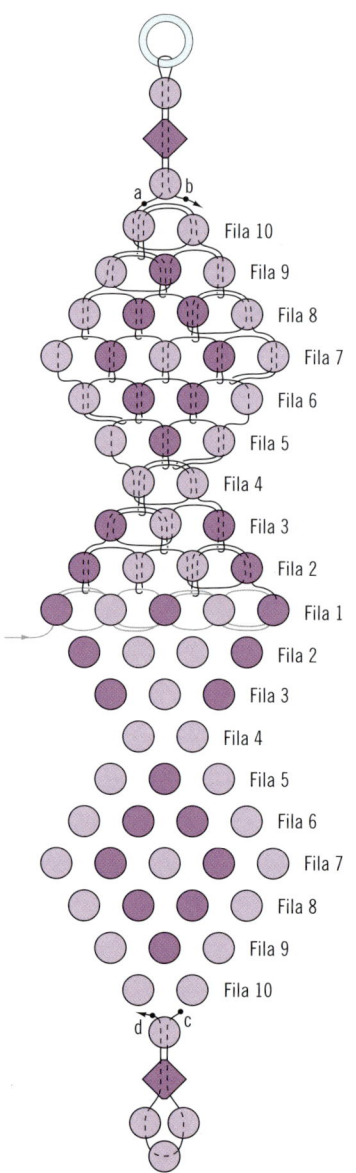

El uso de formas y acabados de cuentas diferentes crea una apariencia engañosamente complicada para este puño hecho con puntada herringbone plano. Pero es un proyecto muy fácil de coser y el trabajo va muy rápidamente.

elaboración de la base

❶ Enhebre una aguja con 3 yardas (2.7m) de Fireline. Haga una escalera de cuentas (vea "Fundamentos," p. 2 y **figuras 1–3**), alternando una cuenta de cubos y una de triángulos dos veces (cuatro cuentas en total). Deje una cola de 6 pulgadas (15cm).

❷ Dé vuelta el trabajo de modo que el hilo con que trabaja salga de la parte superior del último triángulo a la izquierda (zurdos: trabajen de la derecha hacia la izquierda).

❸ Ensarte un cubo y un triángulo. Baje la aguja por la segunda cuenta de la fila previa y súbala por la tercera (**figura 4**).

❹ Añada un cubo y un triángulo. Baje por la cuarta cuenta (un cubo) de la fila previa (**figura 5**).

❺ Ensarte dos mostacillas de tamaño 11º para doblar la esquina y suba por el último triángulo de la nueva fila (**figura 6**).

❻ Dé vuelta el trabajo de modo que el triángulo esté a la izquierda y sea la primera cuenta de la nueva fila. Repita a partir del paso 3 hasta que el brazalete se acomode a la parte más ancha de su mano.

figura 1

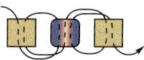

figura 2

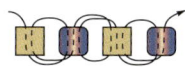

figura 3

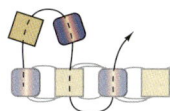

figura 4

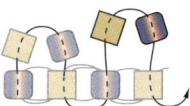

figura 5

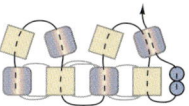

figura 6

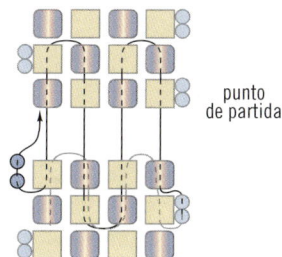

punto de partida

figura 7

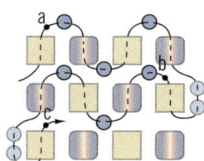

figura 8

juntura de los cabos

1 Conecte los cabos al tejer la cola del extremo del brazalete entre las primeras pocas filas del comienzo del brazalete. Entonces teja la cola de la punta de partida entre las últimas pocas filas del otro cabo. Asegúrese de mantener la correspondencia entre triángulos y cubos en el patrón alternante.

2 El cubo al borde de la última fila no tendrá al lado dos 11°s. Añada estas cuentas mientras teja los cabos (**figura 7**). Entreteja las colas y átelos, usando nudos de medio enganche (vea "Fundamentos"). Corte las colas.

relleno de abertura

1 Enhebre una aguja con 3 yardas (2.7m) de hilo y suba por cualquier cubo de borde.

2 Añada una 11° y baje por el siguiente triángulo de la misma fila.

3 Añada una 11° y suba por el siguiente cubo de la misma fila.

4 Añada una 11° y baje por el último triángulo de la misma fila. Ahora baje la aguja por las dos 11°s en el borde y suba por el cubo de la siguiente fila inferior (**figura 8, a–b**).

5 Repita del paso 2 (**figura 8, b–c**) hasta que se hayan llenado todas las aberturas. Entreteja el hilo y átelo como se hizo arriba. Entonces corte las colas. ●

– Anna Nehs

materiales
- 5–7 gramos de cuentas de cubos de 4mm
- 5–7 gramos de mostacillas triangulares (triángulos) de tamaño 5°
- 5–7 gramos de mostacillas de tamaño 11°
- hilo para pescar Fireline a prueba de 6 libras
- agujas para cuentas, #10

Brazalete entrecruzado

Me encanta lo fácil que es tejer la puntada en ángulo recto con la técnica a dos agujas. El problema es que el hilo para cuentas no es bastante fuerte como para sostener este dibujo. Entonces sustituí un alambre flexible para ensartar por el hilo. Ahora mi hermoso brazalete es fuerte y fácil de hacer sin hilo ni agujas.

grupo entrecruzado

❶ Prepare el broche al sujetar una anilla dividia a cada extremo.

❷ Ensarte 11 cuentas cilíndricas y una parte del broche en el centro de 2 yardas (1.8m) de alambre flexible.

❸ Cruce ambos filamentos por una cuenta pulida al fuego (PF) de 4mm (**foto a**).

❹ Ensarte una PF en cada filamento y cruce los alambres al pasar por una cuarta PF (**foto b**). Vuelva a pasar los filamentos por las cuentas PF de al lado. Entonces crúcelos por la primera PF del grupo de nuevo (**foto c**).

❺ En cada filamento, ensarte dos cuentas cilíndricas. Luego crúcelos al pasar por otra cuenta cilíndrica (**foto d**).

❻ En cada filamento, ensarte dos cuentas cilíndricas más y crúcelos al pasar por la cuarta PF (**foto e**).

conectores de grupos

❶ En cada filamento, ensarte siete cilíndricas. Omita los tres últimos cilíndricas y vuelva a pasar el alambre por el cuarto cilíndrica antes del extremo (**foto f**) para formar un lazo. Añada tres cilíndricas a cada filamento y cruce los filamentos al pasar por una PF (**foto g**).

❷ Alterne los grupos entrecruzados con los connectores de grupos hasta que llegue al largo descado. Termine con un grupo entrecruzado.

último toque

❶ Ensarte cinco cuentas cilíndricas en cada filamento. Añada la otra mitad del broche y cruce los filamentos al pasar por una cuenta de grapa (**foto h**).

❷ Pase uno de los filamentos por los cinco cuentas cilíndricas, la cuenta PF final, los otros cinco cilíndricas, y por la cuenta de grapa para reforzar el lazo. Pase el otro filamento por cinco cilíndricas, si es posible.

❸ Comprima la cuenta de grapa (vez "Fundamentos," p. 2) y corte las colas. ○

– Anna Nehs

materiales

- 2 gramos de cuentas cilíndricas (Delicas) o de mostacillas de tamaño 11º
- alambre flexible para ensartar, .012
- **40–48** cuentas facetadas pulidas al fuego de 4mm
- 2 anillas dividias
- broche de palanca
- cuenta de grapa

Herramientas: cizallas, alicates de grapas o alicates de punta encadenada, alicates para abrir anillas (opcionales)

Brazalete de ventanilla

El tejido con puntada cuadrada da la impresión de haberse hecho al telar, pero se hace sin telar. Para este brazalete de fácil confección, se alternan secciones de puntada cuadrada sólido con espacios de cuatro filas de altura. Antes de volver al puntada cuadrado sólido, se cosa una cuenta de seis milímetros en el centro de la abertura.

cinta

❶ Ensarte una aguja para cuentas con 2 yardas (1.8m) de hilo acerado o suavizado. Levante una cuenta cilíndrica y vuelva a pasar por ella en la misma dirección para formar una cuenta de pare. Deje una cola de 12 pulgadas (30cm). Ensarte 10 cuentas cilíndricas de color principal (CP).

❷ Levante dos CP y pase por las dos últimas cuentas de la fila inferior. Vuelva a pasar por las dos nuevas cuentas. Continúe cosiendo con puntada cuadrada dos cuentas a la vez (**figura 1** y "Fundamentos," p. 2). Complete cuatro filas con cuentas CP.

❸ Para la fila 5, cosa dos CP con puntada cuadrada, seis CA (color de acento), y dos CP.

❹ Empiece la primera fila de una ventanilla: Cosa dos CP con puntada cuadrada, entonces una CA. En la siguiente fila cosa una CA y una CP por encima de la primera dos cuentas, luego una CP. Repita este patrón, añadiendo dos cuentas al primer punto y una a la segunda por cuatro filas (**figura 2, lado izquierdo**).

❺ Después de añadir las tres cuentas a la fila 5, ensarte cinco CA y dos CP (**foto a**).

❻ Cosa cuatro filas debajo de las tres cuentas del borde (**foto b** y **figura 2, lado derecha**).

❼ Conecte con puntada cuadrada la tres cuentas del lado de la ventanilla con las tres cuentas del borde de la fila inferior (**figura 3, a–b**).

❽ Zigzaguee por la primeras dos filas al lado derecho (**figura 3, b–c**). Ensarte una cuenta de 6mm y cosa por la tercera fila al lado izquierdo (**figura 3, c–d**). Pase por la segunda fila, la cuenta de 6mm, y la tercera fila a la derecha (**figura 3, d–e**). Vuelva a trazar el miso camino para reforzar la cuenta de 6mm.

❾ Zigzaguee por la cuarta fila y las tres cuentas del borde de la fila superior (**figura 3, e–f**). Repita los pasos 2–9, terminando con cuatro filas de CP cuando el brazalete ya se acomode a su muñeca.

Termine el hilo corto al zigzaguear por algunas cuentas de varias filas. Para añadir hilo, vuelva a trazar los últimos tres a cinco puntos, saliendo de la última nueva cuenta.

término

❶ Ahuse el término como a continuación: Cosa por las dos cuentas finales de la penúltima fila (**figura 4, a–b**), entones pase por dos cuentas más de la última fila (**figura 4, b–c**). Cosa con puntada cuadrada seis cuentas por encima de las seis cuentas que están en el centro de la última fila (**figura 4, c–d**).

❷ Para añadir el broche de botón, pase por las últimas tres cuentas (**figura 4, d–e**). Ensarte una cuenta y pase por el lazo del botón y la cuenta añadida. Pase por la cuarta cuenta de la fila corta (**figura 4, e–f**). Cosa por las dos cuentas debajo de las dos que están en el centro de la fila corta y por la tercera cuenta de la fila corta (**figura 4, f–g**). Vuelva a trazar por el mismo camino para reforzar el botón.

❸ Quite la cuente de pare del extremo de partida del brazalete, y repita el paso 1 para ahusar el extremo.

❹ Cosa todo el camino por la fila corta (**figura 5, a–b**). Ensarte cuentas suficientes para hacer un lazo que se acomode bien alrededor del botón (**figura 5, b–c**). Pase de nuevo por la fila corta. Vuelva a trazar el miso camino 3–4 veces para reforzar el lazo.

❺ Para el ribete, empiece un nuevo hilo o continúe a coser con el hilo del botón. Vuelva a salir por la cuenta del borde de la última fila de ancho entero. Levante tres CA y cosa por la segunda cuenta del borde (**figura 6, a–b**). Salga de la próxima cuenta (**figura 6, b–c**) y repita. Ribetee los dos lados. ○ – *Alice Korach*

materiales

- 7.5 gramos de cuentas cilíndricas (Delicas), tamaño 11º, color principal (CP)
- 3 gramos de cuentas cilíndricas, tamaño 11º, color de acento (CA)
- **8–12** cuentas facetadas pulidas al fuego de 6mm o cristales redondos de 6mm
- botón de mango pequeño
- agujas para cuentas, #10 o #12
- hilo para cuentas Nymo D
- cera de abejas o suavizante Thread Heaven

a

b

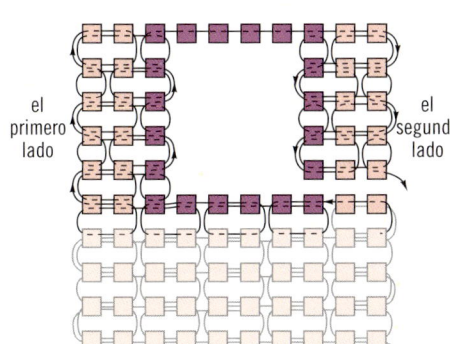

figura 1

figura 2

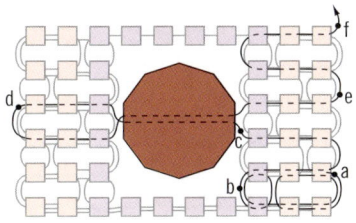

figura 3

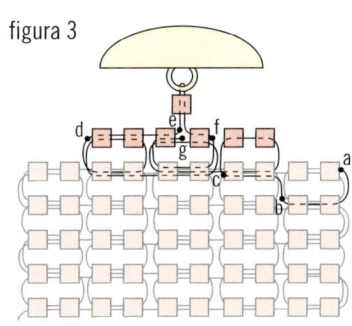

figura 4

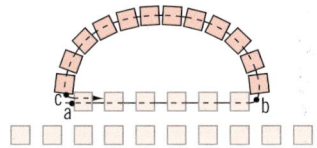

figura 5

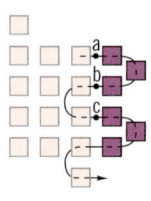

figura 6

Brazalete con cuentas de peyote

Es divertido emplear las mostacillas que sobran para hacer cuentas abaloriadas con puntada de peyote planos en números pares. Se tejen rápidamente y se prestan a mil variaciones. Necesita solamente siete cuentas abaloriadas y unos cristales para un brazalete de 8½ pulgadas (22cm).

cuentas abaloriadas cortas (haga 4)

❶ Enhebre una aguja con 24 pulgadas (61cm) de hilo para cuentas. Ensarte una cuenta cilíndrica, una mostacilla de tamaño 11º, un triángulo, dos mostacillas de tamaño 8ºs, un triángulo, una 11º, y dos cilíndricas. Deje una cola de ocho pulgadas (20cm). Estas cuentas forman las primeras dos filas más la primera cuenta de la tercera fila (vea "Fundamentos," p. 2).

❷ Para empezar la fila 3, omita las dos cilíndricos y pase por la 11º hacia la cola (**figura 1**). Asiente las cuentas cilíndricas una al lado de la otra.

❸ Añada un triángulo, omita el triángulo del paso 1, y pase por la primera 8º.

❹ Añada una 8º, omita la segunda 8º, y pase por el triángulo. Añada una 11º, omita la 11º ensartada, y pase por la cilíndrica (**figura 2**).

❺ Dé vuelta el trabajo de modo que pueda seguir cosiendo de abajo hacia arriba.

❻ Para la fila 4, añada una cilíndrica y pase por la nueva 11º. Añada un triángulo y pase por la nueva 8º. Añada una 8º y pase por el nuevo triángulo. Añada una 11º y pase por la cilíndrica (**figura 3**).

❼ Continúe a dar vuelta el trabajo y añadir la cuenta correspondiente en cada espacio entre las cuentas añadidas de la fila previa, hasta que haya cinco cilíndricas a lo largo de la parte superior y de la parte inferior (**figura 4**).

❽ Rodee la cuenta en un tubo y cosa los bordes juntos, zigzagueando hacia delante y hacia atrás entre las cuentas altas (**figura 5**).

❾ Cuando esté terminado el tubo, entreteja las cola adentro, haciendo varios nudos de medio enganche (vea "Fundamentos") entre las cuentas. Corte las colas.

cuentas abaloriadas largas (haga 3)

❶ Cosa la cuenta larga como la cuenta corta, pero ensarte dos cilíndricas, dos 11ºs, dos triángulos, dos 8ºs, dos triángulos, dos 11ºs, y tres cilíndricas para las primeras dos filas (**figura 6**).

❷ Cosa la cuenta con puntada de peyote, siguiendo **figuras 7–9**.

❸ Cuando haya cinco cuentas a lo largo de la parte superior y de la parte inferior, rodee las cuentas en un tubo, y zigzaguee juntos los bordes (**figura 10**). Termine las colas como antes.

montaje

Comprima un mitad del broche a uno de los extremos de un largo de 12 pulgadas (30cm) de alambre flexible (vea "Fundamentos"). Ensarte un cristal, espaciador, cuenta de peyote pequeña, espaciador, cristal, espaciador, cuenta de peyote larga, y un espaciador (**foto**). Continúe con este patrón hasta llegar al largo deseado, luego comprima la otra mitad del broche como antes. ●

– Anna Nehs

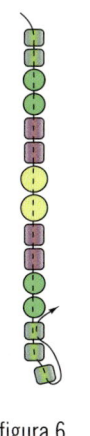

figura 6

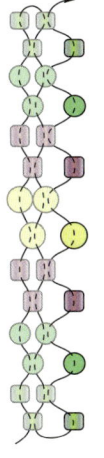

figura 7

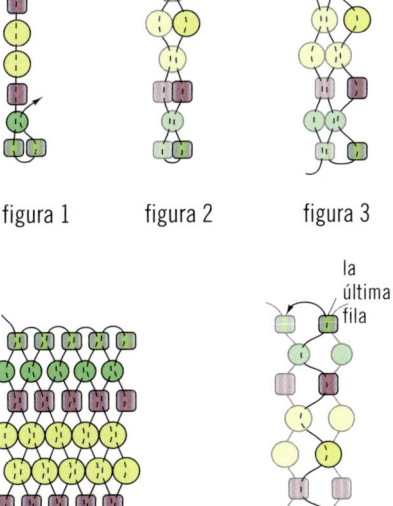

figura 8   figura 9

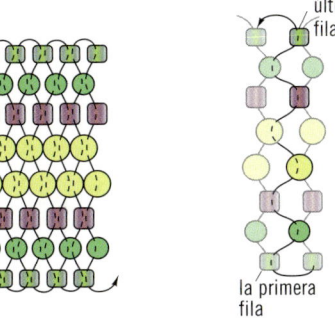

figura 1   figura 2   figura 3

figura 4   figura 5

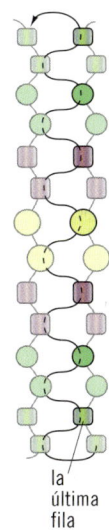

figura 10

materiales

aproximadamente 100 de cada estilo de mostacillas:
- cuentas cilíndricas de tamaño 11º
- mostacillas de tamaño 11º
- mostacillas triangulares (triángulos) de tamaño 10º
- mostacillas de tamaño 8º
- **14** espaciadores de plata de 4mm (2 por cuenta)
- **8** cristales de 6mm
- broche de palanca
- **12** pulgadas (30cm) de alambre flexible para ensartar, .012–.015
- **2** cuentas de grapas
- hilo para cuentas Silamide o hilo para pesca Fireline a prueba de 6 libras
- agujas para cuentas, #10 o #12

Herramientas: cizallas, alicates de grapas, tijeras

Puño de cristal

Originalmente intenté usar hilo para cuentas para este brazalete de tejido de red, y pensé ponerle un broche. Pero cada vez que estuve para terminar, los cristales cortaron el hilo. Entonces decidí usar alambre flexible para ensartar. Después de tejer la cinta, me encantó cuando me di cuenta que la red era suficientemente elástica como para acomodarse por encima de mi mano en un dibujo sin fin.